DAVID EWEN *Introduces* MODERN MUSIC

A History and Appreciation
from Wagner to the Avant-Garde

Other Books by DAVID EWEN

DAVID EWEN *Introduces*

CHILTON BOOK COMPANY
Philadelphia   New York   London

MODERN MUSIC

A History and Appreciation—
From Wagner to the Avant-Garde
By David Ewen

REVISED, ENLARGED EDITION

To the Memory of
MYRTLE PERMAN—
she will never be forgotten

"You've got to learn to *stretch* your ears!"

—GEORGE E. IVES *to his son* CHARLES

"There is no reason why anybody in the music world, professional or layman, should find himself in the position of not understanding a piece of 20th-century music, if he is willing to give himself a little trouble."

—VIRGIL THOMSON

Acknowledgments

The quotations on Impressionism and Expressionism by Thomas Craven in Chapters 3 and 5 come from *Modern Art,* copyright 1934, 1961 by Thomas Craven. Reprinted by permission of Simon and Schuster, Inc.

The quotation on Debussy by Oscar Thompson in Chapter 3 comes from *Debussy, Man and Artist,* copyright 1937 by Dodd, Mead & Co., Inc.

The definition of the twelve-tone technique which appears in Chapter 5 comes from *The Harvard Brief Dictionary of Music* by Willi Apel and Ralph T. Daniel, copyright © 1960 by the President and Fellows of Harvard College. Reprinted by permission of the Harvard University Press.

Contents

DAVID EWEN *Introduces* MODERN MUSIC

A History and Appreciation
from Wagner to the Avant-Garde

Introduction: But Is It Music?

Since 1900, many composers in different parts of the Western world have sprung up like some well organized fifth column to overthrow the status quo in music.

These rebels, these revolutionaries, have been determined to destroy once and for all many, if not all, of the principles by which the making of music has been governed for so many centuries. After sweeping away the ruins, they tried to build a new kind of musical art, with new materials, techniques, and concepts; a musical art freed forever from the tyranny of century-old textbooks and precepts, subject only to its own laws and principles.

The old forms had to be swept away like so many cobwebs. Structures of the past had to be replaced by shapeless organisms, seemingly without a logical beginning, middle, and end. Sometimes these amorphous structures were spacious in design. Sometimes, as in some of the pieces by Anton von Webern, they consisted only of a few notes which took no more than several seconds to perform.

The discipline of tonality, to which composers had so willingly subjected themselves since the days of Bach, was superseded by the anarchy of no tonality at all. This new music roamed about freely from one key to another, no longer tied to the resting point of a tonal center. Lyricism made way for seemingly disconnected snatches of ugly

1

ideas which the German and Austrian atonalists described as "song-speech."

Polyphony now consisted of a marriage of melodies in which each melody was in apparent violent disagreement with the others. First Ives, then Stravinsky, and after that Milhaud produced works in a "polytonal" style in which two or more themes, each in a different key, were joined in an unholy union.

Rhythm had to be unharnessed like some nuclear power. Rhythms in more varieties, combinations, and permutations than even the wildest imagination could have dreamed of a century ago were released by Stravinsky in *Le Sacre du Printemps* (*The Rite of Spring*) a composition which produced an atomic explosion all its own. Olivier Messiaen wrote a huge ten-movement glorification of rhythm, *Turangalîla*. As he himself explained somewhat awesomely, his hour-long work was filled with "nonreversible rhythms, asymmetric augmentations with several rhythmic identities, rhythmic modes, and the combinations of quantitative and sounding elements in reinforcing the values and timbre of each percussion instrument by chords which form the resonance of these resonances." Messiaen further assumed a role as a prophet of rhythm by preparing a rhythm dictionary incorporating the basic rhythms of the Eastern and Western worlds as well as those of Greek music.

Harmonies long sanctified by conservatory rules and textbooks were succeeded by piercing discords—the more the cacophony, and the greater the volume, the better. Dissonant chords no longer demanded the relief of resolution; they were self-sufficient, independent—the replacement for consonance.

Emotion? This was just excess baggage, a useless carry-over from the sentimental Romantic era, now dead. Mu-

2

sic had to be stripped of all feeling, all human experience, and become as cut and dried as a mathematical formula. Indeed, several composers actually did create <u>formulas</u> to govern creation. Arnold Schoenberg devised the twelve-tone technique which has mathematical precision and exactitude. Boris Blacher invented a strict arithmetical series for organizing rhythm and meter, sometimes in strict succession (1, 2, 3, 4), and at other times evolved by having each subsequent number become the sum of two preceding numbers (1, 2, 3, 5, 8). Joseph Schillinger worked out a creative system based on scientific methods. He produced an exact technique for writing music through the application of formulas, charts, and graphs. On one occasion he created a composition derived from the week's stock-market quotations—the rise and fall of these quotations translated into equivalent rise and fall of the melodic line. Heitor Villa-Lobos went one step further. He wrote pieces about a South American mountain range and the New York skyline by tracing the contours of each on graph paper, then retracing the same curves into melodic lines.

The stock market and the New York skyline were only two of similarly off-beat subjects stimulating some of our modern composers. In the Soviet Union, factories, iron foundries, collective farms, the reforestation program, and a peace conference in Geneva all provided material for musical exploitation. Honegger set a moving train and a game of Rugby to music; Leonard Bernstein found musical inspiration in a cookbook, and Milhaud in a catalogue of agricultural implements. Manuel Rosenthal described a lavish musical meal, Stravinsky a poker game, Poulenc fish and marine life. One American even made a musical setting of the instructions preceding the income-tax form. Esoteric settings, far removed from their

3

own everyday experiences—with appropriately esoteric musical idioms—fascinated still other composers. Arnold Bax and Sir Granville Bantock, both Englishmen, were respectively influenced by Celtic lore and the Orient. Two Americans, Colin McPhee and Alan Hovhaness, based many of their compositions on subjects and musical styles relating to Bali, on the one hand, and Armenia, on the other.

New sounds had to be concocted, sounds never before heard in a serious musical creation—grating, shrieking, nerve-wracking sounds. When a composer exhausted the sound potential of known musical instruments, he reached for noisemakers, machines, electronics, even radio static. Satie used a typewriter and a spinning roulette wheel in *Parade*, Ravel a cheesegrater in *L'Enfant et les sortilèges*, Mossolov a shaken steel-sheet in *Iron Foundry*. One Italian modernist specified the need of a "whistler" and a "snorer" in one of his compositions. When Richard Strauss wanted to reproduce the noise of a storm, he invented a thunder and a wind machine for *Don Quixote* and *An Alpine Symphony*. One woman in Berlin, reading that a wind machine was being introduced by Strauss, inquired from a local paper whether it was necessary to bring an umbrella to the concert hall. A wind machine also appears in Vaughan Williams' *Seventh Symphony*, the "Antarctica."

The world of electronics opened up entirely new possibilities for the projection of noises, and distortion of noises. Some musical adventurers in France, Germany, and the United States were quick to explore the completely new electronic world of musical creation. "You hear roars from an air terminal," one American critic wrote in describing such an electronic composition, "background effects from a cheap radio thriller, the stac-

4

cato click of rolling dice, screeching brakes, or the unpleasant vibrato of an electric organ. . . . What value does such a work have as music? Your guess is as good as mine." In the concluding chapter of this book we shall say more about our musical men of electronics.

Edgard Varese (1883–1965), an American, devoted his life to compositions based on dynamic effects, timbres, sonorities of percussions, sirens, electronic instruments, etc. For these experiments Varese concocted the descriptive phrase "organized sound." Varese uses not only musical instruments and machines, but even simulates noises of insects and animals. In *Ionisation*—written for sixteen percussion, friction, and sibilation instruments of undetermined pitch—he uses two fire sirens. In *Hyperprism* the percussion group includes sleigh bells; another composition, *Arcana,* requires five choirs of percussion. Varese aspires, as Nicolas Slonimsky, one of America's leading musicologists, once said, to reach "into the field of musical infinities." But to W. J. Henderson, another American critic, one of Varese's compositions "shrieked, grunted, chortled, mewed, barked. . . . It was just a ribald outbreak of noise." Olin Downes was reminded of "election night, a menagerie or two, and a catastrophe in a boiler factory." Varese's own simple explanation is: "I try to fly on my own wings."

Other innovators uncovered new sounds not through dynamics but through experiments with unusual intervals. As a departure from the traditional use of whole tones and half tones that has governed our scales since Bach proved the feasibility of the "well-tempered" or "well-tuned" clavier, Alois Hába, a Czech, conceived an altogether new type of music by means of quarter tones. In this idiom he wrote operas, string quartets and various other instrumental works, devising his own system of notation, and

5

manufacturing new types of musical instruments capable of performing his works. Hans Barth, an American, also wrote quarter-tone music for a two keyboard, quarter-tone piano which he had invented. The Mexican, Julian Carrillo, not only made notable experiments in quarter-tone music—even to the point of rewriting Bach's *Well-Tempered Clavier* and Beethoven's nine symphonies in quarter tones!—but also created compositions in eighth tones and sixteenth tones, inventing special instruments for this purpose. Carrillo pointed out the vast new world that can be uncovered through this means in the introduction to his *El Infinito musical* (a valuable manual on modern musical theory): "If there is anyone who would like to publish this work, the first chapter will have to present 1,193,232 chords for which it will be necessary to have 14,315 volumes of five hundred pages each."

Was there any excess to which tonal adventurers would not go in their efforts to explore a brave new world of musical sound?

In the early 1920's, Henry Cowell (1897–1965)—then an *enfant terrible,* though later a traditionalist—became famous for his piano pieces performed by hammering fists, elbows, or forearms on the keyboard. He called these violent eruptions of sound "tone clusters." However, tone clusters were not new with Cowell. Charles Ives had used them many years earlier. In the middle 1910's a young man, Leo Ornstein, horrified concert audiences with compositions like the *Wild Men's Dance* which made use of minor-second dissonances called "note clusters." But Cowell used this technique so extensively, that the term "tone clusters" is invariably identified with his name.

6

At one of his concerts in Germany a riot broke out in the hall between those favoring his music and those who were outraged by it. The police were called in to quell the disturbance. But through it all Cowell was so busily—and so noisily—engaged with his smashing sounds that he did not even realize anything unusual was taking place in the auditorium. Needless to say, each of Cowell's public appearances proved a taxing physical feat. Accepting Cowell more in a spirit of fun than art, the managing editor of a New York newspaper sent not his music critic but the sports editor to cover a Cowell concert in Carnegie Hall. And the headline of the review read: "Cowell Wins in Bout with Kid Knabe."

A radical extension of this tone-cluster technique was presented by Toshi Ichiyanagi in a program of avant-garde music in New York on May 15, 1961. In one of his compositions he used a hammer on the piano keyboard, and repeated a single loud elbow-smash chord over five hundred times.

George Antheil, another American bad boy of music in the 1920's, created a furor with a work named *Ballet mécanique*. The composition was scored for airplane propellers, anvils, electric bells, automobile horns, and sixteen player pianos. The cataclysm of sound that emerged from the stage of Carnegie Hall on April 10, 1927, caused one wag in the audience to attach a white handkerchief to his cane and wave it frantically overhead as a symbol of surrender.

If the instrumentation for compositions by Antheil and Varese seems outlandish, then, surely, the last word was had by the young composer, Harold G. Davison, in *Auto Accident*. His score required the following instruments: "Two plate glasses, each resting on a washing bowl or crock, with a hammer or mallet, in readiness to smash

7

them." Then the composer provided his performer with the following instructions: "On page nine, measure four, these plates are to be shattered with the hammer, one on the second count, and the other on the second half of the third count. In the next measure the bowls containing the broken glass are to be emptied on a hard surface [such as a] table or floor."

Hardly less audacious an innovator is John Cage. His earlier works were written for a "prepared piano"—a piano that had been "prepared" by stuffing dampers of metal, wood, rubber, felt and other substances between the strings to permit unusual sounds and sonorities. Each of Cage's pieces required him to "prepare" a piano differently.

From the "prepared piano" Cage went on to far more outlandish experiments. He has written compositions for an audio-frequency oscillator, an electric-wire coil, and regulated recordings of various industrial noises. Some of his works need automobile brake drums, tubs of water, flower pots, electric buzzers, and numerous other devices capable of producing singular noises. In *Water Music,* two containers are utilized, one empty and one full of water; a stop watch regulates when and for how long a time the water is poured from the full container into the empty one. *William Mix* attempts to reproduce city and country noises, electronic sounds, manually produced and wind-produced sounds, and faint sounds audible only through amplification. One of Cage's most novel pieces was featured a few years ago on the Garry Moore television show. It was offered there as a stunt, though the composer himself regards it as a very serious artistic production. In performing this music, Cage runs from one device to another for a succession of sounds—from radios producing static and fragments of programs, to a glass half-filled with water, to a pneumatic pump, to a tape recorder, and so forth.

Cage has also tried to introduce spontaneity and improvisation into the creative process. One of his piano works instructs the performer to drop the manuscript on the floor. The pianist then picks up at random any sheet and proceeds to play it; the composition thus becomes a haphazardly conceived concoction, as the pianist proceeds to pick up one sheet after another. In one of his orchestral works—scored for 'cellos, basses, winds, percussion and piano—Cage does not indicate the individual notes to be played by the men but merely tells them whether to play high or low, loud or soft. (*Zeitmesse* by Karlheinz Stockhausen is similarly without a plan. The score is made up of unrelated musical fragments which the performer can pick out at will, one after another. When the same fragment is repeated the composition is over.)

In view of the almost harrowing noises produced in so many of Cage's works perhaps the most welcome of his creations is a piano piece entitled *Four Minutes Thirty Seconds*. This is a "silent composition" in "three movements," during which the virtuoso sits at his piano all the time and plays—nothing!

Cage has his disciples and pupils, and the most provocative of these is Morton Feldman. Like his teacher, Feldman is the creator of "silences" as well as "sounds." He has never written a completely silent work; rather, he uses carefully calculated periods of silence which interrupt periods of sound—or, as one critic described the process, "spots of sound variously dropped on silence." Feldman has written *Pieces, Extensions, Intersections,* for string quartet, one or more pianos, violin and piano, and so forth. These compositions demand a completely

9

new system of notation: graphs and charts in place of formal notes, bars and dynamic markings. He has devised a new system of figures, numbers and signs to indicate pitch and time values, and such instrumental indications as pizzicato and arco.

Opera has also had its non-conformists, adventurers, and outright anarchists—beginning with Debussy's *Pelleas and Melisande* which represented to Camille Bellaigue, the eminent French critic, "a structureless art" abolishing rhythm and melody and containing "germs, not of life and progress, but of decadence and death." In his Expressionist opera, *Wozzeck,* Alban Berg went on to banish formal melody and rhythm, substituting a strident "song-speech" for singable arias. But to many of Berg's contemporaries—shocked by these yawps and outcries and burps and yelps—this was neither song *nor* speech. "As I left the State Opera last night," reported Berlin critic Paul Zschorlich, after the première of *Wozzeck,* "I had the sensation not of coming out of a public institution but out of an insane asylum."

In Carl Orff's opera trilogy, *Trionfi* (which includes the now frequently performed *Carmina Burana*) the style consists almost entirely of a kind of rhythmic declamation, often without any orchestral accompaniment. Repeated notes make up a good part of the melody, and harmony is used economically.

If Orff sometimes dispenses with melody, normal rhythm and at times even harmony in opera, Boris Blacher has done away with the libretto. *Abstrakte Oper No. 1* has no continuity or plot; emotional states are indicated by such headings as "Fear," "Love No. 1," "Panic No. 1" and so forth. The dialogue consists almost entirely of arbitrary sounds rather than words, and when

10

real words are used at infrequent intervals their meaning is completely unintelligible.

What are these composers trying to do? Are they just charlatans, publicity-seekers, sensation-mongers? Are they scientists instead of creative artists, devising experiments in their own kind of laboratories?—experiments which, in themselves, may not be art but which some day may become the means by which art is created by musicians. Or are these innovators powerful inventive figures, evolving a musical art which, however strange to our ears, will in a future day sound as pleasing, simple and appealing as do Haydn and Mozart?

II

Before such a question can be answered, an important fact must be stressed. Throughout the history of music rebels and iconoclasts have broken down traditional rules, customs, and procedures to open up new horizons for music. Were this not the case, our musical experiences today would still be confined to the unaccompanied polyphonic vocal music that dominated the fourteenth and fifteenth centuries. From century to century, music has been subjected to violent changes, and these changes were effected as often by revolution as by evolution.

From the fourteenth through the sixteenth century, music's first great era, polyphony was the prevailing texture. The music of that age was contrapuntal—unaccompanied, ecclesiastical, and vocal. In counterpoint several different melodies were sung simultaneously. To break away from this style and initiate the homophonic variety, that is music with a single melody supported by a harmonic accompaniment, represented a titanic upheaval. This revolution came about during the Ren-

11

aissance through the efforts of a small group of Florentine intellectuals who aspired to revive Greek drama with music. In the early sixteenth century, a simple declamation—a one-voice melody accompanied by instruments—sounded as weird and without logic and reason to ears so long accustomed to the multi-voiced choral music of the times, as atonality first did in our own day. But the simple device of declamation helped bring on a new musical culture.

Opera's first undisputed master, Claudio Monteverdi, was severely hounded by his contemporaries for his "modernism." He was one of the earliest composers to champion the major-minor tonal system; he was one of the first to introduce dissonance in harmony; he was one of the first to use such completely new instrumental devices as the pizzicato and the tremolo. Many of his colleagues were astounded and shocked by his innovations. Artusi, a noted theorist of Monteverdi's day, remarked bitterly that Monteverdi's music made no appeal to reason. In 1600 another of Monteverdi's critics wrote: "These kind of air castles and chimeras deserve the severest reproof. . . . You hear a medley of sounds, a variety of parts that are intolerable to the ear. . . . With all the best will in the world how can the mind see light in this chaos?" Yet Monteverdi's revolution did represent light, throwing illumination on paths which ultimately led to the music drama.

After Monteverdi, notable pioneers of operas like Jean-Baptiste Rameau and Christoph Willibald Gluck were frequently abused and denounced for daring to depart from clichés and formulas already long established by Italian opera composers. Rameau and Gluck, like Monteverdi, were far ahead of their times in trying to change opera into a musical drama in which music and

12

text were equal partners in an artistic undertaking. Both Rameau and Gluck were opposed to lilting tunes, pleasing duets, ensemble numbers, and pretty choral pieces whose only *raison d'être* was either to exploit a remarkable voice or a set of voices, or else to please the ear of the listener. These bold pioneers also objected vehemently to big scenes, elaborate ballets, and spectacular stage procedures; they preferred to have everything on the stage arise naturally and inevitably from the needs of the play. Finally, both Rameau and Gluck were determined to make music reflect the emotional and dramatic nuances of the stage action and the characterizations, even if it meant producing music that was dramatic and expressive instead of merely melodious. "French melody is no melody at all," insisted Jean Jacques Rousseau about Rameau's operas, "and French recitative is not recitative. I conclude, therefore, that the French have not and cannot have music of their own." The men of the Opera orchestra in Paris jeered loudly when first asked to play Rameau's music which, they said, was so complicated that it did not even provide musicians with an opportunity to sneeze. And the Viennese audiences that first heard Gluck's epoch-making *Orfeo ed Euridice* in 1762 were as baffled by Gluck's musical revolutions as the French people had been by Rameau's.

In the same way that Monteverdi, Rameau and Gluck first changed the course of opera, so other visionaires in music continually revised the concepts of what structure, melody, harmony, and orchestration should be. Each time these revisions were made, a new language was introduced which contemporaries—even some of the learned ones—often failed to comprehend. So revolutionary was the vague tonality in the opening bars of Mozart's *String Quartet in C major* that in listening

13

to it the master, Joseph Haydn (already the greatest composer of his generation), could only shake his head with wonder and incredulity. He remarked: "If Mozart wrote it he must have had a good reason to do so." Indeed, to this day this composition is known as the "Dissonant Quartet," though to us it represents a world of grace and charm.

The radical way in which Beethoven opened his *First Symphony* seemingly in the key of F, then passed on to the key of G before arriving at the C major tonality, and the prominent use he made of brass instruments and timpani, ushered in a new day for symphonic writing. But these procedures seemed like madness to Beethoven's critics. One said this work sounded as if it had been written for a military band; another described Beethoven as a musical ignoramus, a "poorly tutored student." Of Beethoven's use of shattering dissonant chords, in the opening movement of the "Eroica" Symphony, one critic remarked: "Poor Beethoven is so deaf that he cannot hear the discords he writes." After hearing the first movement of the *Fifth Symphony,* Goethe exclaimed: "It is meaningless. One expected the house to fall about one's ears."

About Berlioz, Fétis, the distinguished French critic, wrote in 1837: "I believe that what Monsieur Berlioz writes does not belong to the art which I customarily regard as music." Yet Berlioz is the genius who was among the first to make a permanent break with the classical past and to carry the musical art to Romanticism. Berlioz evolved a new kind of flexible and expansive symphonic structure that was unified by a central thought (or as he described the technique, the *idée fixe*); he was one of the first to try producing a dramatic, programmatic, and pictorial symphonic style; he opened

14

new areas for rhythm, harmony, and orchestration through never before essayed techniques. Consequently, in the early nineteenth century, Berlioz was an innovator no less brazen and fearless than some of our twentieth-century modernists.

There were many in Berlioz' day who thought he represented the end of musical sanity. Yet time and again after that composers were subjected to the most violent attack even when their infringements on the *status quo* were comparatively minor. Liszt suffered derision and vituperation for daring to use the glockenspiel in his *First Piano Concerto*. César Franck's *Symphony in D minor* was soundly abused for adding the English horn to the family of symphonic instruments. (One eminent professor of the Paris Conservatory shouted after the concert: "This a symphony? Who ever heard of writing for the English horn in a symphony?") Tchaikovsky's delightful use of extended pizzicato passages in the Scherzo of his *Fourth Symphony* led Henry E. Krehbiel to remark that "as a symphonic movement, it is about as dignified as one of the compositions which delight the souls of college banjo clubs." Rossini so scandalized the musicians of Milan by opening his overture to *La Gazza ladra* with rolls of two snare drums—each drum in an opposite side of the orchestra—that (according to a familiar story) the concertmaster of the La Scala Orchestra threatened to kill him. Chopin's new approaches to harmonic colorings, tonalities and techniques of piano performance completely changed the course of writing for the piano. But in 1833 Rellstab, a German critic, insisted that Chopin's music (now the very essence of the poetic) was nothing but "ear-rendering dissonances, tortuous transitions, sharp modulations, repugnant contortions of melody and rhythm."

15

The truth of this whole matter is that what one generation may consider ugly and noisy and insane may very well become the essence of beauty to a later era. In his time Franz Schubert was attacked for—of all things—a lack of lyricism. This was because Schubert was so intent upon making his melody express the most subtle and elusive nuance of the poem he was setting, that he arrived at a new kind of expressive and dramatic melody far different from the classical kind found in earlier songs by Haydn and Mozart. Today we recognize Schubert as one of the greatest creators of melody the world has known because our ears are completely attuned to *his* kind of musical beauty. The song composers who followed Schubert (Schumann, Brahms, Hugo Wolf, Debussy) all tried to penetrate ever deeper into the meaning and emotion of their poems. Each arrived at a new concept of lyricism. These composers were also condemned by many critics for failing to create beautiful melodies, yet each of these composers is now recognized as a master.

Is there any opera more melodious than Verdi's *Rigoletto?* This is a work so full of lovable and familiar tunes that some may be tempted to believe it full of "quotations." Yet, in 1858, an unidentified Italian critic bellowed that there was simply no melody in *Rigoletto!* Is there any composer of songs more bitterly accused in his time of avoiding melody than Debussy? But only a half-century later one of these melodies was popular enough to become an American hit-song!

If the concept of beauty in melody can change with time, so can that of beauty in harmony. Because they ventured into new worlds of harmonic sound to realize a richer and more meaningful expression, masters like Mozart, Beethoven, Berlioz, Liszt, Brahms and Richard

16

Strauss were often described as noisy, incoherent, mad. How did a Boston critic react in 1878 to Brahms' *First Symphony?* To him the music was only "noisy, ungrateful, confusing," an "unattractive example of dry pedantry." What was it that another critic said in 1896 of one of the most delightful, witty and ingratiating of all of Richard Strauss's orchestral pieces, *Till Eulenspiegel's Merry Pranks?* "The orchestration is sound and fury signifying nothing, and the instruments are made to indulge in a shrieking, piercing, noisy breakdown most of the time."

One more point is well worth emphasizing. There is, as the cliché tells us, nothing really new under the sun. Some of the idioms and techniques first regarded in the twentieth century as so outlandish and so without basis in precedent or reason, can be found (however tentatively suggested) in the works of earlier masters.

Dissonance? . . . The discords in the first movement of the "Eroica" are as jarring as some found in *The Rite of Spring.* And, as far back as 1770, Charles Burney, the English historian, said that "discord seems to be as much the essence of music as shade in painting."

Polytonality? . . . Stravinsky and Milhaud may have shocked graybeards with this technique, yet polytonality is certainly suggested in many eighteenth-century compositions where a pedal or organ point is sustained throughout a work and thus linked with unrelated tones. And polytonality is forcefully foreshadowed in a canonic passage by Bach quoted in Percy Scholes' *Oxford Companion of Music.*

Syncopation? . . . The works of Bach, Beethoven, Schumann, Brahms are full of it.

The Whole-Tone Scale? . . . Long before Debussy it

17

was used by Mozart, Schubert, Rossini, Berlioz, and Liszt.

Atonality? . . . There are recognizable examples of twelve-tone composition in Liszt's *Faust Symphony*; one musicologist even detected a twelve-tone row in Mozart's *G minor Symphony*; and the last quartets of Beethoven have decidedly atonal implications.

Sprechstimme? . . . The recitatives of Mussorgsky, in which he consciously tried to imitate speech, are the ancestors of song-speech.

Nor is the introduction of outlandish paraphernalia to concoct new sounds, or the use of exotic instruments a phenomenon peculiar to our century. Beethoven wrote *Wellington's Victory* for a mechanical wind band known as the "panharmonicon"; Tchaikovsky interpolated actual booming cannon into the scoring of the 1812 *Overture*; Mozart utilized sleigh bells and a hurdy-gurdy in his German dances; and in his overture to *Il Signor Bruschino,* Rossini had the violinists tap the music stands with their bows.

III

One reason why composers tried new and unorthodox techniques was to open new vistas for the musical art. But another force has also been operating, sending composers into revolt against existing institutions. That force can perhaps best be summed up by the old bromide that for every action there is a reaction. Or, to change the image, music history is a pendulum swinging now to one extreme, now to the other, before finding a resting point midway between the extremes. After one style has been carried to excess, composers invariably appear to react decisively against that style with a far different kind of music. After this reaction has spent itself, a compromise is usually reached with a style assimilating tendencies and mannerisms of both extremes.

18

We already have had occasion to remark that the polyphonic era was the first important one in music. As the years passed this style grew ever more complex and subtle under the influence of masters like Josquin des Prés, Vittoria, and Palestrina. Eventually composers were impelled to break away and try something new: something that was, by contrast, simple, one-voiced, harmonic. Thus the reaction to polyphony brought on homophony—a single melody against a harmonic accompaniment. Music could now move back from the intricate to the elementary, from the esoteric to the universal. Thus the pendulum swung to the opposite extreme of polyphony, and when it finally came to rest, a middle ground was reached with the masterworks of Bach and Handel.

The age of Bach and Handel has been designated by historians as "baroque." The Baroque period was followed by the Classical era, with the works of Haydn and Mozart as its apex. In Classicism, order, discipline, symmetry, formality, and precise structures were combined with an objective approach and an emotional restraint. After Classicism had progressed to an extreme in its strict adherence to law and order, reaction proved inevitable. It came with the licenses of Romanticism. Forms became flexible, and new structures were invented; style grew freer; technique achieved elasticity. Emotion, subjectivity, fantasy, and emphasis of the poetic element governed the creative impulse. Romanticism reached its climax with Berlioz, Schubert, Schumann and Liszt. Then another middle ground was reached which combined elements of Classicism and Romanticism; this middle ground found its expression in the music of Johannes Brahms.

A good deal that has happened in twentieth-century music is the result of history's pendulum swinging freely now to one extreme, and now to the other. The greatest single influence upon the twentieth century was Wagnerism, a tidal wave that swept over the entire world of music in the closing decades of the past century. Different composers broke with Wagner in different ways and each of these break-throughs represents some current or cross-current in contemporary music-making.

Wagner was one of the greatest revolutionists in music. His world was opera, and in that world he fashioned a new art—the music drama which he tried to make a "synthesis of the arts." His ideal was a super-art in which every element—music, poetry, drama, scenery, acting— was just a part of a monumental whole. He wrote his own poetic dramas filled with symbolism and allegorical allusions pointing up his own social and political thinking. He clarified his own ideas of staging, scenery, and costuming. He wrote his own music. He was gifted in every department, but a genius in only one—music. With a musical technique equalled by few before him; with an inspiration that never seemed to fail him when he summoned it for a big scene or a great emotion; with a capacity for innovation which brought new dimensions to harmonic and contrapuntal writing, to thematic development, to tonality, to orchestration, he made his music express the loftiest sentiments, the noblest concepts, and the most sensual moods of his stage plays.

Music had to be as dramatically and poetically expressive as his inexhaustible invention could make it; tone had to serve his most searching aims as a poet and a man of the theater. He used a Gargantuan orchestra because his musical ideas were Gargantuan, and he endowed his music with colors, nuances and dynamics new to the operatic theater. From his orchestra players he demanded such virtuosity that for a long time they insisted his music was unplayable. He gave his orchestra an importance it had never before enjoyed in the opera house; the orchestra became the human voice's equal in his overall musical scheme.

Wagner had to evolve a new harmonic language to project the subtlest and most elusive suggestions. He used suspended ninth chords, six-four chords in protracted cadences, and chromatic harmonies which introduced a new type of dissonance through continual modulations until all sense of a consistent tonality was lost.

To achieve integration and unity he worked out an elaborate scheme of continual, uninterrupted melody. Wagner's kind of melody was so wide in its expressive range and so technically demanding on the voice that singers of his day said it was beyond their capabilities. He also worked out a new technique of leading motives. Each motive represented some character, situation, mood, or emotion. These leading motives recurred throughout the opera, often magically transformed, often combined in the most complex and subtle contrapuntal textures.

He was a giant who thought and worked in gigantic terms. It took him over a quarter of a century to create *The Ring of the Nibelungs,* a monumental cycle of four music dramas, each of which (except for the first, a prologue) required about four hours for performance. As he worked on this vast project, he never wavered in his belief in himself and his mission. What matter if voices and orchestra players of his day could not meet the demands made by his exacting music? In time musicians and singers would acquire the necessary technique! What matter if the stage of that day could not cope with his advanced demands or his concept of an

21

ideal opera performance? In time there would be a special theater built to do justice to his far-sighted ideas! Meanwhile there was work to be done, a dream to bring to life—not only *The Ring of the Nibelungs,* but also other mighty musical epics, such as *Tristan und Isolde, Die Meistersinger,* and *Parsifal.* For all he knew, as he worked so passionately, none of these works would be performed in his own lifetime. But he kept on working, confident of his ultimate victory, confident that his music was truly (as he himself called it) the "art of the future."

For a long time he was the object of vilification and vituperation such as few composers ever experienced. The powerful Viennese music critic, Eduard Hanslick, one of his most bitter antagonists, described the music dramas as "formlessness elevated to a principle, a systematized non-music, a melodic nerve fever written out on the five lines of the staff." Leading critics in France, Germany, Austria, and England called him a "madman" and his music "a monstrosity"; "the anti-Christ, incarnate of art"; "the enemy of melody, seeker after the unorthodox, corrupter of art, eccentric by nature"; "a disease who contaminates everything he touches—he has made music sick." His immortal drama of love and death, *Tristan und Isolde,* was described as "advanced cat music. . . . It can be produced by a poor piano player who hits the black keys instead of the white keys, or vice versa." The incomparable comedy, *Die Meistersinger* was said to be a "horrendous *Katzenjammer*" which "could not be accomplished even if all the organ grinders of Berlin would have been locked up in Renz's Circus, each playing a different waltz."

He had violent enemies, but he also had passionate disciples who knew he was a prophet of the *new* music; musicians like Hans von Buelow (whose wife he stole)

22

and Franz Liszt; patrons of all kinds, including the mighty King of Bavaria, Ludwig II. They promoted his music in every way they could. And it was through the bounty of the King that many of Wagner's music dramas were finally heard in Munich. After that, Wagner brought one of his most cherished dreams to realization with the building of a Festival Theater in the Bavarian town of Bayreuth. There his mighty *Ring* cycle was given in its entirety for the first time with the quality of performances he desired. Now Bayreuth is the shrine of Wagner's music dramas to which music lovers stream from all parts of the civilized world.

For vastness of artistic concept, for newness of musical language, for independence of musical thought, Wagner dominated the closing nineteenth century like a Colossus. He might be hated or worshiped; but to ignore him was impossible. The spell of Wagner was inescapable; it was felt by every composer who followed him. There were those who tried to write as he did (and not necessarily for the stage). In following in his giant footsteps, these men carried German Romanticism to a point beyond which it could go no further. Then there were those who reacted violently against his superstructures, his harmonic and melodic extravagances, his determination to make music express ideas and concepts well beyond the boundaries of tones. Such composers, breaking with Wagner, helped to swing the musical pendulum to the extreme which opposed German Romanticism. We shall see that many of the trends of the twentieth century represent just such a violent reaction against Wagner.

CHAPTER 1

The Wagnerites

S ome composers carried Wagner's torch while he was still alive; many others carried this torch long after his death. All adopted his aesthetics, his ideals and his personal creative mannerisms not merely for music dramas but for orchestral compositions and songs as well. These composers liked to employ huge structures and vast vocal and instrumental forces. They utilized elaborate harmonic and contrapuntal schemes and doted upon big sonorities and dynamics, and over-rich colorings. They liked to express highly sensual or theatrical moods or to speak of philosophical, meta-physical, literary or spiritual concepts. Their speech was filled with dramatized or pictorial tonal images. Wagner's harmonic idiosyncrasies, Wagner's chromaticism, Wagner's way of writing for large brass choirs and divided strings was also *their* way of writing.

When Wagner was still alive, a Viennese composer became identified as the "Wagner of the symphony." He was Anton Bruckner (1824–1896), a humble, naive man who was a peasant at heart. Bruckner believed in only two things outside his own music: Wagner and God—and there were times when he confused the two. He was a composer of choral and organ music, and a church organist, when in 1863 he heard Wagner's *Tannhäuser*. Here he found a musical religion. Henceforth he worshiped at the Wagnerian shrine with all the humility of a true believer. After attending the première of *Parsifal*, Bruckner fell on his knees before Wagner, kissed his hand, and exclaimed: "Master, I worship you!"

Bruckner tried to write symphonies the way Wagner wrote music dramas. He used large structures, dramatic and passionate utterances; his music is filled with flights towards the sublime and the grandiose. More than that, Bruckner copied some of Wagner's own methods in harmony and orchestration, and on occasion even used thematic material that had more than a passing resemblance to some of Wagner's. Bruckner's *Third Symphony* was not only dedicated to Wagner but is filled with Wagner-like speech. The slow movement of his *Seventh Symphony* is touched with tragedy for as Bruckner wrote it he had a premonition of the master's imminent death.

Bruckner's immediate successor in symphonic music in Vienna was Gustav Mahler (1860–1911), also a perfect Wagnerite. One of the greatest conductors of his generation, Mahler was sophisticated and immensely cultured. He had studied philosophy at the University, and all his life had been an omnivorous reader of great literature. Cosmic problems tormented him; even as a composer he grappled with them.

Like Bruckner (and Beethoven before that) Mahler completed nine symphonies. All of them were superstructures using large orchestral forces and filled with Wagnerian conventions in harmony and instrumentation. Many of Mahler's symphonies are in five or six movements, requiring an hour to an hour and a half for performance. The oversized orchestra included many instruments not generally found in traditional symphonic works. The gigantic *Second Symphony*, the "Resurrection," requires (with the usual complement of strings) four flutes, four piccolos, four oboes, two

25

English horns, five clarinets, two E-flat clarinets, a bass clarinet, four bassoons and double-bassoons, six horns (four off-stage), six trumpets (four off-stage), four trombones, a tuba, two sets of timpani, a bass drum, one or more snare drums, cymbals, small and large tam-tams, a triangle, a glockenspiel, three bells, a *ruthe* (bundle of sticks), two harps, an organ,—and in addition to all this another timpani, bass drum, cymbals and triangle "to be sounded from a distance." This giant score also calls for a soprano, alto, and mixed chorus! In the *Eighth Symphony,* so many singers are required (eight solo voices, a double choir, and a boys' choir) that the work has been dubbed the "symphony of a thousand voices."

Mahler tried to make music convey ideas which belong more rightfully in the province of philosophy and metaphysics (just as Wagner had introduced social and political concepts in *The Ring of the Nibelungs*). Continually in his nine symphonies Mahler wrestled with the meaning of life and death, of the universe and nature, of eternal love and fate, of suffering, and resignation, and of resurrection. He used tones the way philosophers used thoughts, to speak of Faustian struggles after knowledge. In the mighty *Eighth Symphony* he probed into the profound philosophical implications of Goethe's *Faust* and tried to translate them into musical sound.

Mahler's symphonies are the last word in German or Wagnerian Romanticism. Beyond his symphonic structures, his huge orchestral forces, and his efforts to express the cosmic, the symphony could progress no further. After Mahler, many composers of orchestral music who wished to walk in Wagner's shoes had to seek out other forms, directions, and means.

Then there was a third Viennese composer—Hugo Wolf (1860–1903)—who was essentially a composer of songs and who is often identified as the "Wagner of the Lied."

His adulation of Wagner was second only to that of Bruckner. Wolf was still a conservatory student when he heard a Wagnerian drama for the first time, this initiation also taking place with *Tannhäuser* as it had with Bruckner. "I find no words for it," he exclaimed. "The music of this great master has taken me out of myself." Since Wagner was then in Vienna, at the Hotel Imperial, the fifteen-year-old Wolf spent hours outside the hotel hoping to catch a glimpse of the master. He not only saw Wagner but even spoke to him, an experience he never forgot. Never again did he meet the master face-to-face, but his associations with Wagner's music lasted until the end of Wolf's life, often taking place at Wagner's shrine in Bayreuth. When Wolf heard *Parsifal* he was so shaken that for hours after the performance he sat on a bench in the street dazed, his head buried in his hands, "completely removed from the world" as a friend revealed. In 1881, when Wolf came to Salzburg as an assistant conductor, he carried a bundle under each arm: under one arm was his clothing; under the other, a bust of Wagner. When he learned about Wagner's death in 1883, he "went to the piano and played the funeral music from *The Twilight of the Gods*," as one of his friends recalled. "Then he shut the piano and went—silently. . . . In the evening he reappeared, in a subdued and deeply sorrowful mood. 'I have wept like a child,' he told me."

As a composer of the art-song (Lied)—and one of the greatest since Schubert—Wolf followed many of Wagner's musical principles with complete dedication. He would never have been able to penetrate as he did into new realms of lyric and dramatic writing but for Wagner,

27

his idiom and style having been shaped by Wagner's. Wolf tried to fuse melody and word so that song might become almost something "spoken." The melody, at times with the character of declamation, was so closely married to the text that it invariably appeared as if poem and melody were the work of a single person. His melody required new kinds of modulations, new kinds of harmonic accompaniments, new intervallic relations and progressions so that he might better be able to seek out the essence of the poem he was setting. Only a poet steeped in the Wagnerian tradition—one who had completely comprehended the Wagnerian dream of making word and tone one—could have brought to these poems that newer melodic line in which we catch anticipations of later and more daring schools of music.

Bruckner, Mahler and Wolf were, for the most part, children of the nineteenth century. But in the twentieth century there were also many composers who were under the spell of Wagner. The most significant of these was Richard Strauss.

It is a crowning paradox that Strauss, the apostle of Wagnerism, should have been the son of a man who stood at the head of Wagner's enemies. Franz Strauss was one of Munich's most important horn players. He was a member of the orchestra for Wagner's music dramas when they were introduced in that city. He was also the central force in most of the conspiracies and intrigues that sprang up against Wagner, and he made no effort to hide from Wagner the contempt he felt for his music. At one rehearsal he rose from his seat and stalked angrily out of the pit shouting that he simply would not play such outlandish music. When the news of Wagner's death was announced to the orchestra men, Strauss stubbornly refused to stand in silent homage. Franz Strauss died in 1905, and until his last day he denounced Wagner and Wagnerism. But he lived to see his son become not only one of the world's foremost conductors of the Wagner music dramas but also a composer who walked proudly under Wagner's artistic banner.

Richard Strauss was born in Munich on June 11, 1864. Since his mother was the daughter of a prosperous brewer, the Strauss family was as wealthy as it was cultured, and the boy's remarkable flair for all things musical could be nursed and developed. Richard received a comprehensive training in both academic and musical studies, but it was in the latter that he proved most uncommonly gifted. Before he was seventeen, a string quartet, a symphony, and three songs of his were performed by leading organizations and performers in Munich.

His talent was brought to the attention of Hans von Buelow, one of Germany's leading pianists and conductors, and the director of the renowned Meiningen Orchestra. Von Buelow not only conducted some of Strauss's early orchestral works, but in 1884 hired him as an assistant conductor, initiating for Strauss a career with the baton that was to carry him triumphantly from Meiningen (where he soon succeeded Von Buelow as principal conductor), to Weimar, the Berlin Royal Opera, Vienna and New York. His success as conductor notwithstanding, he kept on producing ambitious musical compositions. A symphony was introduced in the United States in 1884, and one of his string quartets received first prize in an important competition in Berlin immediately thereafter.

In these early works Strauss was the German Romantic whose indebtedness to Brahms was as obvious as his own

29

technical skill and intensity of expression. Then he discovered Wagner, and with it the Northern Star by which to guide his own course. *Tristan und Isolde* and *Die Walküre* (*The Valkyries*) were a revelation. Henceforth he could speak in Brahms's language no longer, and it was Wagner he had to emulate.

His new values as composer were further clarified through conversations with the poet and philosopher, Alexander Ritter, a close friend. Ritter (who married Wagner's niece) held second place to no one in his veneration of Wagner, and he aroused in Strauss the ambition to adopt Wagner's aesthetics and ideals. Ritter convinced Strauss to abandon the kind of objective, absolute music he had thus far been producing within the formal structures of the symphony, string quartet, sonata and concerto; he also veered Strauss towards the creation of music filled with dramatic, programmatic, and poetic ideas. Ritter induced Strauss to seek out a form of orchestral music more flexible than the symphony; he was thinking specifically of the symphonic or tone poem which Franz Liszt had brought into being to carry over into orchestral writing some of Wagner's dramatic principles.

Strauss's first work in the new manner came immediately following a visit to Italy in 1886. *Aus Italien* (*From Italy*) was a symphonic poem based on realistic tone pictures of Italian life. When first performed in Munich in 1887, it was a fiasco. This was due mainly to the fact that Strauss's excursions into dissonance and new tonalities to heighten his expressive powers proved bewildering to a nineteenth-century audience. Strauss was one of the first composers to bring a new importance to discords, and *Aus Italien* was his first composition to do so. Dissonances, as we have already remarked, had been used by many composers before Strauss, but were always re-lieved through resolution with consonances. With Strauss, and later modernists, dissonances were self-sufficient. Even Hans von Buelow was taken aback by this kind of unorthodoxy. "Does my age make me so reactionary?" he inquired after hearing *Aus Italien*. "I find that the clever composer has gone to extreme limits of tonal pos-sibilities . . . and, in fact, has even gone beyond these limits without real necessity." Franz Strauss, Richard's father, shook his head sadly, heartbroken to witness how the poison of Wagner had infected his son.

But, despite such an unfavorable reception to his new style, Strauss had no intention of turning back. He would continue writing programmatic and realistic tone poems constructed from harmonic and instrumental designs first suggested by Wagner. As Strauss himself explained, *Aus Italien* was to be "the connecting link between the old and the new."

The "new" was sounded with a series of incomparable tone poems which made Strauss one of the most contro-versial, as well as one of the greatest, orchestral com-posers since Wagner's day. First came *Macbeth* in 1887. After that followed *Death and Transfiguration*, *Till Eu-lenspiegel's Merry Pranks*, *Thus Spake Zarathustra*, *Don Quixote*, and *A Hero's Life*. Here, it seemed, music had progressed as far as it could go in realistic writing, in cacophony, in the use of brash sonorities and flaming orchestral colors (often through unorthodox instruments recruited into the orchestra for special effects), in the exploitation of sensual harmonies, and in the fantasti-cally complex and adroit transformations and develop-ments of leading motives.

There was a good deal in these tone poems to outrage the musical and aesthetic sensibilities of Strauss's contemporaries: the piercing cacophonies in the battle scene of *A Hero's Life,* and those in *Till Eulenspiegel* describing the havoc wrought by this mischief-maker in a public market place; the realism in which the bleating of sheep and the howling of the wind is recreated in *Don Quixote;* the sensuality of Strauss's overrich orchestrations and harmonizations in *Don Juan;* the introduction of such unusual instruments as a wind machine in *Don Quixote;* the egocentricity with which Strauss identified himself as the hero in *A Hero's Life* by quoting some of his compositions in the "A Hero's Mission of Peace," and his identification of music critics as the hero's "adversaries."

The carping critics intensified their attacks on Strauss as, with each succeeding tone poem, they were shocked by the kind of music they heard. Louis Elson, an American, wrote: "If such modulations are possible, then the harmony books may well be burnt at once." Richard Aldrich, the critic of *The New York Times,* commented: "Strauss . . . deliberately affronted the ear with long continued din and discord . . . consciously used ugliness in music to represent conceptions of ugliness." Even highly distinguished musicians were upset. César Cui of the Russian nationalist school, had this to say: "His method is to overwhelm the listener at once. That is why he makes his violins scream, his flutes hiss, his trumpets blare, his cymbals crash. A free-for-all, everybody for himself, resulting in a terrible cacophony and noise in which one is lost. . . . This is not music, this is a mockery of music." And Debussy, himself no minor iconoclast, described one of Strauss's tone poems as "an hour in an insane asylum."

We no longer hear in these Strauss tone poems noise, ugliness, or bad taste. Instead we are consistently made conscious of Strauss's incomparable dramatic surge and

32

sweep, the grandeur of his elocution, the wizardry of his thematic development and orchestration, and his uncommon capacity to express non-musical ideas in tones.

Strauss's bent for realism, and his flair for sensuality and eroticism, were even more pronounced in his operas. If the tone poems upset the equilibrium of their audiences, then Strauss's operas scandalized them.

Strauss began his career as an opera composer innocently enough. His first opera was *Guntram,* in 1894. He was his own librettist; his play was based on an old German legend; his theme was redemption. On all these counts, the hand is that of Wagner. The music for the opera was also much like Wagner's. *Guntram* was a failure. So was Strauss's second opera, *Feuersnot,* in 1901, in which (as in *A Hero's Life*) Strauss once again unashamedly identifies himself with the hero and does not hesitate to indulge in some self-glorification.

Then Strauss turned to a text which could support his extraordinary gift for realism and sensuality. The text was *Salome,* a decadent and erotic poetical drama by Oscar Wilde based on the Bible story. Salome, daughter of Herodias, is in love with the prophet, John the Baptist. When he rejects her, her love turns to hatred, and she becomes determined to destroy him. She offers to dance for the king if, in return, he grants her one wish. Salome performs her celebrated "Dance of the Seven Veils," then reveals that her price is the head of John the Baptist, on a tray. When the head is brought to her, she indulges in such a revolting dance around it that the king orders her death.

Some of the methods, some of the harmonic and orchestral devices, and the use of a leading-motive technique all reveal Wagner's influence on Strauss. But in

33

many other respects, Strauss's writing is identifiably his own. At every point in the score he is able to match Wilde's sensual moods with sinuous melodies, orgies of orchestral and harmonic colors, abrupt and rapidly changing rhythms, and a striking literalness in translating stage action into musical sound. "The Dance of the Seven Veils" is no less provocative or tantalizing in music than it is visually on the stage. First the orchestra erupts with shrieks and primitive rhythms. Then comes the first dance, languorous and exotic, after that passionate and intense; the rhythms suggest the sinuous movements of Salome's body. The second dance is more sensual still. This is a slow and ecstatic melody for the strings. After that the savage mood of the opening phrases returns and is built into a shattering climax.

Both the play and music were so lurid that in the early part of the twentieth century *Salome* was regarded as a violation of existing moral codes. In Vienna and in London the censors refused to allow it to be performed. When *Salome* was first given in Dresden, in 1905, and later introduced in Berlin, it was denounced in no uncertain terms as "repulsive" and "perverted." The American première at the Metropolitan Opera on January 22, 1907, aroused an even greater tempest of public and critical protest. One physician wrote to *The New York Times:* "I say after deliberation that *Salome* is a detailed and explicit exposition of the most horrible, disgusting and unmentionable features of degeneracy that I have ever heard, read of, or imagined."

Two of New York's foremost critics had this to say:

"There is not a whiff of fresh and healthy air blowing through *Salome* except that which exhales from a cistern" (Henry E. Krehbiel).

"Richard Strauss' music is aesthetically criminal or at

34

least extremely coarse and ill-mannered. His music often suggests a man who comes to a social reception unkempt, with hands unwashed, cigar in mouth, hat on, and who sits down and puts his feet on the table. No boor ever violated all the laws of etiquette as Strauss violates all the laws of musical composition" (W. J. Henderson).

Clergy joined with the press in denouncing the Metropolitan Opera for having dared to mount such a sacrilegious work. The outburst of fury finally led the directors to remove the opera from the repertory after a single performance. Not until about a quarter of a century later did *Salome* return to the stage of the Metropolitan.

Strauss followed *Salome* with *Elektra*—an opera even more sordid in its realism, more sensual in mood, and more shocking in moral tone than its predecessor. Here the libretto was prepared by Hugo von Hofmannsthal (who became Strauss's favorite librettist) from the celebrated Greek tragedy of Sophocles. Queen Klytemnestra, in league with her lover, Aegisthus, murders the king, Agamemnon. Elektra, daughter of Agamemnon and Klytemnestra, vows vengeance. However, it is her brother, Orestes, who succeeds in killing their mother and her lover. Jubilant that her mother has at long last met the punishment due her, Elektra performs a corybantic on her father's grave, then sinks to her death.

The play which had decidedly psychoneurotic overtones, was grim with depravity. And so was Strauss's music. It rocked with a demoniac frenzy and quivered with emotional hysteria. More shattering than ever grow Strauss's cacophonies, more sensual and lush his harmonies, more hypertensioned his moods, more agonized the cries that stood for arias. This music, said one critic, was "an orchestral riot that suggests a murder scene in a

Chinese theater"; another said of its melodies that they "spit and scratch and claw at each other like enraged panthers."

Moral codes, as well as our conception of what constitutes beauty in music, change with passing generations. Today the horror and shock of *Salome* and *Elektra* are gone. When, for example, *Salome* finally came back to the Metropolitan, in 1934, it met a far different reception than the one accorded it a quarter of a century earlier. Olin Downes said in his review of *Salome* which appeared in *The New York Times* that "the opera as an opera, aside from its sensational reputation . . . fascinated and impressed the audience. Its effect no longer lies in its novelty, but in something quite else, namely, its convincing intensity and inspiration."

Both *Salome* and *Elektra* now are frequently given by leading opera houses everywhere, and there are not many who doubt that they represent twin peaks in twentieth-century opera. As we listen to these operas today we are overwhelmed by their dramatic force, by the many pages of compelling theater, by passage after passage of soaring eloquence, and by the extraordinary fusion of text and music. *Salome* and *Elektra* are ever emotional experiences that leave audiences exhausted after the final curtains.

Strauss had travelled as far as humanly possible in realism and sensuality. The opera that followed *Elektra* was strikingly different. *Der Rosenkavalier,* introduced in Dresden in 1911, was a comic opera somewhat in the style of Mozart and Johann Strauss, II. It is sentimental and tender on the one hand, light of heart and satirical on the other. The setting is the Vienna of Empress Maria Theresa. The central characters are Princess von Werd-

36

enberg, a woman of stately character, and her cousin, Baron Ochs, a fat, lecherous fellow around whom most of the opera's comedy revolves. The Princess is in love with Octavian, a boy many years her junior. The Baron is courting Sophie, the daughter of Faninal, a wealthy man. Tradition dictates that a silver rose be dispatched to a prospective bride. At the suggestion of the Princess, Ochs enlists the services of Octavian to perform this mission. Octavian and Sophie meet and fall in love, and receive the blessings of the magnanimous and sympathetic Princess. The Baron, meanwhile, is made the helpless victim of a comical prank in a disreputable hotel where he thinks he is having a rendezvous with a fetching wench.

From the ultra-realism of *Elektra* we here pass on to a musical idiom and manner that is poignant, wistful, gay, ardently lyrical, and intensely human and compassionate. The heart of the score is a series of waltzes— often played at symphony concerts in a special adaptation written by the composer. These are in the style of Johann Strauss, II, though, to be sure, with a more modern harmonic and melodic vocabulary, and a richer and more varied orchestral palette. But there are other unforgettable musical pages as well: the extended monologue of the Princess where she contemplates her lost youth and fading beauty (one of the most poignant scenes in all contemporary opera); the incomparable trio in which the Princess stands ready to give up Octavian and permit him to pursue his love for Sophie; and the ecstatic love duet of Sophie and Octavian that follows.

With *Der Rosenkavalier* Strauss began his retreat from modernism. After all, by 1911, there were many composers in the public eye whose unconventional and daring writing was beginning to make even Strauss sound old-hat! Henceforth, Strauss would be increasingly romantic, and sometimes he would even venture into the classical world of Couperin and Lully. Toward the end of his life, his evolution as a composer came full circle with concertos and orchestral pieces in which he reverted to the neo-Romanticism of Brahms. In his last composition, the *Four Last Songs,* he returned for the most part to the Wagnerian fold.

If he was no longer an innovator, he was still a genius commanding respect for his technical virtuosity, freshness of musical thought, and over-all charm. Strauss was the dean of twentieth-century music and a creative figure who had lived to see himself honored by the entire world. In America, where he appeared as a guest conductor, directing his own works, audiences sprang to their feet in homage to a master as soon as he appeared on the stage. In Vienna, the government presented him with a tract of land near the Belvedere Palace so that he might build there a permanent home for himself. In Germany he was the *Meister* who had no rival for public adulation. At Garmisch-Partenkirchen in the Bavarian Alps near Munich, where he maintained permanent residence, pilgrims came to pay him tribute.

During the turbulent era in Germany just before World War II when the Nazis first came to power, his many admirers lost their veneration—for the man rather than the artist. At first Strauss allied himself completely with the aims and principles of the Third Reich and assumed the post of President of the Music Chamber. But the excesses of the Nazis—of which Strauss himself eventually became a victim when he was soundly taken to task for having dared to collaborate with Stefan Zweig, a Jew—disillusioned him completely. He was removed from all official positions and allowed to withdraw into retirement in Garmisch-Partenkirchen where for a while (because of his opposition to the war) he was under house arrest. After the war, a denazification court of the American occupation forces exonerated him completely of being a Nazi. On his eightieth birthday, the entire world of music paid him homage, Germany included. He died a few months after that at his home in Garmisch-Partenkirchen on September 8, 1949.

II

Strauss's realism was just one of several roads leading from Wagner to twentieth-century music. Another road was mysticism, its high priest being Alexander Scriabin. Scriabin was Russia's first important composer of piano music—the "Russian Chopin" as he is sometimes called. Truly Chopinesque are his early sonatas, preludes, and etudes—in elegance of form, poetic expression and exquisite lyricism. But it was not long before Scriabin became hypnotized by the wizard Wagner. Under this influence Scriabin aspired to write large orchestral compositions with Wagner-like harmonies and instrumentation. To heighten the expressiveness of his musical vocabulary, Scriabin devised a new type of chord to which he gave the label, "Mystery Chord." It was constructed from fourths rather than thirds (C, F-sharp, B-flat, E, A, D). He went on to conceive a vast artistic edifice which he called the "Mystery." The inspiration for this edifice was Wagner's *Parsifal*, but Scriabin's "Mystery" was more grandiose and visionary than anything Wagner had contemplated. In essence it was not only a synthesis of every possible art, but also a world philosophy, new social thinking, and a new religion. Here was the first attempt in music to tap theosophical ideas and draw from the occult sciences. As one critic said, Scriabin's art now was "but a means of achieving a higher form of life"; or as Scriabin himself once explained, "art must unite with philosophy and religion in an indivisible whole to form a new Gospel which will replace the old Gospel which we have outlived."

Born in Moscow, on January 6, 1872, Scriabin was a highly sensitive, and in some respects an eccentric, child. His feelings expressed themselves in extravagant responses. When he first fell in love with the piano he would kiss it continually as if it were a human being; whenever his piano had to be tuned, repaired, or moved he suffered the physical torment of one seeing his beloved operated upon by a surgeon. Later on, when Chopin became his first musical god, Scriabin not only played that master's music continually and talked about it indefatigably, but even assumed some of Chopin's personal mannerisms. He never went to sleep before making sure that a volume of Chopin's music was under his pillow.

Financial difficulties and the death of Alexander's stepmother, broke up the Scriabin household. Young Alexander went to live with his grandmother, who shared an apartment with one of the boy's aunts. The two women doted on Alexander, pampered, spoiled, and overprotected him. They did not allow him to play with other children or to go into the street unaccompanied; and they worried to death every time he became physically indisposed. They succeeded in making him a self-centered, introspective and socially uncommunicative lad who developed a neurotic fear of the outside world. Scriabin's lifelong hypochondria made him wear gloves as protection from germs and use all kinds of quack medicines.

His first musical impressions came from an opera performance when he was just five years old. Forthwith he began to build a little theater of his own for the performance of operas in which he sang all the roles. After that he lived almost entirely for music, especially for the piano, and spent hour after hour absorbed in improvisation. Though he hated systematic study, preferring to express himself in music without impediments of any kind, he did manage to get a competent preliminary training at the piano from Conius and Zverev. He studied harmony with Taneiev, and later on attended the Moscow Conservatory.

Like Robert Schumann before him, Scriabin soon became fired with the ambition of becoming one of the world's great pianists. And, once again like Schumann, he tried all kinds of artificial exercises to develop digital dexterity to the point of suffering paralysis of the muscles. But he refused to give up, keeping on with his finger and muscle exercises until a certain amount of flexibility was restored. He won a gold medal for piano playing at the Conservatory, and in 1894 he gave a successful piano recital in St. Petersburg.

That concert made a forceful impression on Belaiev, one of Russia's most powerful music publishers. Belaiev now stood ready not merely to manage Scriabin's future concerts, but also to publish his compositions. A concert tour in 1896 brought Scriabin impressive successes in many of Europe's leading capitals. At the same time, the first of Scriabin's works published by Belaiev were enthusiastically received by some of Russia's leading musicians.

After Belaiev's death, Scriabin found another potent and generous patron to promote him and his music—the world-famous conductor, Serge Koussevitzky. Koussevitzky was founder and director of a publishing house which now issued most of Scriabin's major compositions. And, as conductor, Koussevitzky proved indefatigable in introducing and presenting Scriabin's orchestral compositions. When Scriabin finally became obsessed with the mission to create his "Mystery," Koussevitzky endowed him with a generous income to enable him to carry on his work without financial worries.

From the smaller piano pieces which Belaiev had published, Scriabin progressed to the larger forms: a piano concerto in 1897; his *First Symphony* in or about 1900. The finale of that symphony provided the first important clue to the growing dimension of Scriabin's thinking. It was a large choral movement intended as a mighty religious paean to art. Thus Scriabin was not only beginning to move within imposing structures, but also (like Mahler before him) to use those superstructures for the projection of ideas pregnant with philosophy and mysticism.

He was first drawn to philosophic thought by attending meetings of the Philosophic Society in Moscow just before 1900. Two years after that he read Nietzsche and began to identify himself with Nietzsche's Superman. At that time he planned but never realized an opera about a Superman like Wagner's Siegfried, a hero who would conquer through the powers of his art. From philosophy Scriabin progressed to theosophy and occultism. The deeper he penetrated into these fields the more strongly did he feel impelled to find some way to interpret these abstruse ideas and concepts in music.

In his *Third Symphony,* entitled "The Divine Poem," which was completed in 1903, he tried to trace the evolution of the human spirit through pantheism to the final affirmation of the divine ego. In the first movement the conflict between man's slavish subservience to a personal god and his eternal quest for freedom is depicted; in the second, man surrenders helplessly to physical pleasures; and in the third, the spirit frees itself from its constricting bonds and soars to the joy of free activity (or, as the composer put it, to the joy of "divine play").

Scriabin's most famous work for orchestra is the *Fourth Symphony*, "The Poem of Ecstasy," written in 1907. Its subject is the joy of creative activity, the ecstasy that comes from unrestricted action. Five principal melodic themes are enlisted to symbolize, in turn, yearning, protest, apprehension, will, and self-assertion.

The destiny of all mankind, the struggle of man against the world around him and his ultimate victory through the assertion of his creative will is the message of Scriabin's *Fifth Symphony*, "Prometheus." Man is represented musically by the piano; the Cosmos, by a giant orchestra. Seeking new areas for heightening and expanding his creative expressiveness, Scriabin here made an experiment to marry colors to sounds. He invented a color keyboard which projected a succession of hues on a screen while the music was being played. When "Prometheus" was performed for the first time the way its composer conceived it, the procession of colors proved so distracting that the music came off only a sorry second best. Since then the practice has been to perform the symphony without the benefit of accompanying colors.

Scriabin planned "Prometheus" as a kind of preliminary study for the gigantic artistic and theosophic vision that had by now been absorbing his thoughts for several years. "The Divine Poem," "The Poem of Ecstasy," and "Prometheus" had only scratched the surface of those monumental concepts Scriabin hoped to project through his music. What Scriabin aspired for was the summation in music of the history of man from the dawn of time to the final cataclysm which Scriabin considered inevitable. The perfect Wagnerite, Scriabin hoped to use music, poetry, drama, scenery and costumes in a single artistic creation; but he also sought to combine with these elements the dance, perfumes, and colors. He concocted for his text a new kind of language made up of sighs and exclamations, expressing feelings which heretofore had never found an appropriate vocabulary. As he dreamed of this Gargantuan vision, he grew increasingly ambitious. He wanted his "Mystery" (for this is the name he gave his project) to be performed in India in a specially constructed globular temple at the side of a lake. He would have only those in attendance who were true believers of his cult.

For ten years he dreamed, planned, talked, sketched. At the same time he acquired from a travel agency whatever information was available about India. During this time he also gathered some of the paraphernalia (including a sun helmet) necessary for living in India. But all that he managed to get down on paper was his text, and some musical sketches for a preamble entitled "Propylaea." "Propylaea," the entrance to the Acropolis in Athens, was Scriabin's symbol for the beginning to all arts and religion. He was confident he would live to complete his "Mystery," just as he was unshakable in his conviction that once he wrote this "Mystery" and had it performed, the end of the world would follow.

He never realized this vast dream. A small carbuncle on his upper lip developed into gangrene of the face. He died from this infection in Moscow on April 27, 1915. The "Mystery" died with him. Not so the wonderful library of music he had created for the piano early in his career; nor his three last symphonies, all of which are among the richest fruits of post-Wagnerian Romanticism.

44

CHAPTER 2

The Eccentrics

RICHARD Strauss's realism and orgiastic orchestral colors, Mahler's superstructures and inflated orchestral forces, and Scriabin's new gospel had carried post-Wagnerian Romanticism to an extreme. The time was ripe for the pendulum of music history to swing back sharply. Several composers, repelled by the emotional and structural extravagances of their contemporaries, simply had to produce a different kind of music that was simple and unpretentious. A music which refused to take itself seriously and was filled with mockery, levity, irony, and wit.

Such a revolution against Wagner and his successors took place in twentieth-century France with one of music's greatest humorists and eccentrics—Erik Satie. Satie represented a complete rupture with the stuffy Romanticism that had preceded him. "He had," as Virgil Thomson once said, "the firmest conviction that the only healthy thing music can do in our century is to stop being impressive."

It is not difficult to understand why so many of Satie's contemporaries were bewildered by him and his music, and were altogether incapable of recognizing their genuine significance. These contemporaries were inclined to regard Satie as a charlatan, a poseur, a buffoon. Here was a supposedly serious musician who was earning his living playing pop tunes and ballads in Montmartre cabarets; who was not beyond writing music-hall songs for popular entertainers, nor for that matter introducing popular styles in his supposedly serious creations. And, as if this were not enough to damn him, here was a creative artist who insisted upon making a mockery of artistic dignity, a shambles of high artistic purpose.

Satie often gave outlandish titles to his serious pieces of music: "Desiccated Embryos," "The Dreamy Fish," "Flabby Preludes for a Dog," "Disagreeable Sketches," "Sketches to Make You Run Away," "Cold Pieces," "Three Pieces in the Shape of a Pear." Within these compositions Satie liked to interpolate the most whimsical instructions to the performer. At one point in a piece he urged the pianist to put his hands in his pockets. One of his phrases, he explained, was to be played "dry as a cuckoo, light as an egg"; one section, he said, must sound "like a nightingale with a toothache." On one occasion he quoted Chopin's "Funeral March" from the *Piano Sonata,* but in doing so he also indicated in his music that this passage was taken from "a famous Schubert Mazurka." Occasionally, Satie would append the most ridiculous programs to explain his musical intentions. "This is the case of the lobster; the hunters descend to the bottom of the water; they run. The sound of a horn is heard at the bottom of the sea. The lobster is tracked. The lobster weeps." Or he would include strange "asides" to his audiences: "Those who do not understand [the music] are asked to be respectfully silent and to show an attitude of complete submission and inferiority."

He was, in short, a musical pixy, a boy who refused to grow old. Carl van Vechten once called him a "shy and genial fantaisite, part-child, part-devil, part faun." But, though few in France knew it at the time, he was also a powerful force in music despite his strange attitudes and peculiar mannerisms and behavior. He was a pioneer in his unorthodox harmonic writing; in his use of meters and rhythms; in his experiments with barless notation. He was, indeed, the first of France's twentieth-century modernists. But most important of all, he was the one, above all others, who led music away from the post-Wagnerian Romanticism. Satie was human, down-to-earth, and witty where other musicians were pretentious and grandiose; he was fresh and simple where they were affected and complicated. *They* liked to regard themselves as high priests of art, and kept up the legendary concept of the long-haired composer creating masterworks in a cold garret. Satie was what W. S. Gilbert would call "a commonplace" and a "matter-of-fact" young man; the Romanticists were "intense" and "soulful-eyed" young men, "ultra-poetical, super-aesthetical, out-of-the-way" young men. Satie enjoyed popular music and the night spots of Montmartre. The kind of music he liked to write was of the everyday variety. The Romanticists prized grandeur, bigness, majesty, eloquence, and formidable messages of all types. Satie, on the other hand, sought, as Thomson wrote, "quietude, precision, acuteness of auditory observation, gentleness, sincerity, and directness of statement." Many of the later French composers who were either his contemporaries or successors were able to write the kind of music they did, and to adopt their kind of musical principles, only because of Satie. With Satie came an invigorating breath of fresh air, and a revitalizing burst of warm sunlight into the dank and stuffy living room of the post-Wagnerian epoch. Satie represented youth and rejuvenation for modern music, where ultimately post-Wagnerism could lead only to decadence.

Satie was born on March 17, 1866, in the town of Honfleur in the Calvados region of France. The town organ-

47

ist gave him his first music lessons and instilled in him a passion for the polyphonic art of the past. When Satie was thirteen, he entered the Paris Conservatory where his bent for medieval plainchant, modal music, and also polyphony was in marked contrast to the passion other students had for Romanticism and Wagner. During his conservatory days Satie wrote somewhat esoteric and dissonant pieces of music. His teachers did not regard him highly, and he returned the compliment. After about a year Satie called it quits, brushed the dust of academicism off his shoes, and went on to shift for himself in music as best he could.

Immediately he started to write the most unusual and bizarre piano pieces, as strange in their sound as in their subject matter. First came *Ogives* in 1886; then, in 1887-8, the three *Sarabandes;* after that, *Gymnopédies* in 1888, and *Gnossiennes* in 1890. In *Sarabande* his daring use of the chords of the ninth in anticipation of Debussy proved electrifying. In *Gymnopédies* Satie dared to write music that was simple and forthright. "Gymnopedia" was an ancient Spartan festival in which naked youths celebrated their gods through song and dance. The three dances in *Gymnopédies* were clear, unemotional, economical, pure in melodic line, and transparent in harmonic texture. Yet they were also filled with the most unusual progressions and harmonic combinations. In *Gnossiennes,* Satie made his first experiments with barless notation, and with continually repeated melodic phrases against a persistent, fundamental bass.

Satie earned his living playing the piano at *Le Chat Noir* in Montmartre. During this period he interested himself temporarily in occultism and mysticism by joining The Society of Rosicrucians, a religious sect made up of reformers. Satie became its official composer, in which

48

capacity he wrote incidental music for two obscure plays by the Society's high priest, Joseph Péladan. Satie did not remain long with the Society. It soon tried controlling and directing his musical thinking and style—and this Satie would not tolerate.

His temporary alliance with religion and mysticism notwithstanding, Satie continued writing outrageous piano compositions with exotic and whimsical titles using ever bolder techniques. When, in 1903, Debussy happened to mention to Satie that Satie's piano pieces were without form, Satie countered by writing "Three Pieces in the Shape of a Pear"—tangible proof that his music *did* have a form of sorts. Satie's titles grew more and more quixotic as did his directions to performers and program annotations.

His personality was as eccentric as his music. In 1898 he went to live in a second-floor room in the Arceuil district of Paris where he remained for the rest of his life. No human being was permitted access to these quarters, in which Satie lived in monastic seclusion. Yet, in other respects, he was no ascetic. When he inherited a legacy he quickly spent all the money on a dozen velvet suits, one hundred stiff collars, and a closetful of shirts—and then lived for months in semi-starvation on the meager salary he drew as cabaret pianist.

But to most of the Parisians who knew him, the most eccentric thing about him was the fact that he went back to formal music study just before his fortieth birthday. Dissatisfied with his technique, and determined to master theory and counterpoint, he enrolled in the Schola Cantorum. For three years he diligently attended the classes of Vincent d'Indy and Albert Roussel with students many years his junior.

This intensive period of study enabled Satie to under-

49

take creative assignments more ambitious than heretofore. He now produced important works in the large forms: a satirical ballet, *Parade,* in 1917; a lyric drama, *Socrate,* in 1918; the opera *Le Piège de Méduse,* in 1920. To the end of his days he remained a humorist, a pixy, an eccentric, and above all else, an innovator. In *Le Piège de Méduse* he had a stuffed monkey perform a dance between the scenes. In *Parade* he became one of the first foreign composers to make use of American jazz. No less daring was his scoring which required the services of a typewriter, dynamos, fire sirens, a discharged revolver, the sound of waves simulated by tubs of water, and airplane motors as well as the conventional instruments of the orchestra. *Parade* created a scandal when first performed. One Parisian critic denounced Satie as an impostor and a fraud; Satie replied with an insulting letter. The critic dragged Satie to court for defamation of character. Found guilty, Satie was sentenced to eight days in jail (a sentence, however, that was suspended).

He also remained the rebel against excesses of all types —even excesses for which he had been responsible. He, who had previously poked fun at and mocked the abuses of post-Romanticism and Wagnerism, lived long enough to do a similar service to the preciousness and oversensibilities of Impressionism, the levity of the "French Six," and the stark bareness and austerity of the "Arceuilists"— though he himself had virtually been the godfather of these respective "schools" of contemporary music.

Erik Satie died in Paris on July 1, 1925. Olin Downes, the music critic of *The New York Times,* met Satie in the composer's last years and described him as "an amusing old man, a dilettante of the future, who wore a blue, shiny suit, a gleaming eyeglass, and misleading whiskerage, and ate his food in a mincing and derisive manner."

An "amusing old man," perhaps, but an artist whose impact upon the music of his time was cataclysmic. "The performance of *Parade*," said Darius Milhaud, "will stand in the history of French music as a date equally important with that of the first performance of *Pelleas and Melisande*." Milhaud might have added that Satie's first eccentric pieces for the piano were the cradle of modern French music.

II

America also had an individualist and eccentric, a contemporary of Satie—though each was completely oblivious of the other. Working in obscurity and seclusion, producing composition after composition which remained unheard for many years, completely uninterested in what other composers were writing in other lands, this American also made a permanent break with the Romantic past and served as a bridge into the future. Like Satie, he combined humor, whimsy and personal idiosyncrasies with the most advanced and iconoclastic musical idioms. But even more so than Satie, he anticipated some of the revolutionary methods which other, and later composers, made famous. He used polyrhythms before Stravinsky, atonality before Bartók and Schoenberg, polytonality before Stravinsky and Milhaud, quarter-tones before Alois Hába, and tone clusters before Leo Ornstein and Henry Cowell. And long before Aaron Copland and Roy Harris established an authentically American identity in music, he was able to create *American* music.

The name of this remarkable composer is Charles Ives, born in Danbury, Connecticut, on October 20, 1874. His father was a musician who gave him his first lessons in harmony, counterpoint, instrumentation, and music appreciation. After receiving a Bachelor of Arts degree at

51

Yale, Ives served as organist and choirmaster of the Danbury Congregational Church in 1887, and of the Central Presbyterian Church in New York in 1900.

In 1900 he became a clerk for the Mutual Life Insurance Company. Six years after that he formed an insurance agency of his own (Ives and Company, agents for Washington Life Insurance Company) which became one of the largest of its kind in the country. Thus Ives achieved great success as a businessman; and he remained a businessman for thirty years. Certainly there was nothing of the eccentric or the recluse about him as day by day he attended to his affairs and sought out new accounts. It would have come as a shock to his business associates if they had discovered that this efficient, practical and calculating insurance salesman was, in his alter ego, a serious composer.

For almost half a century, Ives regarded his creative process as an intimate function in which nobody but himself could be interested. He did not want to make money from his music. He did not court fame or seek applause. He had no intention ever of giving up business to become a full-time composer. When he finally did retire in 1930, it was only because of his failing eyesight and weak heart. He long felt that it was creatively and morally healthier for a serious artist if his art were just one phase of his life, instead of the be-all and end-all of his existence. He insisted that a composer could draw wisdom and strength from business. "My business experience revealed life to me in many aspects that I might otherwise have missed," he once confided to a friend. "I have experienced a great fullness of life in business. The fabric of existence weaves itself whole. You cannot set an art off in the corner and hope for it to have vitality, reality, and substance. There can be nothing exclusive about a substantial art. It comes directly out of the heart of experience of life, and thinking about life, and living life. My work in music helped my business and my work in business helped my music."

His music was the result of an irresistible inner compulsion. And what a driving force that was! His wife once revealed that when Ives's business hours were over, he would rush to his piano to work on his compositions, sometimes forgetting dinner. He kept at his music seven evenings a week, during all the four seasons, at times until the early hours of morning. He never went anywhere, or did anything else, during those hours. His manuscripts kept accumulating. It never seemed to bother him that what he was putting down on paper was a dark secret, known only to his wife and a few close friends.

Incapable of opportunism and innocent of expediency, Ives never tried to get his works performed. Surely, never before or since was a composer so completely indifferent to an audience. It may have been that he knew that his writing was much too unorthodox for public consumption. It may have been that his extraordinary reticence, where his creative life was concerned, made him guard his isolation jealously rather than allow public attention to shatter it. And so, though all of Ives's important works were completed by 1920, and most of them before 1910, not one of his significant compositions was performed publicly until about 1930. His masterwork, the *Third Symphony*, completed forty years earlier, received its world première on May 5, 1947; his *Second Symphony*, written between 1897 and 1902, was heard for the first time on February 22, 1951. Before World War II, about all that was known of Ives's production was the *Concord Sonata* for piano, which John Kirkpatrick introduced in New York on January 20, 1939; and the *Three Places in New England,* for orchestra, first performed on January 10, 1931, Nicolas Slonimsky conducting. Yet when first heard, each of these works made a profound impression. When Lawrence Gilman reviewed the *Concord Sonata* in 1939, he described it as "the greatest music composed by an American, and the most deeply and essentially American in impulse and implication."

Then suddenly and unexpectedly—at the dusk of his life—Ives achieved full recognition. He was given the Pulitzer Prize in music for his *Third Symphony* and a special citation from the New York Music Critics Circle; and he was elected a member of the National Institute of Arts and Sciences. Performances of his neglected works now grew numerous; the critics and magazine writers began discussing his personality and his music; photographers began to beat a path to his door. In success Ives, aged seventy-five, remained the same man he had so long been—sublimely indifferent to acclaim and applause. He refused to talk to interviewers, to pose for photographs, even to attend performances of his works. He permitted only a handful of his most intimate friends and relatives to shatter the privacy he had built up on his farm in Connecticut. The battered hat, rough shirt, mended sweater and faded dungarees which for years had been his uniform, still reflected the asceticism of a man who had either disciplined himself to reject the so-called good things of life, or who had never been tempted by them. Thus, at the climax of his strange career, Ives remained completely in character. And he stayed in character until he died in New York City, on May 19, 1954, at the age of eighty.

54

The need to work in seclusion, away from the glare of public recognition, and freed from all possible associations with a listening or writing public, was not just the idiosyncrasy of a strange man. It was an artistic necessity. Only a man who wrote for himself could rid himself as completely of inhibitions as Ives did. In the bassoon part of one of his orchestral scores, Ives added the Satie-like instruction that "from here on, the bassoon may play anything at all." In his *Violin Sonata* there emerges, inexplicably and suddenly, a theme for a trumpet solo! In a song for voice and piano there mysteriously arises a brief line for violin obbligato. These are essentially the excursions of an artist who desired complete freedom of movement.

Similar examples of absurdity and whimsy overflow in his various works. In the *Second String Quartet,* Ives affectionately nicknames his second violin "Rollo." At one point, where there is an extended rest for the second violin, the following note is appended: "Too hard to play—so it just can't be good music, Rollo." As a footnote to one of his songs, Ives wrote: "This song is inserted . . . to clean up a long-disputed point, namely, which is worse, the music or the words." In "Essays Before a Sonata," published as a programmatic analysis of his *Concord Sonata,* Ives explained: "These prefatory essays were written by the composer for those who can't stand his music—and the music for those who can't stand the essays. To those who can't stand either, the whole is respectfully dedicated." In the preface to *114 Songs,* Ives wrote: "Some of the songs in this book cannot be sung. . . . An excuse for their existence . . . is that a song has a few rights, same as other ordinary citizens. . . . If it happens to feel like trying to fly where humans cannot fly—to sing what cannot be sung—to walk in a cave on all fours—or to tighten up its girth in the blind hope and faith and try to scale mountains that are not—who shall stop it?"

In all his music Ives tried to fly where no composer had flown before. Since he was writing for neither audience nor critic, nor for money or personal glory, but exclusively for his own artistic satisfaction, he did not hesitate to give his creative impulses full freedom of expression. And so, in his obscurity and solitude, Ives went his lonely way in his music. "I found," he said, "I could not go on using the familiar chords, and so I found something else."

Ives's iconoclasm was the heritage of a remarkable father. George E. Ives, a bandmaster during the Civil War, also tried to find new horizons for music. He was always experimenting either with acoustics or a system of quarter tones. An authenticated story related how he made his son, Charles, sing "Swanee River" in one key while he himself played the accompaniment in another, to train the boy to new sound relations. "You see, my son," he explained, "you've got to learn to *stretch* your ears." Many years later, Charles Ives re-echoed his father's sentiments when, hearing some severe criticism about the dissonances used by an American composer, he shouted: "Don't be a goddamn sissy! This is strong music! Try to use your ears like a man."

Despite the formal training he had received at Yale from Horatio W. Parker, Charles Ives yielded to an irrepressible urge to uncover new sounds when he started writing music. In one of his earliest works, "Song for the Harvest Season," written when he was twenty, we find startling polytonal combinations (a decade before *The Rite of Spring!*). This song is set for voice, cornet, trombone and organ; the music for each of these is written in a different key. A string quartet and his *First Symphony*, in 1896, abandoned the traditional concepts of harmony and rhythm. His courage and individuality grew by leaps and bounds as he kept on writing. In his songs, completed during the first years of the twentieth century but published in 1920 as *114 Songs*, he opened vistas undreamed of at the time by anybody else. In "Majority" tone clusters appear, as the composer instructs the piano accompanist to use fists and a ruler in hammering outlandish chords; one of these chords encompasses fourteen white keys, another ten black keys. "The Cage" is completely atonal, and the rhythmic design is so free that no two consecutive bars have the same time values. Dissonant chords prevail in "The Children's Hour," still more polytonal combinations of voices are heard in "Rough Wind." In three war songs and five street songs, Ives made a conscious effort to use popular American materials with serious intent. Thus many of the later provocative tendencies of twentieth-century music are forcefully foreshadowed.

The *Third Symphony* was written between 1901 and 1904. Inspired by camp meetings once prevalent in Danbury, Connecticut, the symphony derived many of its melodies from actual hymn tunes. Structurally, the work is unusual in that it presents slow movements for the first and third parts, and unusual chord progressions and cross-rhythms throughout. It is most significant in its strong, direct, and authentic American accents.

Ives began writing *Three Places in New England* the year he completed the *Third Symphony*, but he did not finish it until 1914. Whereas New England hymns had been the stimulus for the *Third Symphony*, in *Three Places* it is New England geography that stirs the composer's imagination. Of technical interest is the remarkable use of polyrhythm in the part describing the approach to town of two village bands, each playing a different melody in a different tempo. Of aesthetic appeal is the subtle impressionistic tone painting of the "Housatonic at Stockbridge" with which the trilogy ends.

In the now-famous (though once notorious) *Concord Sonata* (1909–15), Ives drew the essence of his musical thought from the school of Concord writers. The four movements are respectively entitled "Emerson," "Hawthorne," "The Alcotts" and "Thoreau." Each re-creates, using the most advanced and experimental devices, the composer's impressions of the celebrated author. The essence of Emerson's transcendental philosophy is captured in the mystery and revelation of the first movement. Hawthorne's "fantastical adventures into the half-child-like, half-fairylike phantasmal realms" (Ives's own words) are reflected in the demoniac music of the second movement. A more idyllic mood is created by the music about the Alcotts and Thoreau.

The *Concord Sonata* is not only free in its self-expression but inventive in its unusual technical procedures. In the "Hawthorne" section, a ruler, or a strip of wood is used by the pianist to play an expansive two-octave cluster. In the "Alcott" music, the first four notes of Beethoven's *Fifth Symphony* are quoted (the Alcott children used to play Beethoven's music indefatigably). In the "Thoreau" part Ives suggests "a flute may play throughout the page" because Thoreau "much prefers to hear the flute over Walden."

Ives's *Fourth Symphony* is made up of music which the composer had used in other non-symphonic compositions, together with a new last movement consisting of a jumble of ideas, various materials, and completed sections found in desk drawers and notebooks. It took musicologists two years to make order out of chaos. When they were through, the world was the richer for a remarkable American symphony which was finally heard in 1965. In the first movement Ives seeks out the "what" and "why" which the spirit of man continually asks. It ends with a choral setting of the hymn, "Watchman, Tell Us of the Night." The second movement is loosely derived from the "Hawthorne" movement of the *Concord Sonata*, while the third movement (a double fugue) is adapted from a movement from the *First String Quartet*. The finale represents the victory of the human spirit which has met and conquered all challenges.

If Ives was an ultramodern long before ultramoderns came into their own, he was also an indigenous American composer at a time when most Americans were copying Wagner, Brahms, Strauss, and Debussy. Ives, with a sublime disregard for what was taking place across the ocean, was creating music whose spirit and breath reflected American experiences and backgrounds. Almost anything American seemed to serve his musical fancy: American culture of the New England writers; American customs as realized in revival meetings, camp meetings, town meetings, or barn dances; American scenes like those in picturesque New England; American history; American holidays; American politics; and American songs.

With his ungovernable spirit, Ives was led to create a music which, in its severity, independent movement, and brusque originality, could have arisen only in America. For, as Lawrence Gilman once remarked, Ives's music "is as indubitably American in impulse as Jonathan Edwards; and, like the writing of that true spirit and mystic,

59

it has at times an irresistible veracity and strength and uncorrupted sincerity."

One of his favorite ways to achieve a national profile for his music was to borrow thematic material from American popular songs and national ballads. He started this practice with his *Symphony No. 2*, where can be heard snatches of "Columbia, the Gem of the Ocean" (a tune to which Ives was particularly partial and which he used in later compositions), Stephen Foster's "Old Black Joe" and "De Camptown Races," and some barn-dance melodies. In later works he interpolated other Foster songs, as well as such popular songs and ballads as "Battle Hymn of the Republic," "Turkey in the Straw," "Yankee Doodle," and "Marching Through Georgia." But he consciously distorted these melodies to suit his own artistic aims; sometimes he would set one, two or more of these tunes discordantly over one another. The themes fly off in all directions as if an explosion had taken place. Frequently the melodies cannot be recognized. But what emerges is not just a hodge-podge of sounds but, as in the remarkable finale of the *Fourth Symphony*, an expression thoroughly American—"a real work," in Leonard Bernstein's words, "original, eccentric, naive, and as full of charm as a New England village green."

It is this intrinsic Americanism that gives Ives's music its significance, and assures its permanence in our cultural heritage. That Ives was one of the first to use various modern techniques identified with other and later composers is, after all, a historical curiosity to fascinate the student of musical history. But the real importance of Ives's music does not lie with this curiosity. Ives did much more than create new techniques. He created an American art. And, for this reason alone, he deserves a place with the foremost composers of the twentieth century.

CHAPTER 3

The Impressionists

AMONG those who visited *Le Chat Noir* regularly, and enjoyed listening to Erik Satie play music-hall tunes, was an intense black-eyed young man who looked like a Syrian—a man with a swarthy pallor, an aquiline nose, jet-black hair, a lethargic manner, and a soft voice. He was Claude Debussy, then still a young and unrecognized composer searching eagerly for an artistic identity. He had recently returned from Rome where he had spent several years as a recipient of the Prix de Rome.

It was not long before Debussy and Satie became friends. Debussy liked Satie's pixyish ways, both in and out of music, and was amused by his eccentricities. But what impressed Debussy most of all about Satie was the way in which he was liberating music from the tyranny of textbook rules, and thereby achieving a new music, free in style and unconventional in technique. As Debussy listened to Satie's music and heard him propound his ideas, he knew he had found a kindred spirit.

As a student at the Paris Conservatory Debussy mortified and, at times, astounded his teachers with his strange and unusual compositions. Debussy could not understand why it was always necessary to resolve seventh chords; why parallel fifths and octaves had to be avoided like the plague; why contrapuntal parts could not be written in parallel instead of contrary motion. And

61

so, in his exercises he deliberately violated the basic laws of the conservatory. Time and again Émile Durand, his professor of harmony, would slam down the lid of the piano angrily as his student veered off on a strange course in his improvisations at the keyboard. One day in 1882, when Léo Delibes, professor of composition, was out of the classroom, Debussy came to the front of his class to teach his fellow students a new concept of harmony and composition. He played a work for them on the piano filled with dissonances, strange progressions, startling tonalities, and forbidden devices. When Delibes returned precipitously and heard this demonstration, he became so infuriated that without further ceremony he ejected Debussy from the class.

Yet, for all his rebellious attitudes, Debussy was a brilliant student who managed to win the highest honor in composition—the Prix de Rome. Even so, he remained the arch heretic. A Prix de Rome winner was required to despatch to the conservatory directors various compositions (called *envois*) as proof of progress. Those returned by Debussy were so strange and exotic in idiom, and so advanced in style and thought that the academicians in Paris denounced them in no uncertain terms as "incomprehensible and impossible to execute." Debussy's answer was: "I can only make my *own* music."

Come what may, he decided to make his *own* music, and for this reason he refused to complete the full three year period required by the Prix. Back in Paris, still groping for a definite direction and a crystallized style, he met and befriended Satie who, for all his strange ways, had the same kind of artistic independence as Debussy. Satie's unconventional ideas, consequently, struck a highly responsive chord in the younger man. But Debussy had no wish to write Satie-like pieces in a gro-

62

tesque or whimsical vein. Debussy's temperament required sterner stuff than this, more attuned with his own sensitive, effeminate nature. What he sought was a style in which the new sounds, colors and idioms with which he was continually experimenting could be fused into an eloquent and sensitive art.

He found that style in Impressionism.

Impressionism was a term coined in the mid-nineteenth century for a school of French painters that included Manet, Monet, Renoir, Sisley, Cézanne, Degas, and Seurat. In 1867 some canvases by Édouard Manet were exhibited in Paris. At that time the catalogue explained that Manet's artistic aim was the rendering of "impressions." At about the same time Claude Monet did a canvas of a sunrise at sea entitled *Une Impression*. From one of these two sources—probably from both—came the word "Impressionism" to identify a new way of painting. Thomas Craven has defined the Impressionist movement as "a view of Nature through a peephole; an eyeful of Nature; a snapshot of a little fragment of the visible world." He also described it as "an indirect method of recording sensations of light and color." Degas put it another way when he said that his aim was "to observe his models through a keyhole."

All the Impressionist painters tried to create subjects or images not as others saw them, but rather as *they*, the painters, saw them. What was important to the Impressionist was the feeling or impression that the subject or image aroused. The conventional way the subject or image looked was not important. The emphasis, therefore, was not on the subject itself, but on its shape, design, color and light values. The technique of Impressionism was (once again to quote Craven) "a flimsy contrivance to ensnare effects of natural light in pretty webs of complementary colors." Skies may be blue or gray, but if the sky suggested to an Impressionist's feelings deep purple, why then he painted skies deep purple. In painting grass, for example, the Impressionist did not use a prepared green as his predecessors had done, but little touches of blue and yellow, leaving the process of blending the colors to the eye of the beholder.

The parallel movement in French literature that took place at this same time was known as Symbolism. The main spokesman for this school was Stéphane Mallarmé. Like the Impressionist, the Symbolist poet tried to appeal to the senses rather than to the intellect. Where the Impressionist emphasized light and color, rather than subject matter, the Symbolist emphasized the sound of words rather than their meaning. In short, just as the Impressionists freed painting from the bondage of conventional subjects treated in a conventional way, so the Symbolists liberated poetry from the limitations imposed upon it by language and tradition.

In Paris cafés, Debussy met many of the leading Impressionists and Symbolists. He saw their paintings and read their poetry; he listened to their theories; he became a member of a group which met each Tuesday evening to discuss art and aesthetics. It was from the Impressionists and the Symbolists that Debussy finally realized his mission as a composer: He would achieve in music what the Impressionists were doing in painting and the Symbolists in poetry.

Thus Debussy arrived at a new kind of music—a music no longer concerned with dramatic force or programmatic realism or emotion per se, but with colors, nuances, moods, sensations, atmospheres. Chords became for him a means of projecting color and thus were used individually for their own specific effect rather than for their relationship to chords that preceded or followed them. Unresolved ninths and elevenths moving about freely without concern for a tonal center evoked for Debussy a world of shadows and mystery, just as the forbidden fifths, the avoidance of formal cadences, and the use of rapidly changing meters and rhythms helped him create elusive moods and evanescent sensations. A new kind of melody—sensitive, refined, seemingly remote—was realized through the use of exotic Oriental scales, church modes, and, most of all, through the whole-tone scale. The last—though appearing in the works of earlier composers—is always identified with Debussy, for it is Debussy alone who used it so extensively and with such extraordinary artistic effect. The whole-tone scale (as its name indicates) is made up entirely of whole tones, the octave being divided into six equal parts. Its unusual intervallic structure is uniquely suited for melodies of a nebulous and hauntingly strange character.

Thus, Debussy became music's first great painter, the first to arrive at new textures, sensations, images and nuances in sound. Oscar Thompson put it exceedingly well when he described Debussy as a "poet of mists and fountains, clouds and rain; of dusk and of glints of sunlight through the leaves. He was moonstruck and seastruck and a lost soul under a sky bespent with stars. . . . He felt faint vibrations as he heard the overtones of distant bells. He was conscious of the perfumes of a summer's day and he could scent in fancy the odors of an Andalusian sky. There was . . . in all a wealth of fantasy as if he not only saw but heard the dancing of shadows on velvet feet."

Debussy was born on August 22, 1862, a few miles outside Paris, in Saint-Germain-en-Laye. Such was the poverty in the Debussy household that to relieve the economic pressure the child had to go to live with an aunt. This in the end proved fortuitous: the aunt was not only a fine musician who recognized Claude's phenomenal musical talent, but also possessed the wherewithal to give it proper nourishment. First she had Madame Mauté de Fleurville (a onetime pupil of Chopin) teach him the piano. Then, when Debussy was eleven, she had him enrolled in the Paris Conservatory.

After graduating from the Conservatory seven years later, Debussy worked for two summers as household pianist for Mme. von Meck, the wealthy Russian patroness who had played such an important role in Tchaikovsky's life. Beginning in 1882, Debussy started devoting himself to composition with complete dedication. Sparked by a love affair he wrote, between 1880 and 1882, several haunting songs including *Clair de lune* (not to be confused with the far more celebrated piano piece of the same name), *Mandoline* and *Apparition*. None were as yet Impressionistic, though the last was a setting of a Mallarmé poem. But they already betrayed Debussy's natural bent for the sensitive and the delicate.

In 1884 Debussy received the Prix de Rome for a cantata, *L'Enfant prodigue*. He was not happy in Rome. For one thing he was separated from the woman he loved; for another, he disliked everything Italian. When the directors of the Paris Conservatory added insult to injury by criticizing his music violently, he knew he had had enough. He returned to Paris precipitously, became infected with the new ideas then filling the atmosphere, and slowly crystallized his own musical style and thinking.

But before he came to and embraced Impressionism, he had been strongly attracted to Wagner. He had studied

Tristan und Isolde painstakingly and was smitten by Wagner's creative power and originality. In 1888 and 1889 he visited Bayreuth—one more pilgrim come to the shrine. But it was not long before this adulation made way for revulsion. "Don't you see," he finally asked, "that Wagner with all his formidable power—yes, in spite of his power—has led music astray into sterile and pernicious paths?" His own sensitive nature needed a musical medium more exquisite, more objective, more controlled, more suggestive than the cataclysmic surge and sweep of Wagner's language and ideas.

Debussy's first masterworks in the Impressionist style came between 1893 and 1894: the *Quartet in G minor* and the exquisite orchestral prelude, *Prélude à l'Après-midi d'un faune (The Afternoon of a Faun)*. The latter was a highly sensitized tone portrait of a Symbolist poem by Stéphane Mallarmé. A faun is lying in a state of half sleep, deliciously recalling the nymphs that had come to him in a dream. Fully awake, he becomes emotional as he tries recalling that vision. Then languidly he once again lapses into drowsiness and returns to his dream world. A solo flute, with which the prelude opens, immediately evokes the misty, half-real world of the faun. A passionate song for oboe and a monologue for solo violin maintain the nebulous feeling until, toward the end, the music dissolves like scattered mist.

From this time on, Debussy committed to music his moody, dreamy, atmospheric impressions of many things: of clouds, festivals and sirens in *Three Nocturnes* for orchestra; of the sea, now gentle and playful, now stormy and elemental in power in *La Mer;* of footsteps in the snow, an engulfed cathedral, a girl with flaxen hair, in his incomparable piano preludes; of moonlight, in the

universally beloved *Clair de lune* for piano, a movement
from the *Suite bergamasque;* of Chinese pagodas, gardens
in the rain, and reflections in water in the *Estampes* and
Images, for piano.

If any single work may be regarded as the quintessence
of Debussy's Impressionist art—and consequently his masterwork of masterworks—it is *Pelleas and Melisande,* still
the greatest Impressionist opera ever written, and one
of the most significant works of the twentieth century.
Maurice Maeterlinck's symbolical drama in verse, set in
a nebulous world of legend in which the characters move
like shadowy figures in a dream, was perfectly suited to
Debussy's style. In a mythical kingdom, Golaud, son of
King Arkel, meets Melisande at a fountain. He is so be-
witched by her beauty that he takes her back to his castle
and marries her. Then Pelleas (Golaud's brother) and
Melisande fall in love with each other. In a fit of jealousy,
Golaud kills Pelleas. Soon afterwards Melisande dies
after having given birth to a child. Golaud is at her side
begging for a forgiveness which can never come.

The marriage of Maeterlinck's text and Debussy's music is as perfect as any to be found in opera. To realize the
remote, amorphous nature of Maeterlinck's drama, Debussy not only enlisted all the tools available in his Impressionist shop but devised some altogether new ones to
meet the specific demands of opera. Like Wagner, he
avoided set arias and ensemble numbers, substituting for
them a fluid flow of uninterrupted musical sound. But
where Wagner had continually erupted into sensual lyricism, Debussy resorted to a declamation that sounded like
exaggerated speech. Debussy never reached in his opera
for those big, climactic scenes which Wagner developed
with such overpowering effect. In fact there is little action in *Pelleas.* The entire opera is poised on a single

level of understatement, its main impact coming from unbroken moods of the utmost sensibility, and the most tenuous kind of atmosphere. There is little emotional stress, and even less dramatic conflict; all is suggestion and nuance.

The première of *Pelleas and Melisande* (in Paris on April 30, 1902) was charged with the electricity of dissension, and dramatized by the violence of controversy and scandal. Maeterlinck had expected his wife, Georgette Leblanc, to play the part of Melisande, but the director of the Opéra-Comique selected (with Debussy's consent) the glamorous new Scottish-American soprano, Mary Garden. Once Maeterlinck learned that his wish had thus been flouted, he did everything he could to discredit the opera and its première. In fact, he even threatened Debussy with physical violence and, on one occasion, challenged him to a duel. Maeterlinck published an open letter hotly declaring that the production was against his will, that Debussy's opera was an "enemy alien to me," and that he wished "its failure should be resounding and prompt." He did more than this, too. On the day of the dress rehearsal he distributed a satirical brochure about the opera outside the theater. This was the spark which set off an explosion within the opera house.

As if all this were not bad enough, other no less disturbing problems beset composer and director. The manuscript of the opera had been copied so sloppily that at the initial rehearsals the men of the orchestra were playing, and the singers were singing, wrong notes; Debussy was at wit's end to make the necessary corrections. Then the scenic designers rebelled. They said that the thirteen scene changes were impractical; Debussy had to write several orchestral interludes to give the stage hands time to make these changes. There was even trouble with the

69

censor who insisted upon deleting several episodes he regarded as immoral.

The première finally did take place on the scheduled day and hour—but not without further incident. Maeterlinck posted as many stooges as he could find in different parts of the theater to create noisy disturbances. At the second performance, the director of the Opéra-Comique countered by filling the balcony with sympathetic students to outshout Maeterlinck's allies. Not until the seventh performance was the furor in the audience completely dissipated.

In their own way, Parisian music critics perpetrated some violence of their own in print. They just did not understand Debussy's musical style, nor what the opera was trying to say. "Morbid," "spineless," "a musical hashish" were some of the epithets they threw at the new work. A London critic, sending his dispatch from Paris, called it a "refined concatenation of sounds. . . . The composer's system is to ignore melody altogether; his personages do not sing, but talk in a sort of lilting voice to a vague musical accompaniment of the text. . . . The effect is . . . almost amusing in its absurdity." Arthur Pougin said: "Rhythm, melody, tonality, these are three things unknown to Monsieur Debussy and deliberately disdained by him." Camille Bellaigue wrote: "No one is better qualified than the composer of *Pelleas and Melisande* to preside over the decomposition of our art. The music of Monsieur Debussy leads to the emaciation and ruin of our essence. It contains germs not of life and progress, but of decadence and death."

But the critics were wrong. *Pelleas* was one of those masterworks that singlehandedly changed the destiny of opera. This was a new kind of musical drama. Its impact was as overwhelming as Wagner's operas had been a half-century earlier. Many composers found a new direction and purpose through *Pelleas;* most of the subsequent changes in twentieth-century opera could hardly have taken place if *Pelleas* had not been written.

Largely because of *Pelleas,* Debussy became a cult among French musicians, who now regarded him as the greatest composer of his generation, and proclaimed Impressionism a new musical dogma. He became a familiar figure in Paris cafés, easily identified by his flowing cape and broad-brimmed felt hat, and always surrounded by fawning disciples.

If he knew the sweet taste of appreciation and recognition immediately after *Pelleas,* he was also to know the gall of neglect. During his last years, as a victim of cancer, he had to undergo serious operations which left him, as he himself once said, "a walking corpse." The outbreak of World War I gave him such pressing financial problems that often he could not pay for food and fuel. And there were few to do him honor. Nevertheless he kept on working, not on the high level on which he had previously functioned, but with the same integrity and high purpose, and completed three sonatas.

He died in Paris on March 25, 1918. Because the war was still on, few knew about his passing, and only a scattered handful cared enough to be present at his funeral.

II

No single composer affected the music of the twentieth century more than Debussy. Composers great and small tried writing the way he did, sometimes at one phase of their careers, sometimes during their most fruitful and productive periods. Impressionism, for example, profoundly influenced such important French creative figures as Florent Schmitt (1870–1958), Albert Roussel (1869–1937) and Paul Dukas (1865–1935); such English musicians as Frank Bridge (1879–1941) and John Ireland (1879–1962); such Americans as Martin Loeffler (1861–1935) and John Alden Carpenter (1876–1951).

One of the most significant Impressionists outside France was the Englishman, Frederick Delius. Born in Bradford, on January 29, 1862, the son of a prosperous wool merchant, Delius (for all his apparent musical inclinations) originally planned a mercantile career. For a while he worked in his father's establishment. But an ungovernable wanderlust made him restless for travel and adventure. He finally prevailed on his father to buy him an orange plantation in Solano, Florida, a wild, primitive area along the St. John River. There, detached from the world, Delius spent several languorous years in isolation. His only diversion was making music. For a six-month period he studied harmony and counterpoint with Thomas F. Ward, an organist from Jacksonville, whom he had induced to come to Solano.

After leaving Solano, Delius spent some time in Jacksonville, singing in a synagogue choir, and after that in Danville, Virginia, where he taught music in a woman's school and gave private lessons to the daughters of wealthy families. His savings enabled him to return to Europe in 1886 and attend the renowned Leipzig Conservatory as a pupil of Jadassohn, Sitt and Reinecke. There he gave convincing proof of his talent as a composer with the orchestral tone poem, *Florida*. This made such a favorable impression upon Grieg (then visiting Leipzig) that he used his influence and powers of persuasion to get Delius' father to support the young man while he tried making his way in music.

For about eight years Delius made his home in Paris.

There he completed three operas, some songs and chamber music, the tone poem *Over the Hills and Far Away,* and the orchestral nocturne *Paris: The Song of a Great City.* While in Paris he met and married Jelka Rosen, a cultured girl from a wealthy family, who brought him financial security, emotional stability, and the encouragement and stimulation he needed for composition. They set up a permanent residence in a villa in the little French town of Grez-sur-Loing, where Delius stayed for the rest of his life. He withdrew from the society of people—for whom, truth to tell, he had a good deal of contempt—to lead a solitary existence of contemplation and work. Creatively he thrived in this monastic seclusion. In 1901 he completed his opera, *A Village Romeo and Juliet* which he described as a "lyric drama in six pictures" but which one commentator considered as a kind of a tone poem with a play for program. "The Walk to the Paradise Garden," one of its orchestral interludes, is often given at symphony concerts. Between 1903 and 1907 Delius produced several of his most significant choral works including *A Mass of Life* and *Sea Drift.* And between 1907 and 1912 he wrote his finest orchestral tone poems with which he won greatness and recognition. The latter came gradually, first in Germany, after that in England, and finally in the rest of the music world— and largely through the devoted efforts of several important conductors (and most notably of all Sir Thomas Beecham) who recognized his genius and were indefatigable in performing his music until it finally achieved worldwide acceptance.

After World War I, Delius was a pathetic victim of complete paralysis and total blindness. He accepted this shattering tragedy with incomparable calm and resignation. "I have seen the best of earth," he said, "and done

73

everything that is worth doing. I am content. I have had a wonderful life." He maintained contact with the world of ideas by having his wife, and one or two friends, read to him regularly. And he continued producing major musical works by dictating them, note by note, to a young amanuensis and disciple, Eric Fenby, who came to live with him.

In the fall of 1929, there took place in London, through Beecham's efforts, a one-week festival of Delius' music. For this occasion, the composer was brought back to England by ambulance, and wheeled into the concert auditorium in his wheelchair. "This festival," said Delius, "has been the time of my life." It was his last public appearance. He died in Grez-sur-Loing on June 10, 1934, and was buried in the local cemetery. But one year after that his body was brought to Limpsfield, in southern England, to be reburied in the churchyard.

Among Delius' most frequently performed compositions are the three tone poems in which his Impressionist writing is most sensitive and exquisite: *On Hearing the First Cuckoo in Spring, Summer Night on the River,* and *In a Summer Garden.* Here he used the Impressionist's equipment in his own way to create a mood or picture whose spell remains unbroken from beginning to end. In *On Hearing the First Cuckoo in Spring* a phrase simulating the distant call of the cuckoo is expanded into a page of haunting beauty and serenity which reveals to us how deeply the composer was affected by nature; a second melody, also in an idyllic vein, was derived from a Norwegian folk song. *Summer Night on the River* conveys an unforgettable impression of boats, embraced by darkness and the mist, rocking gently in the waters; the mystery of a summer night unfolds in an eloquent song in the 'cellos around which other sections of the orchestra weave delicate arabesques. *In a Summer Garden* was inspired by Delius' own garden in Grez-sur-Loing in full bloom. The music is touched with our ineffable sadness "in the presence of beauty," and, as Arthur Hutchings has noted, "our reflection that it must fade as the flowers."

III

The one who can most rightfully be said to be Debussy's heir is one of his countrymen—Maurice Ravel. Debussy was still alive when, in 1907, Ravel became the target for annihilating attacks from Parisian critics who judged him to be just an imitator of Debussy. The immediate cause for this onslaught was the première of Ravel's *Histoires naturelles,* a curious composition—its text, by Jules Renard, being some caustic poems about a peacock, kingfisher, guinea hen, and cricket. Ravel's music was in a similarly mocking vein. Some important critics were outraged by a work they regarded as just "a café concert with ninths." Some found it "labored and unmusical," others said it was "a collection of laborious rarefied harmonies—and successions of involved and complicated chords." What angered critics most was that Ravel appeared to be copying Debussy's personal stylistic mannerisms. As Pierre Lalo said, in Ravel there could be detected "the unmistakable echo of Debussy's music."

But there were also some perceptive musicians and critics who saw the forest and not just the trees. They realized that while Debussy had influenced Ravel, the latter was not just a Debussy imitator but Debussy's heir. These musicians realized that Ravel was using Debussy as a starting point from which to proceed in his own directions, led by his own drives and impulses. M. D. Calvocoressi, Henri Ghéon, Georges Jean-Aubry, and Laloy were some of these who rose stoutly to Ravel's defense by pointing out in Ravel's music a love of classical symmetry and order, a virility of style, irony and wit and intellectualism and precision in place of vagueness—traits rarely, if ever, encountered in Debussy. If this was Impressionism—as, indeed it was—it was actually *post*-Impressionism, Impressionism of a later vintage, Impressionism with a new flavor and texture.

For months the Parisian newspapers were crowded with the pros and cons of what soon became known as *l'affair Ravel*. Nor did the accusations against Ravel completely die down until he had finally succeeded in producing some masterworks of his own in which his personality was established unmistakably: compositions like the *Rapsodie espagnole* for orchestra; *Gaspard de la nuit* for piano; the one-act comic opera, *L'Heure espagnole;* the *Mother Goose Suite,* written both for the orchestra and for four-hand piano; and most significant of all, the music for one of the crowning works in contemporary ballet, *Daphnis and Chloe.* Now the critics could say: "Monsieur Maurice Ravel has created an orchestral language which belongs exclusively to himself" (Jean Marnold). Now they could describe him as "a painter, a goldsmith, a jeweler" (Emile Vuillermoz).

Ravel was born in Ciboure, in the Basque region of southern France, on March 7, 1875. A musical child whose interest had been stimulated by his father—an engineer who loved music deeply—Ravel began studying with Henri Ghys, composer of the popular *Amaryllis,* in 1882, and soon after that with Charles-René. For fifteen years, beginning in 1889, Ravel attended the Paris Conservatory where he was both a consistently brilliant pupil and a rebellious one. One Conservatory professor had

76

a particularly far-reaching influence upon him: Gabriel Fauré. Fauré knew how to encourage the young man's need for independent thinking and his restless search after new musical sounds. Under Fauré, Ravel completed two individual compositions: *Sites auriculaires* for two pianos, and the overture *Sheherazade*, both performed in Paris between 1898 and 1899, and both dismal failures. After that came a poignant and evocative piece for the piano (later orchestrated by the composer) which still is among his most popular pieces, *Pavane pour une Infante défunte*. (Its melody was lifted by American popular writers in 1939 for the successful "pop" tune, "The Lamp Is Low.") This work, coupled with another equally remarkable one, *Jeux d'eau*, was introduced at a concert of the Société Nationale in Paris in 1902 and brought Ravel his first success. An unqualified masterwork, the *String Quartet in F major* (dedicated to Fauré), followed two years later; one French critic remarked that this work "placed its author . . . in the foremost rank of French musicians."

In or about 1904, Ravel and some of his friends (including Florent Schmitt, Stravinsky, and Manuel de Falla) formed an artistic cult, the *Société des apaches*. An *apache*, of course, is a member of the Parisian underworld; the term was used by Frenchmen to describe every kind of social outcast. Ravel and his friends regarded themselves as musical outcasts or outlaws because of their passionate dedication to innovation and experiments. These musical *apaches* met first in a Paris studio and subsequently in a studio in Auteuil. They talked, argued, played each other's music. All-night sessions were not unusual. "We were happy, cultured, and insolent," was the way one of the members described the group. One of Ravel's greatest works for the piano, *Miroirs,*

77

was introduced at one of these sessions. The increasing originality of Ravel's thinking and style, the daring of his harmonic writing, and the perfection of his post-Impressionist style were all revealed in this work which was so strongly affected by his contacts with the musical *apaches*.

This *apache* influence is evident in several other Ravel masterworks written after 1905. Some were in a Satie-like vein of irony, mockery, and laughter: the *Histoires naturelles* and *L'Heure espagnole*, for example. Some reflected Ravel's fascination for everything Spanish: the *Rapsodie espagnole* and *Alborada del gracioso*. Some were in the style of fantasy as in the *Mother Goose Suite*. And some were eloquent Impressionist pictures that were extensions of Debussy. In the last category we find what is probably Ravel's greatest work, and one of the most important ballets produced in France in the twentieth century, *Daphnis and Chloe*.

Ravel wrote this music on a commission from Serge Diaghilev, the brilliant impresario of the Ballet Russe. The scenario, the work of Michel Fokine, was based on a Greek pastoral. Daphnis, stretched out before a grotto of nymphs, dreams about his beloved Chloe. She appears with her shepherdesses, wearing a crown which Pan had presented her in remembrance of the nymph, Syrinx, whom all the Gods loved. Daphnis and Chloe now mime the story of Pan and Syrinx. More and more agitated grows their dance, as Daphnis suddenly begins to perform a melancholy tune on a flute fashioned from a stalk. Finally Chloe falls into the arms of Daphnis before the altar of the nymphs. When Daphnis vows eternal fidelity, girls dressed as bacchantes, and a group of young men, join in a joyous and tumultuous dance.

78

To this score Ravel brought all his technical wizardry, all his powers as a magic colorist, all his sensitivity for projecting the most subtle and elusive atmospheres. Like the Debussy prelude about the afternoon of a faun (of which it is a legitimate offspring), this music evokes with haunting beauty the unreal world of nymphs and satyrs. "The score," Jean Marnold said in his review, following the première of the ballet in Paris on June 8, 1912, "abounds in tableaux of the most exquisite plastic beauty; among these the appearance of the gracious nymphs in the twilight shadow of a dream is a page without precedent or model in the whole of music. . . . Never has the magic of picturesque sonority reached such an intensity."

The music for *Daphnis and Chloe* is a familiar item today on symphonic programs by virtue of two suites (or, "series of orchestral fragments" as Ravel himself described them) which the composer derived from his ballet score.

During World War I, Ravel tried to enlist in the army and air corps. After being turned down for physical reasons, he joined a motor corps with which he served at the front. After the war, he bought "Belvedere," a beautiful villa in the small French town of Montfort l'Amaury, which became his home from then on. Here he worked on his compositions with his customary meticulous attention to detail and dedication to the highest principles. He entertained his friends, and he spent reflective hours in his library and garden. His everyday life was shared by a servant who took care of him with almost maternal solicitude (Ravel never married), and by a family of Siamese cats on whom he lavished excessive tenderness, and to whom he liked to talk in "cat language" which, he insisted, they understood. (Debussy had also been a lover of cats, and invariably had one as a companion.)

During this period Ravel wrote many Impressionistic compositions. These included a delightful stage fantasy, *L'Enfant et les sortilèges,* in which furniture and toys come to life to taunt a mischievous boy; a remarkable orchestral fantasy, *La Valse,* in whose misty images we can discern a ball in a Viennese imperial court in or about 1855 set against a waltz melody growing from an embryo into a vibrant living organism; a violin sonata in which Ravel experimented with the "blues" idiom; a remarkable work in a pseudo-Spanish idiom that literally took the world by storm, *Bolero.* His last compositions, completed in 1931, were two piano concertos (one of them for the left hand alone) in which American popular jazz styles are once again employed.

If *Daphnis and Chloe* is Ravel's greatest work, then *Bolero* is his most popular. Ida Rubinstein, a famous French dancer, asked him to write this music for her, and she introduced it with phenomenal success in Paris on November 20, 1928. But it was at symphony concerts that this music went on to become one of the most celebrated concert pieces since 1900. It had a kinetic appeal which was irresistible. A single melody in two sections grows and develops both in volume and in changing orchestral colors for about seventeen minutes. As the theme passes now to one section of the orchestra and now to another, it grows louder and louder, more and more brilliant, until, at last, a thunderous climax is proclaimed by the full orchestra.

When *Bolero* was heard for the first time in America— Toscanini conducted it in Carnegie Hall—one of the greatest demonstrations ever seen in that auditorium was let loose. Then *Bolero* was played by virtually every other American orchestra; it was immediately released in six different recordings; it was adapted for every possible instrument or combination of instruments (including a jazz band!); it was featured in a Broadway revue and in a night club show; it even lent its name to a movie starring George Raft.

In the fall of 1932, Ravel suffered an accident in a Paris taxicab. At first his injuries seemed minor, but as the months passed he began to lose his powers of coordination. Then partial paralysis set in. In 1935 his physical deterioration necessitated an operation on his affected brain. Ravel never survived that operation. He died in the hospital on December 28, 1937.

CHAPTER 4

The "Everyday" Men

THE Impressionist school was not the only school affecting French music in the early twentieth century. There was also the group that clustered around and developed from César Franck—which, like its patron saint, brought to music a kind of religious consecration, a feeling for the spiritual, an unwavering idealism. If the Impressionists helped carry music to an extreme in nebulousness and preciousness, the Franckists were also extremists in their sanctimoniousness, pretentiousness, and scholasticism.

The inevitable reaction to the extremes of both these schools came with the "French Six" or *Les Six*. This group of six young Frenchmen had sympathy for neither the Impressionists nor the Franckists. "The Six" expressed their disdain in little, unpretentious pieces of music, slight in structure, and filled with impish, tongue-in-cheek attitudes, and other light, gay moods. "The Six" believed in *une musique de tous les jours*—everyday music. They stood in sharp contrast to those who regarded themselves as high priests of their art.

The "French Six" differed from other modern groups or schools traveling under a single artistic banner. In other instances, composers banded together for the purpose of carrying out set principles. The "French Six" did not come together for any such purpose, nor, for that matter, for any purpose whatsoever. They did not follow a single style of composition. In fact, the six men wrote a good deal of music in many veins other than the light and jaunty one in which they expressed their rebellion against Impressionism and Franckism. The force coalescing "The Six" into a single group was not an artistic motivation, but a synthetic process in the person of one of Paris's leading music critics. On January 16, 1920, Henri Collet reviewed in *Comedia* an album of piano pieces containing the work of six Frenchmen: Georges Auric, Louis Durey, Arthur Honegger, Darius Milhaud, Francis Poulenc, and Germaine Tailleferre. Collet drew a parallel between the famous nineteenth-century Russian nationalist school, known as "The Five," and the six French composers. "Russian music," he wrote, "cultivated by the illustrious Five—Balakirev, Cui, Borodin, Mussorgsky, and Rimsky-Korsakov—united in their aims, became the object of universal admiration. . . . The Six Frenchmen . . . have, by magnificent and voluntary return to simplicity, brought about a renaissance of French music, because they understood the lesson of Erik Satie. . . . The different temperaments of the six composers jostle without jarring, and their works, individual and distinct, reveal a unity of approach to art, in conformity with the spokesman of the group, Jean Cocteau."

One week later, Collet published a second article on French music in which he discussed the personalities and achievements of *Les Six Français* or "The French Six." This label henceforth stuck to the group, though each member did not particularly relish being artistically associated with the others.

Collet was not altogether accurate in maintaining that the six French composers revealed "a unity of approach to art." Actually they did nothing of the sort. From time

to time, each of the six men produced compositions that
bore no spiritual affinity or stylistic resemblance to the
works of the other five. But it was quite true that all six,
at one point or another, wrote simple, easily comprehended compositions that were down-to-earth. These
compositions had catchy tunes and rhythms; if texts or
scenarios were used they usually were outlandish in
theme and quixotic in development. This was the common ground on which the members of "The Six" stood
for several years, and it was from this ground that they
launched their attacks against Impressionism and Franckism.

II

Throughout a rich, long, prolific career which has
yielded hundreds upon hundreds of compositions, Darius Milhaud has employed many styles in every possible
form. As an ultramodernist he was one of the first to use
polytonality extensively. He has written Hebrew music—
even a religious service; Provençal music; music of the
French West Indies; music that exploited the classic
dances of the sixteenth and seventeenth centuries. He
has written a good many symphonies, string quartets
and operas combining a variety of styles from the romantic to the modern, from the esoteric to the popular—
sometimes within a single work. But the music with
which he first achieved worldwide recognition, or—if you
will—notoriety, was that in the insouciant manner which
carried music from the high ivory tower of Impressionism and Franckism to the common man in the street.
Milhaud wrote large and small works in which the tango,
the shimmy, the blues, jazz, ragtime, and music hall tunes
were used, sometimes for humorous or ironic effects,

sometimes to introduce surprise, and sometimes with the most serious artistic intent.

Milhaud was unusually sensitive to the influence of poets. Three of them led him away from Debussy's misty and unreal world. The first poet was Francis Jammes, author of the text for Milhaud's first opera, *La Brebis égarée,* completed when Milhaud was still a Conservatory student. Jammes, as Milhaud himself once confessed, led him "out of the symbolists' fog and revealed to me a new world, to be captured merely by opening one's eyes." Until now a passionate disciple of Debussy (as so many other young Frenchmen were at the time), Milhaud was soon able to free himself from the lure of Impressionism and wander off freely into the green pastures of Satie's whimsy and impishness. The second French poet was Paul Claudel (who was also a diplomat). Because of Claudel, Milhaud started writing music that either imitated or used popular musical styles of North and South America. The third French poet was Jean Cocteau, a nonconformist in living as well as in art. Cocteau had a particular weakness for satire, for "fresh-air realism" and for fantasy. Through his unorthodox poems and texts, which Milhaud set to music, he was able to encourage similar light moods and feelings in the young composer.

Milhaud was born on September 4, 1892, in Aix-en-Provence, a town in the sun-drenched regions of Provence made famous by Van Gogh's painting. (Some of the old dance melodies of this district were used by Milhaud in one of his finest and most popular orchestral works, the *Suite provençale.*) Milhaud's music study took place first with local teachers; then at the College of Aix; and from 1909 to 1914 at the Paris Conservatory with

85

Paul Dukas, Charles Widor and André Gedalge. Milhaud was an outstanding student, winning prizes in virtually every department, and undertaking the most ambitious projects for composition. His earliest works were Impressionistic. With the opera *La Brebis égarée*, he took his first step away from Impressionism. The second step away from Impressionism was taken with his incidental music for *Protée*, a satirical play by Paul Claudel. Here Milhaud's style drifted toward popular areas, as he made a skillful use of the tango and other South American dance rhythms.

Both the opera and the music for *Protée* were written while Milhaud was attending the Conservatory. The outbreak of World War I brought his Conservatory schooling to an abrupt end, and frustrated Milhaud's ambition to win the Prix de Rome. By this time, his association with Paul Claudel had flowered into such friendship that, in 1917, when Claudel was appointed France's Ambassador to Brazil, Milhaud accompanied him as a Legation attaché. This South American visit not only afforded Milhaud a first-hand opportunity to learn the country's popular songs and dances but also to become acquainted with American jazz, then becoming extremely popular throughout Latin America.

In South America Milhaud completed a major score—the music for a farce in pantomime, *Le Boeuf sur le toit*. Jean Cocteau had written the highly offbeat scenario—but only *after* Milhaud had completed his score. Cocteau placed his action in an American speakeasy, the hangout for a strange assortment of American characters—a Negro boxer, a Negro dwarf, a bookie, and a woman with paper hair. A brawl ensues. A policeman come to quell the riot is decapitated by a revolving electric fan. The dwarf, after singing a romance to the lady, refuses to pay his bar bill. When some of the characters leave the speakeasy, the bartender calmly goes about the business of restoring the head of the policeman to its body. Then, revived, the policeman presents the dwarf with a two-foot bill for payment.

Though background and characters were American, Milhaud's style came not from jazz but from popular Brazilian music. Brazilian songs and dances also were the source for a remarkable orchestral suite, *Saudades do Brasil,* which also exists in a version for the piano. A *saudade* is a "nostalgic recollection." In this twelve-movement work, Milhaud recalls Brazil through the rhythms of Brazilian dances.

One of Milhaud's most remarkable works in a popular style is the Negro ballet, *La Création du monde (The Creation of the World),* in 1922. This was one of the first large-scale serious works to employ jazz—preceding Gershwin's more popular *Rhapsody in Blue* by two years; it is still one of the best jazz works in a symphonic idiom. The scenario describes the world's creation through the eyes of an aborigine. Dancers (who walk about on stilts) represent herons. Animals caper about on a darkened stage on all fours. Out of this mass, human beings slowly begin to emerge. We soon recognize a Negro Adam and Eve, who embrace in a sustained kiss. The score begins with a haunting American blues for the saxophone, and includes a fugue based on a jazz motive; throughout, the music is rich with syncopations and ragtime.

These and other similar excursions into wit and irony by way of unconventional and offbeat subjects made Milhaud popular in Paris after his return from South America in 1919. Further publicity came his way when the title of "French Six" was attached to him in conjunction with five other rebellious spirits in music. Milhaud continued writing other compositions with down-to-earth, popular, and unorthodox approaches. *Le Train bleu*, in 1924, was a "danced operetta" dealing with gigolos and girls at a fashionable beach. *Les Mariés de la Tour Eiffel*, a ballet in 1921, was the only instance in which Milhaud joined forces with his colleagues of "The Six" for a common artistic effort.

A good many critics found the kind of music Milhaud was producing for these more popular efforts refreshing and invigorating after the hothouse atmosphere of Impressionism. Others looked askance and described Milhaud as a "sensation monger" and a "vulgarian." But whether damned or praised, Milhaud was frequently performed, and discussed, thereby becoming one of the most provocative figures in French music since Satie.

On occasion, in later years, Milhaud paid hasty revisits into popular areas, as in the *Suite provençale*, the *Scaramouche* suite for two pianos, and the *Suite française*. Nevertheless Milhaud had grown weary of his former levity, and was impelled by a severe artistic conscience to seek out more serious, sober, and flexible kinds of self expression. And so he completed all kinds of major works—symphonies, quartets, operas, song cycles, as well as shorter works in every possible shape and form. A masterful use of modern idioms and techniques was here combined with a personal lyricism and at times a deeply affecting emotion.

With the death of Ravel, in 1937, Milhaud's position as France's first composer was not seriously questioned. He had by then become, as Virgil Thomson later wrote, "one of the most completely calm of modern masters . . . by adding . . . depth and penetrating and simple humanity to his gamut." To Boris de Schloezer, the Russian-born authority on contemporary French music,

Milhaud was "after Stravinsky, the most richly endowed and the most powerful musician of our times . . . [who belongs] to the race of great creators."

During World War II, Milhaud lived in the United States where he made numerous appearances as guest conductor, lecturer, and pianist besides serving as a member of the music faculty at Mills College, in Oakland, California. Though stricken by a crippling attack of arthritis, which made him a prisoner to a wheelchair or to two canes, he continued writing remarkable music in a truly formidable outflow of compositions—including his *Second Piano Concerto*, his *Second 'Cello Concerto*, his *Third* and *Fourth Symphonies*, and his *Fourteenth* and *Fifteenth String Quartets*. The last two are unusual in that they can be played separately as string quartets or can be combined as a string octet. Though he had to conduct from a seated position, he continued appearing with the foremost American orchestras.

After the war, Milhaud paid his first return visit to France. Since then he has been dividing his year and his activities between his native land and the United States.

Arthur Honegger and Francis Poulenc were two other members of "The Six" who progressed from levity to sobriety, from trivialities to profundities. Nevertheless, they did not fail to make a profound impression upon the French musical thought of their time with some of their earlier slight efforts.

Honegger was perhaps the one member of "The Six" least interested in the kind of musical trifles the others enjoyed dispensing. Honegger's most significant composition in the lighter vein is a pleasing little *Concertino for Piano*—a simple, lyrical, bouncy, syncopated, and at times, jazzy composition. But before he wrote this concertino in 1924, Honegger had become famous for something quite different—a powerful oratorio with an almost Handel-like grandeur, *Le Roi David,* first heard in Switzerland in 1921, and a few years later given with huge success in Paris, Zurich, Rome, and New York. During this period Honegger had also achieved a measure of notoriety with a provocative piece of music, so cacophonous and jarring that he was instantly numbered with the *enfants terribles* of the day. This work was *Pacific 231* in which the composer—reflecting a lifelong passion for locomotives—went to painful extremes to reproduce the sounds and motion of a moving train through shattering dissonances, nervous rhythms, and abrupt chords.

Although Honegger was born in France and maintained his permanent home there, he was all his life a Swiss citizen, by virtue of his parents. They came to the coastal town of Le Havre to set up a business establishment. Here the composer was born on March 10, 1892. A Bach cantata and some excerpts from Mozart's *The Magic Flute* heard in his boyhood aroused his ambition to start music study so that he, too, could write an opera. Nevertheless for a long while he seriously contemplated a career in business. When he was sixteen he entered his father's establishment. But his heart lay with music and not with commerce, a fact his father reluctantly submitted to when he allowed the boy to enter the Zurich Conservatory. In 1912, Honegger was transferred to the Paris Conservatory where he was Milhaud's fellow-student. Four years later Honegger made his bow as composer when some of his songs were introduced in a Paris concert hall, and a piano piece was played by Andrée Vaurabourg at a soirée. (Andrée had been Honegger's classmate; later on she became his wife.) By 1920, Honegger's name had begun to attract attention by being linked with those of the other "Six." But in the next half dozen years he asserted his own artistic personality and independence with works like *Le Roi David* which was far removed from the kind of writing for which "The Six" had become so famous.

Honegger's real creative personality was more accurately reflected in *Le Roi David* than in the little piano concertino. It was this personality which he allowed to unfold in his later works. Most important of all were the symphonies Honegger completed during and after World War II. Not Gallic wit or charm do we find here, nor razor-edged satire but a dramatic and virile style, sometimes acidulous and astringent, but often touched with an encompassing humanity and a kind of spiritual exaltation.

The *Second Symphony* was written while Paris was occupied by the Nazis during World War II. Throughout the work we are plunged into the mood of despair that at the time had seized most Frenchmen, and particularly Honegger, a member of the Resistance movement. But there is also a note of defiance in this symphony, and it ends not on a note of sorrow but with an exultant paean, prophetic of ultimate liberation.

Honegger's *Third Symphony* commemorated the fiftieth anniversary of the Boston Symphony. Subtitled *Liturgique,* it has been described as the search of the human spirit for serenity in a world of unrest. The subtitles to each of the three movements (*Dies Irae, De profundis clamavi* and *Dona nobis pacem*) suggest a strong religious identity. The *Fourth Symphony* uses quotations from old songs popular in Basel, Switzerland, and for this reason has acquired the name *Deliciae basilienses (Basel Delights).* The *Fifth Symphony* has

91

come to be known as *De Tre Re* (*Of the Three D's*), because the note D is a unifying element, heard at the conclusion of each of the three movements.

Honegger's *Fifth Symphony,* completed in 1950, was his last. He had been in poor health for a long time. Indeed, when he paid his second visit to the United States in 1949 to conduct a master class in composition at the Berkshire Music Center in Tanglewood, he was physically incapable of fulfilling this obligation. After 1950 his health deteriorated, making sustained creative work difficult. He died in Paris on November 27, 1955.

Francis Poulenc's brevity and wit revealed themselves most forcefully in some of the earlier works with which he gained membership in "The Six" and popularity in French music. One was *Rapsodie négre* (*Negro Rhapsody*), a setting of a Negro poem in gibberish, supposedly the work of a native Liberian, but actually a hoax concocted to meet the then prevailing vogue for all things Negro. Poulenc took this hoax at face value. Placing tongue squarely in cheek he wrote a score full of spice and satire for a poem that begins with the following lines: "Honoloulou, poti lama, Honoloulou, Honoloulou, Kati moki, mosi boulo, Ratsku sira, polama!" The *Negro Rhapsody* came in 1917, long before "The Six" had been officially baptized by Collet. The work was such a "roaring success" that the career of the eighteen-year-old composer was vigorously launched. After that Poulenc wrote *Le Bestiaire* (*The Bestiary*), a song cycle vividly and humorously describing six specimens of animal and marine life. This, in turn, was succeeded by music for *Les Biches,* a witty ballet produced by Diaghilev, adapted from French popular songs. After that

92

came a charming little concerto for harpsichord and a two-piano concerto, in both of which the thematic material resembled music-hall tunes.

Poulenc continued to tap this satirical and lighthearted vein for a long time. But just before, and soon after, World War II, he created large works rich in emotional content and poetic expressiveness, at times dramatized by a tragic undercurrent. In 1943 he wrote a violin sonata in memory of Federico Garcia Lorca, a poet killed during the Spanish Civil War of the 1930's, in which his "speech" is in turn vehement and turbulent, lyrical and tender. Poignancy, and at times, tragedy, are encountered in songs written in the 1930's and 1940's —some of the best songs created in France since Debussy. And tragedy pervades Poulenc's greatest work for the stage—the opera, *Les Dialogues des Carmélites,* introduced with outstanding success at La Scala in Milan in 1957. The period is the French Revolution, the setting Paris. Sixteen nuns are commanded to dissolve their order. Rather than do this, they proudly meet their death at the guillotine. For this deeply emotional and profoundly religious subject, Poulenc created a score that was continually lyrical but which progressed toward its shattering dramatic climax with a relentless tread. *Les Dialogues* was first heard in the United States in 1957, then in 1958 was telecast over the NBC network when it was awarded the New York Music Critics Circle Award. Poulenc died in Paris on January 30, 1963.

The other three members of "The Six"—Georges Auric (1899–   ), Louis Durey (1888–   ), and Germaine Tailleferre (1892–   )—have remained for the most part effervescent wits. Durey and Tailleferre have long since fallen by the wayside and are almost never performed anymore. Auric has preferred to concentrate his efforts on music for motion pictures, the popular theater, and the ballet. Americans will surely remember Auric for his hit song, the title number in the motion-picture biography of Toulouse-Lautrec, *Moulin Rouge.*

"The Six" were not the only ones in France leaning toward lighter moods and styles. Many other composers were similarly disposed. The most significant of these has been Jean Françaix. Françaix—born in Le Mans in 1912—was a child prodigy who began improvising when he was four, and completed his first composition at ten. After attending the Paris Conservatory, he came to prominence before his twentieth birthday with a *Bagatelle,* for string quartet, introduced at the modern-music festival in Vienna, and his *First Symphony,* performed in Paris by the Orchestre Symphonique under Pierre Monteux.

Françaix' reputation was solidly established between 1934 and 1936 with a piano concertino and a piano concerto, each with the kind of terse, tart statements within slender structures that, a decade earlier, had characterized so many works by "The Six." It was with the *Piano Concerto* that Françaix made his American debut in 1938, when he appeared as soloist with the New York Philharmonic. On that occasion, one of the music critics in New York referred to him as "the white hope of French music." As that white hope, Françaix later completed several fine operas, one of which, *L'Apostrophe,* was introduced at the Holland Festival in 1951. So sparkling were both the text and the music that the New York correspondent reported that "even the non-French speaking section of the audience was lured into laughter by the caprices of the score."

This trend toward "everyday music" by "everyday composers" was not an exclusively French phenomenon. A parallel movement swept across Germany in the 1920's and early 1930's where it was designated as *Zeitkunst,* or "Contemporary Art." Followers of this cult liked treating racy modern subjects, filled with all sorts of contemporary allusions and references, in a timely and provocative musical style. In such a vein Paul Hindemith wrote a controversial opera, *Neues vom Tage* (*News of the Day*), first produced in Berlin in 1929 where it shocked audiences and critics out of their senses. The farcical subject involved a marital dispute in which the couple becomes the "news of the day" through their efforts to get a divorce. When they arrive in court they do not want to separate. But the public now expects them to get a divorce, and a divorce is what they get. Within this general plot structure are found all kinds of amusing and provocative episodes. The heroine, seen taking a bath, sings a hymn in praise of hot water. Stenographers chant to the accompaniment of clicking typewriters. The protagonists engage in a lusty fight, accompanied musically by the sounds of smashing crockery. A chorus of men at the registrar's office announce births, deaths, marriages, and divorces. Everything is topsy-turvy in this opera. Other operas might have a love duet, but this one has a hate duet. Others might feature a wedding march, but this one has a divorce ensemble. Through it all we hear music written with broad strokes generously spiced with the colorations and rhythms of jazz.

In line with this "Contemporary Art" Hindemith also created a whole library of music with popular content for mass appeal. For these pieces the term *Gebrauchs-musik* (Functional Music) was concocted. *Gebrauchs-musik* consisted of "practical music" for amateurs—operas and instrumental compositions for performance by schools and colleges in which the audience could sometimes participate. This music also embraced pieces for animated cartoons, radio, movies, pianola and brass band. "Practical music" also included music with political or social implications intended for large and generally unsophisticated audiences. Thus, Hindemith produced compositions for various mechanical instruments; a score for *Felix the Cat*, a motion-picture cartoon; functional instrumental and choral pieces of all sorts; and, in 1931, an opera for children, about children, to be performed by children—*Let's Build a Town*. Explaining his purpose in creating these compositions, Hindemith said in 1927: "It is to be regretted that in general so little relationship exists today between the producers and consumers of music. A composer should write today only if he knows for what purpose he is writing. The days of composing for the sake of composing are perhaps gone forever. On the other hand, the demand for music is so great that composer and consumer ought most emphatically to come at last to an understanding."

Despite this pronouncement, and despite his many attempts at *Zeitkunst* and *Gebrauchsmusik*, Paul Hindemith became after 1930 one of the most complex, esoteric, and original musical creators. He gave the lie to his own dictum that "the days of composing for the sake of composing are perhaps gone forever." The far more serious endeavors with which this composer became one of the supreme creative figures in twentieth-century music will be discussed in a later chapter.

Another exciting and sensational German example of *Zeitkunst* in a jazz idiom was *Jonny spielt auf!* (*Johnny Strikes Up the Tune*), an opera by Ernst Křenek (1900–). When introduced in Leipzig in 1927, it took the city by storm, then went on to conquer all of Germany, and the rest of the music world. In less than two years it was performed in over one hundred European theaters and translated into eighteen languages. Johnny, the central character, is a Negro jazz-band leader who wins hearts and starts feet tapping whenever he strikes up a popular tune with his band. He inspires a mass performance of the "Charleston" at the North Pole and in the end bestrides the world like a conqueror, still playing his intoxicating and irresistible jazz. In setting this unusual text, Křenek deliberately set out to write a jazz opera with "rhythms and atmosphere of modern life" interpreting "this age of technical science." His score overflows with blues melodies, jazz harmonies and rhythms, and music-hall ballads. After *Jonny*, Křenek wrote two more operas in a jazz idiom, but neither one matched its popularity. Then Křenek left jazz for good, first to assume a Romantic and almost Schubertian lyricism in various chamber music and orchestral compositions, and after that to embrace the twelve-tone technique to which he has since remained faithful.

Nobody was more successful in producing *Zeitkunst* or in becoming an "everyday" composer than Kurt Weill, born in Dessau, Germany, on March 2, 1900. After attending the *Berlin Hochschule für Musik* and studying privately with Ferruccio Busoni, Weill started out as an ivory-tower composer of avant-garde music in the most advanced idioms. His career ended in New

York where he had become one of its most distinguished composers of musical comedies and musical plays. In between these two polar points of composition—and while he was still a German—he wrote operas in a new format which he dubbed "song plays." "I want," he said in explanation, "to reach the real people, a more representative public than any opera house attracts. I write for today. I don't care about writing for posterity." And so, he tried to make opera an everyday form of stage entertainment for the masses, with music that belonged more legitimately in the European music hall than in the opera house. Ballads, popular tunes, current dances like the tango and the shimmy, jazz devices like the blues and ragtime, all found their way into his operas.

One of Weill's most sensational song-plays was *The Rise and Fall of the City Mahagonny* (text by Bertolt Brecht), first seen in Germany in 1930. Stink bombs were thrown into the theater at the première; boos and shouts of disapproval disrupted the performance. Even fist fights ensued between those who liked the opera and those who denounced it. During that whole first-night performance the manager of the theater insisted upon keeping the lights on in the theater to avoid possible disaster. As it was, one man was shot and killed.

Brecht's play was unusual, irreverent, and at times obscene. It is set in Mahagonny, a fictional town in Alabama. Three ex-convicts, fleeing from the law, establish in this city a new kind of society in which people can do whatever their hearts desire without any of the limitations imposed upon them by ethics, morality, or the law. The only thing in Mahagonny that was unpardonable was the lack of money. Thus Brecht drew a caricature of modern society, laying bare the corruption, decadence and materialism of modern living. "First, for-

98

get not, comes devouring food," explains one of the choral numbers; after that, the song says, come love, boxing, and drink, in descending order of importance. Weill's music also consisted of jazz episodes, ditties and popular songs of the Tin Pan Alley variety. Of the last, the most popular was "Alabamy Song," in gibberish English.

The greatest artistic and popular success of Brecht and Weill, came with *Die Dreigroschenoper (The Three-Penny Opera)*, a work that literally circled the globe. It opened in an intimate and unpretentious little theater in Berlin in 1928, before an audience that had been forewarned by rumor that this little opera was just a "dud," filled with "unsingable music" and a text generously sprinkled with "filthy lines." "Then," as Lotte Lenya recalled (at that time appearing in the leading female role of Jenny), "after the *Kanonen* song, an unbelievable uproar went up, and from that point on it was wonderfully, intoxicatingly clear that the public was with us." After that, *The Three-Penny Opera* infected Berlin like a contagious disease. Everywhere one went one heard its tunes; there was even a bar opened named the *Dreigroschenoper* which featured the music of the opera exclusively. And Berlin was not the only place to be thus affected. During its first year, the opera was given over a thousand times by more than one hundred German theaters; in five years it was seen ten thousand times in Central Europe, and translated into eighteen languages. It was made into a fine German movie directed by G. W. Pabst.

Nor did its history end there. In 1954, it was presented off Broadway with a text revised by Marc Blitzstein, but with Weill's music left intact. It lasted there over six years—one of the longest runs ever accumulated by any

American musical production. After that it toured the country in performances by several national companies. In that time one of its principal songs, "Mack the Knife" twice became a national hit: In 1955 it received over twenty recordings and was at the top of the Hit Parade for several weeks. In 1959, it helped establish the career of young Bobby Darin, whose new recording of that song sold over a million discs.

The Three-Penny Opera was a modernization of the venerable ballad opera of John Gay, *The Beggar's Opera,* but with a completely new score. The latter, first produced in London in 1728, was a political travesty which pointed up the political corruption of the times and the callousness of the upper English classes to poverty and human suffering. The main characters were drawn from the lowest strata of English society—thieves, highwaymen, a beggar, and so forth. The music by John Christoph Pepusch consisted for the most part of adaptations of tunes, airs, and ballads then popular in England. What these authors wanted to do, of course, was not merely to write a political and social satire, but to mock at the pretensions of the Handelian-type opera then so greatly in vogue in London.

So successful was *The Beggar's Opera* that it created a passion for this new genre—the ballad opera. Over a hundred ballad operas were produced in London between 1728 and 1738. Serious Italian operas were thrown completely into the shade by these more popular stage productions.

In the late 1920's, *The Beggar's Opera* was revived in Berlin. It was this production that gave Brecht the idea to rewrite it along modern lines and make it a commentary on the social and political decadence in post World-War I Germany. He enlisted the cooperation of Kurt

Weill who, to give the play a genuine twentieth-century flavor, wrote a lively and unusual score made up of Tin Pan Alley tunes, sentimental ballads, the blues, a shimmy, and vivacious choruses. When the older musical forms were utilized—such as a canon, a chorale, or a formal opera aria—they were usually dressed in a jazz or Tin Pan Alley garb to point up, as it were, the contradiction between the old and the new. Thus in text and in music *The Three-Penny Opera* was the rebel voice of a country—singing and whistling in mocking tones as it inched ever closer toward the abyss of the swastika and the second World War.

Though Weill was the top composer of the German musical theater in 1933, he had to flee when the Nazis came to power, since he was a Jew. He finally came to America, became an American citizen and soon was one of Broadway's most successful composers. He wrote scores for *Lady in the Dark, Knickerbocker Holiday, Street Scene,* and *Lost in the Dark,* as well as many other musicals. Toward the end of his life, in 1947, he completed a one-act American folk opera, *Down in the Valley.* He died in New York City on April 3, 1950.

IV

It is singularly appropriate to find Marc Blitzstein modernizing Weill's *The Three-Penny Opera* and making it a triumph of the American musical theater. For Blitzstein, who was a composer as well as a librettist and lyricist, was Weill's American counterpart as an everyday composer of song-plays. Born in Philadelphia in 1905, Blitzstein (like Weill) received a comprehensive musical schooling at the Curtis Institute, and later privately with Nadia Boulanger and Arnold Schoenberg. Then, once again like Weill, he started out professionally as a

101

composer of avant-garde music. Such were the dissonances and jarring sounds of his esoteric compositions that one Philadelphia critic was tempted to describe them as full of *"Donner und Blitzstein."* But as the Depression deepened and aroused the social and political consciousness of many Americans, Blitzstein felt a need to make his music an instrument for social propaganda, and at the same time to simplify and popularize his style so he might be able to speak to the common man. And so he wrote a *Three-Penny Opera* of his own, calling it *The Cradle Will Rock.* He wrote his own text, building it around the efforts of workers in Steeltown to form a union despite the obstructionist tactics of the employers and other town leaders. Eventually, the workers triumph and the union comes into being. Though designated a proletarian opera, *The Cradle Will Rock* is actually a Kurt Weill-like song-play. Weill-like is Blitzstein's highly appealing musical texture, made up of patter songs, parodies, ballads, torch songs, the blues, pop tunes, recitatives, and chorales.

When first produced, *The Cradle Will Rock* was given oratorio style, that is, without costumes or scenery. The characters stood on a bare stage, wearing their everyday dress. There was no orchestra. The composer sat on the stage at the piano, playing his score, and between scenes giving the audience an informal commentary on what is taking place in the play.

And thereby hangs a tale—one of the most dramatic and unusual in the history of opera performances. A production of the WPA Federal Theater (a government subsidized agency to provide work to actors and writers), *The Cradle Will Rock* was scheduled for a formal première (scenery, costumes, orchestra and all). Then, as this writer has had occasion to explain in *The Story of*

America's Theater, "soon after the dress rehearsal, in June of 1937, such pressure was brought to bear on the Federal Theater by powerful government officials and agencies against a play with a pronounced left-wing slant, that the decision was finally arrived at to cancel the production. But the cast did not receive notification of the cancellation until a few hours before curtain time on opening night. A feverish search ensued to find a nearby empty theater in which the play could be given without government auspices. Luckily that theater was found, and the cast and audience were transferred there. Since the scenery belonged to the Federal Theater, and no funds were available to pay the men in the orchestra, both had to be dispensed with. . . . Strange to say the play gained in dramatic force and emotional impact through this untraditional presentation, and *The Cradle Will Rock* became a box-office attraction. A producer was now found ready to finance a regular run on Broadway, which began on January 3, 1938. Still presented without scenery, costumes, or orchestra—but this time through choice rather than necessity—*The Cradle Will Rock* stayed on Broadway for about four months. It was also performed in other parts of the country, and was recorded in its entirety."

A decade after this première, *The Cradle Will Rock* was revived in New York by Leonard Bernstein, who conducted a concert version of the opera with the New York City Symphony. The opera was so generously hailed by critics and the audience, that once again it was brought to Broadway, but with much less success than originally; this revival lasted only thirteen performances.

For a while, Blitzstein continued writing song-plays on provocative political or social subjects; *I've Got the Tune* for radio in 1937; *No for an Answer* in 1940

103

(closed down by the city authorities soon after its première because of its controversial left-wing slant). After that Blitzstein abandoned the political arena to write compelling musical dramas in which some of the popular elements of his earlier song-plays are wedded to the most serious and ambitious techniques of musical-dramatic writing, as well as to some of the advanced idioms of the avant-garde composer. Among these later stage works are *Regina* in 1949, based on Lillian Hellman's play, *The Little Foxes;* and, a few years after that, *Juno,* adapted from Sean O'Casey's *Juno and the Paycock.*

Blitzstein was working on a new opera based on the provocative Sacco and Vanzetti case of the 1920s, when he was murdered in Fort-de-France, in Martinique, on January 22, 1964.

CHAPTER 5

The Expressionists

IF Satie and Impressionism were reactions against Wagnerism, and if "The Six" and *Zeitkunst* were reactions against Impressionism, then Expressionism is the reaction against Wagnerism, Impressionism, the levities of "The Six" and the functionalism of *Zeitkunst* and *Gebrauchsmusik*. As a matter of fact, Expressionism rebelled against everything that had been governing musical creation for generations. For while the new harmonic and tonal language of Wagner, Debussy, Ives, Milhaud, and Stravinsky had been an amplification and revision of older systems, the vocabulary of Expressionism was a complete break with the past through the creation of altogether new methods. Expressionism was revolution, not evolution.

Expressionism bears the same relation to music that Abstractionism does to painting. The abstract painter sought a pure and absolute art, governed by its own laws, and divorced from all sense of reality. "I paint what I *think*," Pablo Picasso once said, "not what I *see*." In amplification, Thomas Craven, the American author of *Modern Art*, has written of Picasso: "He believes that art is a purely material thing; that is to say, a picture is a composition in the same sense that a pile of neatly arranged bricks is a composition; that its value is measured simply and solely by the skill, the orderliness and the novelty of the arrangement; that a picture represents

105

nothing; that even when dealing with the human form, it does not communicate emotions inseparably connected with figures; that it is not a symbol charged with human implications, an instrument employed by artists to express their experience with life; that, in short, the material constituents—the actual mud and oil—when arrestingly consolidated, contains the true esthetic values."

The expressionist, paraphrasing Picasso, might well say: "I write the kind of music I *think*, not what I hear." The sensual perception is not important, only the thought processes. The expressionist composer tries to strip music of all possible feeling, emotion, and human relationships. He wants to get down to the barest essentials. He seeks a logic of thought as exact as a mathematical formula. He strives for the full freedom of anarchy. Through a strict adherence to dissonant chords unrelieved by consonance; through the absence of any basic tonality; through the freedom of his melodic line to move at will horizontally and vertically—through all this the expressionist has freed music once and for all from the long-held concepts of harmony, counterpoint, and melody.

Atonality—the absence of tonality—is his basic tool. Since Bach, a musical composition has been identified as being in a specific key, say C major or D minor. This means that the basic tone of that key (the tonic) dominates the other eleven notes of the chromatic scale. The other eleven notes revolve around that basic tone, and are dependent upon it. But the expressionist who writes atonal music abandons this practice by eliminating keys. In atonal music each of the twelve notes of the chromatic scale is independent of the other, and is unrelated to any focal point.

106

II

Arnold Schoenberg is the apostle of Expressionism. Like Debussy, he started out as a disciple of and true believer in Wagner, before overthrowing the old gods and promulgating a new faith of his own.

He was born in Vienna on September 13, 1874. While attending public school he studied the violin and 'cello by himself. Without any formal training, he soon started putting down musical ideas on paper. By the time he was sixteen he had come to the conclusion that more than anything else he wanted to become a professional musician. Seeking guidance, he came to Alexander Zemlinsky, a distinguished Viennese composer and teacher, who was so impressed by the boy's compositions that he forthwith took him under his protective wing. He began teaching Schoenberg harmony and counterpoint, found for him a job as 'cellist in one of Vienna's lesser orchestras, and introduced him to a circle of dedicated musicians.

By 1897, Schoenberg had completed a string quartet, his first large-scale work. His indebtedness to Wagner was evident in the sensual lyricism and indulgence in chromatic harmonies. Thus the Wagner camp had claimed young Schoenberg just as it had done so many other of the younger Viennese musicians; and for a long time Schoenberg remained faithful to it.

When that first string quartet was introduced in Vienna it was well received. This was Schoenberg's first pleasant association with audiences and critics—and it was also destined to be his last for many years to come. Although his next few compositions were still steeped in Wagner, were still essentially romantic in feeling and traditional in technique, they encountered hostility.

107

These works included an orchestral tone poem, *Pelleas and Melisande; Verklaerte Nacht (Transfigured Night)*; and some songs. When *Transfigured Night* was heard for the first time at the turn of the twentieth century, the antagonism Schoenberg was henceforth to experience erupted forcefully for the first time. To present-day ears there is nothing here to cause surprise or offense. But this music rubbed Viennese sensibilities the wrong way, and evoked a response of stamping and hissing. "From that time on," said Schoenberg, "the scandals never ceased."

Transfigured Night and *Pelleas and Melisande* also aroused the anger and aggressiveness of Viennese music audiences. The former was completed in 1899 as a string sextet, and in 1917 was transcribed for string orchestra. Here Schoenberg is the Wagnerian who brings intensity and passion to a glowing poem by Richard Dehmel. The poem describes a walk by a man and a woman through a moonlit grove. She confesses that she has loved another man. Her partner is all-forgiving. They sink into each other's arms, then continue their walk through the wondrous night.

Pelleas and Melisande was no less lush in its harmonic writing, no less sensual in mood, no less a recognizable child of Wagner than *Transfigured Night*. Yet when first heard in Vienna on January 26, 1905, it encouraged catcalls from the audience and hostile attacks from the critics. "Schoenberg's tone poem . . . is not just filled with wrong notes . . . it is a fifty-minute long protracted wrong note," exclaimed Ludwig Karpath. "What else may hide behind those cacophonies is quite impossible to find out. . . . One deals here with a man either devoid of all sense or who takes his listeners for fools."

The *Chamber Symphony* (1907) described as a dou-

ble-faced mirror looking back at Schoenberg's Romanticism and forward to his Expressionism, provoked an
even greater scandal. A dispatch to *Musical America* tells
the story: "If this concert was intended to be a 'memorable occasion' it surely succeeded, for it occasioned
the greatest uproar that has occurred in a Viennese
concert hall. . . . Laughter, hisses, and applause continued throughout a great part of the actual performance. . . . The dispute became almost a riot. The police were sought after and the only officer who could be
found actually threw out of the gallery one noisemaker
who persisted in blowing on a key for a whistle. But the
policeman could not prevent one of the composers from
appearing in the box and yelling to the crowd, 'Out with
the trash!' Whereat the uproar increased. Members of
the orchestra descended from the stage and entered into
the spirited controversy with the audience."

After the *Chamber Symphony*, Schoenberg abandoned
Wagner once and for all and fearlessly embarked on his
own artistic journey. Seeking precision and economy of
thought, complete independence of movement, and abstraction, he began to write a new kind of music: as
logical as a syllogism; its lyric line as austere as the
spoken word; its tonality completely free; its harmonic
language completely dissonant. The last time Schoenberg
now used a central key was in the *Quartet in F-sharp
minor* (1908). After that his music became atonal. He
arrived at the threshhold of Expressionism in 1912 with
Pierrot Lunaire, a set of 21 songs based on poems (or
as the poet specified, "melodramas") by Albert Giraud,
for speaking voice, piano, and four instruments. Once
and for all tonality had been discarded. In this work
dissonance replaces consonance; *Sprechstimme* (a kind
of gliding song-speech in which rhythm and pitch are

rigidly controlled) takes the place of lyricism; thematic material is terse and concentrated; the meter is extremely free. This is absolute music completely divorced from extra-musical meanings, deriving its interest and force exclusively from musical values. Indeed, the music seems to make no attempt to interpret the poems, and at times seemingly is irrelevant to the text. In the nineteenth song ("Serenade") the poem makes mention of a viola while the musical background is scored for 'cello.

The première of *Pierrot Lunaire* in Berlin on October 16, 1912, was the occasion for one of the greatest scandals witnessed in a German concert hall before World War I. Not only did the audience bellow its disapproval after each of the songs, but tried its best to drown out the music with loud, rhythmic stamping of the feet. Fists began to fly as adherents of Schoenberg tried to quell the noise. One critic regarded this music as "the most ear-splitting combinations of tones that ever desecrated the walls of a Berlin music hall." The Berlin music critic, Otto Taubman, remarked simply: "If this is music, then I pray my Creator not to let me hear it again."

Even among the usually staid and undemonstrative music audiences of London the sparks began to fly at a Schoenberg première, this time of the *Five Pieces for Orchestra*, on September 3, 1912. As the concert progressed, the laughter mounted and heated arguments developed. The critic of the *London Daily Mail* described the music as "scrappy sounds and perpetual discord" while the *Daily News* reviewer expressed heartfelt sympathy for the composer who had thus depicted so gruesomely his own experiences in music. Elaborating on the same theme, the critic of *The Globe* said: "The music of Schoenberg's *Five Pieces* resem-

bled the wailings of a tortured soul and suggested
nothing so much as the disordered fancies of delirium
or the fearsome, imaginary terrors of a highly nervous
infant."

The Schoenberg scandals had become such a habit
by 1913 that they erupted with very little provocation.
The *Gurre-Lieder* is a case in point. This work actually belonged to Schoenberg's post-Romantic, Wagnerian period, most of it having been written in 1900–
1901. Many of its pages have an arresting beauty and
a deeply moving emotional intensity. Yet when the
Gurre-Lieder was finally heard in Vienna on February 23, 1913, a veritable tempest was unleashed. At
the rehearsals, the first horn-player attacked the composer with his instrument, then left the hall in a rage
vowing he would never play this kind of music. (Actually after he calmed down he not only played the
work but grew to like it.) At the concert, the shouts
of denunciation drowned out vocal expressions of enthusiasm. A brawl developed. One woman fainted.
Some years later the reverberations of this concert
were felt in the law courts. One man, who had attended the première, had brought suit against another
for assault during the concert. A prominent physician
testified that the music had been so nerve-racking that
it provoked neuroses in its hearers. Yet this supposedly
nerve-racking music was tame stuff, indeed, even for
1913.

All this hostility succeeded in drawing Schoenberg
away from the world of audiences, critics, and public
performances. He surrounded himself with an intimate
circle of friends, pupils and disciples. They founded
in Vienna the Society for Private Performance which—
since it barred all critics, and admitted only those

111

sympathetic to the new style—allowed for a more favorable climate in which the works of Schoenberg and his followers could be heard. On the few occasions when established musical organizations played his works he refused to attend the performance. He would wait until concert audiences and critics caught up with him and understood what he was trying to say. Meanwhile, he would strike out even more boldly into the virgin territory he had been the first to explore.

And so with the single-minded purpose and the passionate zeal of a prophet he looked neither to the right nor to the left, but marched steadfastly toward a still greater revolution. From atonality he progressed to the twelve-tone system with which he has since become so intimately identified.

As Schoenberg plunged ever deeper into the world of atonality he began to realize that the style had brought him not freedom but anarchy. As a creative artist he now felt the need for discipline and order, and a new set of principles to replace the old ones of tonality he had long since abandoned. Thus he came to the "twelve-tone technique" or "row"—or, to use a more formidable designation, dodecaphony. His first tentative experiments in this direction came in 1915 with a Scherzo in which the black and white notes of the octave were used without an established pattern. Soon after that came the *Piano Pieces* (Op. 23) in which he experimented with a technique which he described as "composing with the tones of the basic motive." In contrast to the old way of building themes or melodies from motives, which in turn followed established rules of melodic construction, Schoenberg was already beginning to build entire sequences with motives constructed from twelve basic tones. Thus the

112

idea of writing music around the twelve-tone framework kept simmering within him, sometimes overflowing in his writings. At last in 1922, in the *Suite for Piano,* the basic formula for a twelve-tone system was set for the first time; and it was clearly realized in 1924 in the fourth movement of his *Serenade.*

The twelve-tone system is a complex method of composition. *The Harvard Brief Dictionary of Music* offers the clearest explanation:

> Every composition is based on a so-called *series* or *tone row,* containing all the twelve chromatic tones in a succession chosen by the composer. The chosen order of tones remains unchanged throughout the composition, except for the modifications explained below. The entire composition, therefore, consists of nothing but restatements of the series in any of its numerous formations (horizontal and vertical).
>
> In addition to its original form (S), the series can be used in its inversion (S^i), in its retrograde form (S^r), and in its retrograde inversion (S^{ri}).
>
> The above four forms of the series can be used in transposition to any step of the chromatic scale. Thus the series becomes available in 48 (12 × 4) modifications.
>
> From this basic material innumerable formations can be derived, differing as to rhythm, chordal grouping, polyphonic juxtaposition, etc., and it is with these that the actual process of composition begins. The technical premises explained above are no more restricting (actually, less so) than those of any other method (e.g., the triads and harmonic progressions as employed by Classical composers).

The melodic patterns made possible by this arrangement and rearrangement of twelve tones are virtually infinite: One theorist, Hauer, computed that there are 479,001,600 possible melodic combinations in this technique!

Schoenberg utilized the twelve-tone row with extraordinary skill and ingenuity in his *Third String Quartet* in 1927 and the *Variations for Orchestra* in 1928. But the sounds produced were cold, hard, and repellingly ugly. This new music was the work of a highly analytical brain that handled the problems of composition as if they were mathematical. Human feeling was dispensed with altogether. What the layman heard was a baffling, seemingly disorganized and overcomplicated pattern of musical sounds. Even highly trained musicians listened, perhaps with admiration at the ingenuity, but without affection.

In any event, this was certainly not the kind of music that could finally win for Schoenberg receptive audiences and admiring critics. The first performance of his *Third String Quartet* once again inspired hissing, stamping, laughter. When the *Variations for Orchestra* was given in Berlin, the "give and take of remarks for and against the piece" (as Max Marschalk, the German music critic, reported) "grew to greater dimensions and took more unfortunate forms than we have experienced at a Schoenberg première." Even the usually docile American audiences were provoked. When Leopold Stokowski performed the work in Philadelphia there was such a noisy reaction that the conductor had to address the audience and take it severely to task for its "bad manners."

After the Nazis came to power in Germany in 1933, Schoenberg disavowed his country and, at the same time, returned to the Jewish faith which he had abandoned early in life through conversion. On July 24, 1933, in a Paris synagogue, he went through a ceremony reinstating him as a Jew—his gesture of protest against the savage persecution of Jews which had become a government policy in Germany. In 1933 he came to America, and soon became an American citizen. He set up home in Brentwood, in Southern California and became a member of the faculty of the University of Southern California. Later he joined the faculty of the University of California, and gave private instruction in composition to a few selected pupils. At this point he directed himself to the writing of several new major works. Composition so absorbed his time and energies that in his seventieth year he retired from the faculty of the University of California. However, he kept on teaching a small circle of students (about eight in all) until a month before his death, on July 13, 1951.

A change of nationality, a return to his race, and the impact of world events affected Schoenberg's music. No longer did he create cold, mathematical compositions. As he became concerned with the turbulent world around him, a human equation began to intrude into his mathematics. He now took his subject material and his artistic stimulation from the contemporary world. The *Ode to Napoleon* was basically an indictment of dictatorship. The *Survivor from Warsaw* was a moving and powerful account of the heroic uprising in the Warsaw ghetto of the Jews against the Nazi war machine. Schoenberg even made an attempt at writing functional music, as was the case with his *Theme and Variations*, intended for performance in schools. And in completely abstract works—the *Concerto for Piano*—an infusion of warmth and charm could be detected.

Schoenberg also revised his one-time ascetic approach to the twelve-tone technique. As a teacher he had never imposed his own theories and techniques on his pupils. His students, who came to him to learn the twelve-tone technique from its source, were startled to find the master devoting so much of his time to a dissection of masterworks by Mozart, Bach, and Beethoven. The same broad view now characterized Schoenberg's creative thinking. He no longer felt the compulsion to write exclusively in a twelve-tone row. In some of his last works the idiom is found in random pages; in others, not at all. The range of his compositions, consequently, was immeasurably expanded. On occasion he even felt compelled to revert to the romantic mode of his youthful compositions. The artist had mellowed.

At long last, recognition and homage came to this musical prophet who for so many years had been despised and rejected. In 1947, the American Academy and the National Institute of Arts and Letters conferred on him a Special Award of Distinguished Achievement. His seventy-fifth birthday was celebrated in many principal cities of the United States with commemorative (and often sold-out) all-Schoenberg concerts. Magazines and newspapers published eloquent tributes. Fellow musicians showered him with congratulations and gifts. And one of the world's greatest writers, Thomas Mann, wrote *Doctor Faustus*, a novel whose main character was a composer like Schoenberg, and in which the technique of twelve-tone composition was elaborately described as part of the narrative. Even the critics had come to hail him. Virgil Thomson called the *Five Pieces for Orchestra* "among the most celebrated works of our century." Similarly high praise attended the world premières of the *Ode to Napoleon, Survivor from Warsaw,* the *Piano Concerto,* the orchestral *Theme and Variations* of 1944; the last of these was performed by virtually every important American orchestra within two years of its première by the Boston Symphony under Koussevitzky.

But the greatest tribute of all which Schoenberg lived to witness was the way in which his twelve-tone technique was embraced by famous composers in all parts of the Western world. His pupils and disciples, who never swerved in their allegiance, and whose life work represented the fruition of Schoenberg's theories and beliefs, were not the only ones to employ the twelve-tone system. Famous composers like Ernst Křenek (1900–   ) and Ernest Toch (1881–1964)—both of whom had long since achieved world acclaim with other methods and other styles—became partial to the twelve-tone row late in their lives. (So did Stravinsky, though Schoenberg did not live to see this come to pass.) René Leibowitz (1913–   ) in France; Luigi Dallapiccola (1904–   ) in Italy; Wallingford Riegger (1885–1961), Roger Sessions (1896–   ) and Ben Weber (1916–   ) in the United States— these were some of many composers for whom the twelve-tone row became a basic idiom. With other important composers, the twelve-tone row became a valuable method for special artistic effects within compositions which were not essentially dodecaphonic: Béla Bartók in his *Violin Concerto,* Walter Piston in *The Incredible Flutist,* and Leonard Bernstein in *The Age of Anxiety.*

Of Schoenberg's disciples, Anton von Webern was the one who, in certain respects, was holier than the apostle himself. Webern not only began to favor the rules as established by his teacher, but even went a step beyond him by introducing a twelve-tone *color* system (in his *Symphony*). Each instrument is rarely permitted to play two successive notes, but after sounding a note must wait until the other instruments have made their appearance. If Schoenberg liked conciseness and brevity, Webern could outdo the master by producing a composition (the fourth of his *Five Pieces for Orchestra*) that required only nineteen seconds for performance. If Schoenberg wanted to get down to the barest essentials of harmony and counterpoint, Webern, in his use of isolated tones, could virtually exile harmony and counterpoint from his musical world. If Schoenberg aspired for the most elementary kind of expression, Webern could produce a *Bagatelle* for string quartet in which, as Schoenberg himself once said, "a whole novel is expressed in a single sigh."

Webern was nine years younger than Schoenberg. He was born in Vienna on December 3, 1883, and received a doctorate in philosophy from the University there, where he also took courses in musicology. In the beginning he earned his living conducting theater orchestras. His first composition, a *Passacaglia* for orchestra (1908), was in a traditional post-Romantic style. His association with Schoenberg took place at about this time, and forthwith Webern had come upon his musical identity. His unique style was crystallized in the *Five Pieces for Orchestra*, one of the works given in Vienna in 1913 on a program devoted entirely to the Schoenberg school. That concert, as we have already remarked, caused a riot. One critic, commenting upon Schoenberg's pupils, said: "They may be called 'Ultralists,' though by any other name they could by no means lose any of their fragrance."

Webern's first twelve-tone work was *Three Sacred Songs* (1924). Thereafter he advanced ever more boldly into the world of musical abstraction—significantly so with his Symphony (1928) which marked the beginnings of serialism, a technique embraced by significant composers the world over since the 1950s. (See Chapter 15.)

Webern met a tragic death on September 15, 1945, in Mittersill, Austria. American troops were occupying the town. Webern became the victim of mistaken identity and was shot by a soldier.

At the time of his death, Webern was one of the least performed of the Schoenberg twelve-tone school. Since his death his time has come, as he knew with finality it would. Everything he has written was recorded by Columbia in 1957. Festivals of Webern's music have taken place in Seattle, Washington, and at the Salzburg Festival. An international Webern society was formed in 1962. In fact he has become a cult among the younger generation of composers. Even Stravinsky found in Webern a new inspiration—so much so that, in his old age, Stravinsky stood ready to reject a style he had been using for about forty years to embrace serialism.

IV

Alban Berg is regarded as the Romanticist of the twelve-tone school, since he succeeded in infusing expressiveness and emotion into the harsh, austere sounds of atonality. It was Berg who created what is surely one of the crowning achievements of the Expressionist school, *Wozzeck*—an endurable monument of twentieth-century opera.

Like his teacher, Schoenberg, and his colleague, Webern, Berg encountered derision, sardonic criticisms, misunderstanding, and vehement attacks most of his life. Yet, he had the courage of both Schoenberg and Webern and remained unshaken in his purpose. Berg was convinced that it was *he* who was right, and his critics who were wrong; he knew with an unshakable conviction that the music he was writing had permanent value, would survive, and in time would gain universal acceptance.

Berg was born in Vienna on February 9, 1885. Without any training to speak of, he made his first attempts at composition when he was fifteen. Four years after that he met Schoenberg, and from that moment on Berg knew he wanted to be a composer. To support himself, Berg worked as a government official, but he spent all his free hours studying music, listening to it, and experimenting with composition. His first model was Wagner—an early piano sonata being filled with Wagnerian chromatic harmonies and sensual lyricism. Then he vigorously brushed Wagner aside and stepped fearlessly into Expressionism.

His first significant atonal work was *Five Songs with Orchestra* in 1912, also one of the compositions performed and annihilated at that 1913 concert in Vienna devoted to Schoenberg and his pupils. But Berg did not lose heart. He now began to plan an atonal opera based on Georg Büchner's expressionist play *Wozzeck*.

120

The outbreak of World War I, when Berg served in the Austrian army, interrupted this ambitious project. But when the war was over, Berg returned to his opera with undiminished excitement, finally completing the work in 1920.

The episodes and characters in *Wozzeck* are like distorted reflections from a cracked, uneven mirror. The hero is a poor downtrodden soldier who finds in a drum major a rival for his sweetheart, Marie's, love. Wozzeck's suspicions mount when he discovers her with a pair of earrings which the drum major has given her. He openly accuses her of infidelity, and she defies him. Later on, the drum major boasts before Wozzeck of his friendship with Marie. When Wozzeck turns down his invitation for a drink, the drum major beats the soldier soundly. Now Marie repents of the shabby way she has treated Wozzeck, and offers to take a walk with him. Distraught and incoherent, Wozzeck suddenly turns on her and murders her. He returns to the scene of the crime to try and retrieve his murder weapon, a knife he had carelessly thrown into a nearby pool. Seeing it floating on the surface of the water, Wozzeck jumps into the pool and drowns.

Berg's basic tool is the *Sprechstimme*, or song-speech, with which he replaces all former concepts of operatic lyricism. The voice swoops and soars and plunges to strange intervals, made even more stark and gruesome by the background of harrowing atonal harmonies. A most unusual orchestra is called for to set off this *Sprechstimme*. It is made up of several ensembles —a chamber orchestra, a restaurant-orchestra of high-pitched violins, and a military band. The formal in-

121

struments are supplemented by some less conventional ones, such as an out-of-tune piano, an accordion, and a bombardon (the predecessor of the bassoon).

Within the seemingly formless organization of his opera, Berg interpolated various old musical structures—passacaglia, march, rhapsody, suite, invention, symphony (though none of these is readily recognizable as such). His purpose was to have each of these forms serve as a symbol for what was transpiring on the stage.

The sounds that soar from voices and instruments may prove bewildering in their haunting strangeness and piercing cacophony. The complexity of Berg's forms and techniques might not be readily comprehended. Nevertheless, as this drama of murder and death proceeds to its overpowering conclusion—made continually more tense and compelling through Berg's musical language—it carries an irresistible emotional impact. Whether or not one understands what Berg is doing, or why he is doing it, one readily admits that listening to *Wozzeck* is a shattering experience. Not since *Pelleas and Melisande* has there been an opera in which music and text are so inextricably one.

Why does *Wozzeck* grip even the listener with no theoretical background? The question was once asked by England's most distinguished critic, Ernest Newman, who also provided this answer: "I suppose it is because of the unique oneness of the dramatic situations, the psychology of the characters and the musical expression. The first two of these elements are so consistently irrational that a certain irrationality (as the ordinary listener conceives it) in the music also seems right, especially in view of the fact that what revolts our harmonic sensibility in black and white can be

122

made not only tolerable but gladly acceptable by means of orchestral color." Then Mr. Newman concludes: "The non-technical listener . . . finds himself, perhaps for the first time in his life, taking a vast amount of non-tonal music and not merely not wincing at it but being engrossed by it. That simple fact is the true measure of Berg's achievement; whether the listener can account for his interest or not the fact remains that he is interested in *Wozzeck* throughout, that he feels the music to be not only 'right' for the subject but the only musical equivalent conceivable for it."

As one of the most original operas ever written, *Wozzeck* did not have an easy time winning admirers. In fact, few operas ever confronted such a rain of venom as that which met *Wozzeck* when it was first produced in Berlin on December 14, 1925. The *Neue Freie Presse* remarked: "Whether one sings or plays wrong notes in such an insalubrious style is utterly immaterial." And Paul Zschorlich wrote in the *Deutsche Zeitung*: "As I left the State Opera I had a sensation not of coming out of a public institution but out of an insane asylum. On the stage, in the orchestra, in the hall, plain madmen. . . . In Berg's music there is not a trace of melody. There are only scraps, shreds, spasms and burps. Harmonically, the work is beyond discussion, for everything sounds wrong. . . . I regard Alban Berg as a musical swindler and a musician dangerous to the community. . . . We deal here, in the realm of music, with a capital offense."

Whenever *Wozzeck* was performed in the 1920's, both in Berlin and elsewhere, it created a disturbance, and sometimes even inspired physical violence. The situation was so bad in Prague in 1926 that the authorities called it a menace to public safety and had to withdraw it from the repertory. But being a highly controversial work, one attracting worldwide publicity as well as conflicting viewpoints and curiosity, *Wozzeck* was widely given. (In Vienna, a booklet was published quoting, commenting upon, and analyzing the opposing critical viewpoints inspired by the opera.) In less than a decade it had been given over a thousand times in twenty-eight European theaters. It was introduced in the United States in 1931, in performances directed by Leopold Stokowski in Philadelphia and New York.

From an opera produced mainly for its shock value, *Wozzeck* has risen to the position of a modern classic, whose performances are artistic events of the first importance. When Dimitri Mitropoulos directed a concert version with the New York Philharmonic in 1951, Arthur Jacobs said in *Musical America:* "The work is a masterpiece. . . . At the end, the audience, showing every sign of being deeply moved, called and recalled the conductor to the platform." (This performance was recorded in its entirety by Columbia, and to the amazement of that company sold remarkably well.) When, later the same year, the opera was given at the Salzburg Festival in Austria, Virginia Pleasants reported in the same journal that "it was an enormous artistic triumph." In 1952, *Wozzeck* was given in English at the New York City Opera to be called by Robert Sabin "one of the incontestable masterpieces of twentieth-century music." And when soon after that it entered the repertory of the Metropolitan Opera, *Wozzeck* not only gathered critical accolades but was even played to sold-out auditoriums—the final testimony, if such be needed, that the opera had finally won over not only the critics but the public as well.

124

Berg was never a prolific composer. Only a handful of compositions came after *Wozzeck*. One was the *Lyric Suite;* another, the eloquent *Violin Concerto,* written as a threnody for a young girl. Both are in the twelve-tone technique, and both are charged with compelling emotion. The operatic successor of *Wozzeck— Lulu—*was never completed. Though in many respects *Lulu* was even more stark in its Expressionism, and more advanced in its atonality, it was cheered when an orchestral suite adapted from its score was heard for the first time in Berlin in 1934. The only dissenting voice came from the balcony—a shout of *"Heil Mozart!"* The first stage presentation of *Lulu* took place in Zurich on June 2, 1937. At that time the audience rose to its feet to give the opera a fifteen-minute ovation. Since then, *Lulu* has been acclaimed throughout most of the civilized world as one of the major contributions to twentieth-century opera. It has not only been performed with immense success by many leading opera companies in Europe and America—including presentations at Expo 67 in Montreal in 1967—but it has even been recorded in its entirety three times.

A rehearsal of the orchestral suite from *Lulu* was the last piece of music Berg was destined to hear. Suffering from a tooth infection, and too poor to consult a dentist, Berg was stricken by blood poisoning. He died on Christmas Eve in 1935.

CHAPTER 6

The Primitives

WHILE the Expressionists were thus shaking the music world out of its complacency, a Russian rebel was creating an upheaval of his own with his own brand of avant-gardism. He was Igor Stravinsky, of whom Erik Satie once said: "More than anyone else he has freed the musical thought of today." Like the Expressionists, Stravinsky was opposed to the excesses of Wagner and Debussy. But his rebellion came not in the form of precise, abstractionist and mathematical-like music, but through a reversion to an uninhibited primitivism. He, too, replaced pleasant harmonies with searing dissonances; traditional counterpoint with jarring combinations of disjointed tonalities; spacious melodies with epigrammatic ideas, some consisting of hardly more than a limited number of notes. But most of all, he unleashed a force that was like an atomic explosion through the use of rapidly changing meters, polymeters, varied rhythms and polyrhythms. Rhythm had never been an important element with the Romantics, or with the Russian nationalists, or with Wagner, or with Debussy. But with Stravinsky rhythm achieved full emancipation. And with this rhythm came flaming orchestral colors, a new emphasis on percussion, and brilliant orchestral sound. This was Neo-Primitivism: a return to the dynamic and elementary forces of primitive music.

126

Stravinsky's Neo-Primitive style became fully developed with a ballet describing a pagan rite in old Russia—*Le Sacre du printemps* (*The Rite of Spring*). In this ballet a ritual is taking place—the adoration of Nature by primitive man. In the first of the two sections, "The Fertility of Earth," we witness a barbaric dance ("The Ballet of Adolescents") in which the excitement reaches a fever pitch. Then comes a second ritual, "The Games of the Rival Tribes," a contest between two groups in battle and gymnastics. The earth is then consecrated by the Sage, and a demoniac dance of the earth ensues. The second part opens with a portrait of pagan night, touched with awe and mystery. A dance "of the mysterious circle of adolescents" is succeeded by two ritual dances: "Evocation of the Ancestors" and "Ritual of the Ancestors." Then the sacrifice must take place: a female victim dances to her death. This dance becomes a corybantic. In a last orgiastic outburst, the rite comes to an end.

Explosive rhythms, volatile meters, shattering discords, and orgies of orchestral sound and color create a momentum in which the tensions become almost excruciatingly painful and whose kinaesthetic appeal is cyclonic. This surely was the apotheosis of barbaric music in sophisticated terms. Nobody—not Richard Strauss with Realism, Debussy with Impressionism, nor Schoenberg with Expressionism—shook the music world to its very foundations the way Stravinsky did with *The Rite of Spring*.

It can, therefore, be readily understood why *The Rite of Spring* should have been the instrument for the discharge of such violent, at times uncontrollable, reactions at its première performance. This première took place at the Théâtre des Champs Elysées in Paris

127

on May 29, 1913, in a presentation by Diaghilev's Ballet Russe. The dance and the music had hardly proceeded more than a few minutes when the *grand'-homme* of French music, Camille Saint-Saëns, rose haughtily in his seat, made a bitter remark about the music, and stalked out of the theater. Perhaps encouraged by the reaction of so formidable a musical authority, others now made their feelings known. The Austrian Ambassador guffawed so loudly that his bellows reverberated over the discords of the music. The Princess de Pourtalès left her box shouting: "I am sixty years old, but this is the first time that anyone dared to make a fool of me!" The critic, André Capu, yelled as loudly as he could that Stravinsky was a fraud.

In *Music After the War,* Carl van Vechten further describes what took place at this unprecedented occasion.

"A certain part of the audience, thrilled by what it considered to be a blasphemous attempt to destroy music as an art, and swept away with wrath, began very soon after the rise of the curtain to whistle, to make catcalls, and to offer audible suggestions as to how the performance should proceed. . . . The orchestra played on unheard, except occasionally when a slight lull occurred. The figures on the stage danced in time to music that they had to imagine they heard, and beautifully out of rhythm with the uproar in the auditorium. I was sitting in a box in which I had rented one seat. Three ladies sat in front of me, one young man occupied the places behind me. He stood up during the course of the ballet to enable himself to see more clearly. The intense excitement under which he was laboring, thanks to the potent force of the music, betrayed itself presently when he began to beat rhythmically on the top of my head with his fists. My emotion was so great that I did not feel the blows for some time. They were perfectly synchronized with the music."

But the provocative new work had admirers as well as critics. Maurice Ravel kept shouting the word "genius" into the din. The distinguished critic, Roland-Manuel, was so loud in his praise that somebody near him tore the collar from his neck. Claude Debussy quivering with rage, begged the audience to quiet down and listen to what was being played. One society lady spat in the face of a particularly obnoxious demonstrator, while another slapped the face of a man who was hissing.

As for the principal characters in this drama. . . . The composer Stravinsky, the impresario Diaghilev, the principal dancer Nijinsky all went with Jean Cocteau for a slow, late drive through the Bois de Boulogne to ease their overwrought nerves and tensions. Nobody spoke until Diaghilev suddenly began to quote Pushkin, as the tears flowed down his cheeks. Not a word was said about that evening's scandal. "It was dawn when we returned," recalled Cocteau. "No one can imagine how quiet and nostalgic these three men were."

But the furor did not die down after the final curtain of that première performance. Indeed, it continued in the press for several years more. "The most essential characteristic of *Le Sacre du printemps,*" said Pierre Lalo, "is that it is the most dissonant and the most discordant composition ever written. Never was the system and the cult of the wrong note practised with so much industry, zeal, and fury." Another Parisian critic remarked: "The music . . . baffles a verbal description. To say that much of it is hideous as sound is a mild description. . . . Practically it has no relation to music at all as most of us understand the word." When *The Rite of Spring* was introduced in London, also in 1913, an English commentator said: "A crowd of savages . . . might have produced such noises." And when the orchestral suite was heard in America for the first time, in 1924, an unidentified wit contributed the following lines to the Boston *Herald*:

"Who wrote this fiendish *Rite of Spring?*
What right had he to write this thing?
Against our helpless ears to fling,
Its crash, clash, cling, clang, bing, bang, bing!'"

Who wrote "this fiendish *Rite of Spring?*" Naturally a good deal of curiosity was now aroused concerning its creator, who had become one of the most provocative and highly publicized musical figures in the world. The floodlight of world attention was consequently directed on the man and his personal history.

Stravinsky was born in Oranienbaum, near St. Petersburg, on June 17, 1882, the son of a famous opera basso. Highly musical, Igor received his first instruction at the piano when he was nine. Later on, his first acquaintance with Glinka's folk operas, *Russlan and Ludmilla* and *A Life for the Czar,* through the published scores, and with Tchaikovsky's *Symphonie pathétique* through a performance marked "the beginning of my conscious life as artist and musician."

He attended local public schools, then the University of St. Petersburg for the study of law. But his pursuit of music went on. He studied harmony from a private teacher, and counterpoint from a textbook. Before long he was also moving socially with some of the city's most famous musicians, one of whom was the renowned composer and teacher Rimsky-Korsakov. He also was in frequent attendance at concerts of contemporary French music then presented by a Russian music society. Stimulated by these contacts and experiences he started to write several musical compositions, one of which—a piano sonata—encouraged Rimsky-Korsakov to accept the young man as his pupil.

In 1905 Stravinsky completed his law courses at the University. The idea of practising law, however, never seriously entered his mind, for by now he had become determined to make his way in music. In this resolve he was strongly encouraged by his cousin, whom he married in January of 1906. Under the guidance of his teacher, Rimsky-Korsakov, Stravinsky now completed a symphony and a suite for voice and orchestra, both performed in St. Petersburg in 1908. After that came a brilliant orchestral tour de force, *Fireworks,* written to honor the marriage of Rimsky-Korsakov's daughter, and a *Scherzo fantastique* for orchestra introduced in St. Petersburg in 1909.

The concert at which the *Scherzo fantastique* was heard changed Stravinsky's destiny, for among those present was that remarkable dilettante of the arts, Serge Diaghilev. Before he had founded the world-renowned Ballet Russe with which he made ballet history, Diaghilev had dabbled in various arts. First, he tried his hand at musical composition, but was soon convinced by Rimsky-Korsakov that this was not his forte. After that he founded and edited a magazine of the arts in which he analyzed and propagandized European art movements for Russia. Then he inaugurated an annual art exhibit in Russia to familiarize his countrymen with the latest schools of European painting.

Having devoted himself thus far to the promotion of European culture in Russia, Diaghilev now decided to do a similar service for Russian culture in Europe. In 1906 he arranged in Paris an art exhibit of Russian painting; in 1907 he arranged, in the same city, a series of Russian concerts; and in 1908 he brought to Paris Mussorgsky's monumental folk opera, *Boris Godunov*, with Feodor Chaliapin in the title role.

A casual conversation in a Parisian café, in which Diaghilev boasted to some Frenchmen of the unique distinction of the Russian ballet, inspired him in 1909 to bring to the French capital some of the finest examples of the Russian dance. Thus he founded the Ballet Russe, with Fokine as ballet-master, and with Karsavina, Anna Pavlova, and Nijinsky as principal dancers. From the beginning, Diaghilev was the guiding genius of the company.

In his own way, Diaghilev was as inventive a creator as the remarkable men who worked under him. A dilettante in the finest sense of the word, Diaghilev was, as Arnold L. Haskell once said of him, "a master painter who never painted, a master musician who never wrote or played, a master dancer who never danced or devised the steps of a ballet." Diaghilev had both a penetrating knowledge of each of the arts and a genuine flair for recognizing genius in the raw. Thus he was able to gather around him a company that included not only Russia's greatest dancers and choreographers, but also the foremost living painters and artists for the sets and costume designs, and the most gifted of twentieth-century composers for the music. Everybody who came into contact with him was stimulated by his infallible taste, penetrating intelligence and dynamic personality.

Stravinsky was only one of the many composers who were comparative unknowns when Diaghilev first recognized their creative potential, had them write for the Ballet Russe, then urged them on to formidable creative achievements. Diaghilev sensed latent powers in Stravinsky's *Scherzo fantastique* and contracted the composer to work for the Ballet Russe. Stravinsky's first assignment was the orchestration of two pieces by Chopin for the ballet *Chopiniana*, produced in Paris in 1909. But this was just a stepping stone. In 1910, Diaghilev turned over to Stravinsky a major assignment—the writing of music for a ballet based on an old Russian legend about the Fire-Bird. Stravinsky completed his score in May 1910, and on June 25 *L'Oiseau de feu* (*The Fire-Bird*) was introduced by the Ballet Russe in Paris and became the outstanding triumph of the ballet season.

In the Fokine adaptation of the age-old Russian legend, the Fire-Bird is first captured and then released by Ivan Czarevitch. Grateful that he has thus been set free, the Fire-Bird presents Ivan with the gift of one of his fine feathers. Suddenly a castle comes to view, the abode of Kastchei, capturer of wayfaring strangers; the castle is the prison of thirteen beautiful girls. Protected by the feather of the Fire-Bird, Ivan penetrates the castle, destroys Kastchei, and effects the release of the girls, one of whom becomes his bride.

The Stravinsky of *The Fire-Bird* is still a man greatly devoted to his teacher, Rimsky-Korsakov. There is a good deal of *Le Coq d'or* in *The Fire-Bird:* the love of

133

fantasy, the pseudo-Oriental melodies, the rich harmonic colorations, the interest in Russian folklore. The haunting and lovely "Berceuse" is of the Russian musical past. But there were things in the score of *The Fire-Bird* which were also of the future: the adventures in dissonances and the exercise in cogent rhythms in an episode like "The Dance of the Kastchei"; the primitive force that swept through the entire music; the extraordinarily effective orchestration. There were some who already thought Stravinsky too audacious. The ballerina, Anna Pavlova—scheduled to appear in *The Fire-Bird*—stoutly refused to be associated with this "horrible music." Some remarked that there was too much in the score that was either noisy or vulgar. But a few perceptive musicians heard a new voice in this music. "Mark that man Stravinsky," said Diaghilev after one of the early rehearsals. "He is on the eve of celebrity." Immediately after the première, Debussy rushed backstage to embrace Stravinsky.

Though the composer today regards the score with a good deal of condescension, *The Fire-Bird* is one of Stravinsky's most frequently performed works, through the three different suites which upon different occasions Stravinsky had himself prepared.

The umbilical cord that tied Stravinsky to Rimsky-Korsakov was cut once and for all in *Petrouchka*, introduced by the Ballet Russe in Paris on June 13, 1911. Petrouchka is the uncouth hero of a puppet-show in a Russian carnival. He is in love with the puppet ballerina, who rejects him. Against the colorful, noisy, and swirling background of the carnival, the tragic love of Petrouchka unfolds. He discovers his ballerina with a Moor, and is driven away rudely. Then the Moor pursues him and kills him, much to the consternation of the carnival public. But the pleasure seekers are soon calmed by the police, who remind them that Petrouchka, after all, is not a human being but a puppet.

Stravinsky's score was at turns vividly pictorial (the depiction of the bustle and gaiety of carnival life), subtle and revealing in its characterization (as in the gentle portrait of the puppet-ballerina by the piano, later joined by flute), humorous and sardonic (as in the amusing picture of the heavy-footed dance by the tuba), and vividly national (the Russian dance of the coachmen, and the music for the gypsies). Yet the score said all this in an altogether new voice. Bolder than ever was Stravinsky in his use of unresolved dissonances. His experiments with polytonality were both so brilliant and successful, that from here on this technique would be favored by many modernists. The long flowing melodies of *The Fire-Bird* made way for terse statements, loosely strung together.

This was the music of the future, bold and free. To many of the younger European artists it represented a spearhead with which to attack tradition and formality. In Italy, the futurist Marinetti, paraded the streets of Rome with a banner proclaiming: "Down With Wagner. Long Live Stravinsky."

Immediately after *Petrouchka* came the exciting *The Rite of Spring* to place Stravinsky solidly with the foremost musical modernists of his generation. His influence was felt the world round, his Neo-Primitivism was widely emulated. He pursued this same Neo-Primitive cult with *Le Chant du rossingol* (*The Song of the Nightingale*). This work had three lives—first as an opera, then as a ballet, and finally in its most familiar form, as a tone poem.

135

A change in Stravinsky's personal life was responsible for a radical transformation of artistic outlook. In 1919, after revolution had broken out in Russia, Stravinsky broke all ties with the land of his birth. For the next fifteen years his country was France, and his permanent home was in Paris. He even became a French citizen. Russian music with its elementary savagery, inherent power and brilliant Oriental colors no longer fascinated him. He became increasingly French in his music as well as in his outlook by reaching for a style that was refined rather than powerful and passionate, restrained rather than emotional, delicate and symmetrical rather than of Gargantuan size and proportions. And so rejecting the Primitivism which had made him, in the opinion of many, the first composer of the world, Stravinsky embraced an entirely different way of writing music.

II

Serge Prokofiev was another Russian whose dynamic approach to musical creativity placed him with the Primitives. Born in the Ukraine, in the little town of Sontzovka, on April 23, 1891, Prokofiev was a prodigy whose musical achievements tempted comparison with those of the child Mozart. Prokofiev started writing music when he was five. Three years after that he had written words and music of his first opera. And by the time he was twelve he had completed two more operas together with numerous piano pieces.

He entered the St. Petersburg Conservatory in his thirteenth year, staying there a decade, and working under such masters as Rimsky-Korsakov and Liadov. He was a precocious and brilliant student, but like Debussy, he took inordinate pleasure in harmonies

136

and tonalities frowned upon by textbooks and professors. He was writing music all the time whose rhythmic momentum and outlandish sounds outraged his professors; one of his student pieces, the *Suggestion diabolique* for piano, is still remembered. When his *First Piano Concerto* was given at the Conservatory, Alexander Glazunov, distinguished professor and composer, fled from the hall in horror, covering his ears with his hands as he ran. The discords of another of Prokofiev's pieces were so disquieting that a member in the audience shouted in derision: "Run for it men! We're being attacked by the heavy artillery!" Maxim Gorky, the novelist, reacted to "The Ugly Duckling," a Prokofiev song with weird progressions and an angular melodic line, by saying: "He must have written this music about himself." And when Prokofiev's *Second Piano Concerto* was played, soon after the composer's graduation from the Conservatory, a St. Petersburg paper said: "The . . . Concerto concludes with a mercilessly dissonant combination of brass instruments. There is a regular riot." Nevertheless Prokofiev was graduated in 1914 with diplomas in composition, piano, and conducting; and his *Second Concerto* received the coveted Rubinstein Prize.

One of his most important and controversial compositions in the Primitive style came soon after he had left the Conservatory. This was the *Scythian Suite,* for orchestra. He had been asked by Diaghilev to prepare a ballet for the Ballet Russe. Prokofiev's subject, the ancient race of Scythians and their gods, proved highly distasteful and Diaghilev rejected it. The composer then went on to change his ballet score into an orchestral suite, its première performance taking place in St. Petersburg in 1916 with Prokofiev conducting. Once

137

again Glazunov ran out of the hall; once again the critics were disconcerted. The strangest review of all came from Leonid Sabaneyev in the *News of the Season.* "If one could say that this music is bad, cacophonous, that no person with a differentiated auditory organ can listen to it, he would be told that this is a 'barbaric suite'. . . . So I shall not criticize the music; quite to the contrary, I will say that this is . . . the best barbaric music in the world. But when I am asked whether this music gives me pleasure or an artistic satisfaction, whether it makes a deep impression, I must categorically say: 'No!' The composer conducted with barbaric abandon." The reason why this review is so strange is that it was published *before* the composition was performed. What had happened was that the *Scythian Suite* had been scheduled for a concert which, at the last moment, had been postponed. Sabaneyev, unaware that the concert had not taken place, published his report the following morning. The fact that he had not heard the work he had thus attacked, that he could not possibly even have seen the score since the only manuscript copy was in the composer's possession, stimulated a scandal that reacted unfavorably against the hapless critic but helped arouse considerable sympathy for the abused composer.

Other compositions in a more or less similar barbaric manner followed rapidly, each now considered a work of first importance: the *First Violin Concerto;* the *Third Piano Concerto;* the ballet, *Chout;* the *Second Piano Sonata; Visions fugitives,* for piano. When Prokofiev paid his first visit to the United States in 1918, appearing as pianist in performances of his works, his music was described as "Bolshevism in art" and "Russian chaos." Richard Aldrich said in *The New York*

Times: "He is a psychologist of the uglier emotions. Hatred, contempt, rage—above all rage—disgust, despair, mockery and defiance legitimately serve as models for moods." H. E. Krehbiel, for forty years the principal music critic of the *New York Tribune,* described one piece as "sheerly bestial in its assaults upon the ear and intellectual fancy." The critic of the *New York World* explained: "The recipe for this sort of composition is as simple as that for boiling an egg. Write anything that comes into your head no matter how commonplace. Then change all the accidentals, putting flats in the place of sharps, and vice-versa, and the thing's done."

Even while he was "going Primitive," Prokofiev was perfecting those creative mannerisms which set him apart from the other Primitives. Those mannerisms identified most of his pre-World War I compositions, and became the trade-marks of all his later significant works. His main bent was for what he himself described as "grotesquerie": a kind of whimsy which expressed itself in saucy themes with capricious leaps to unexpected intervals; in sudden alternations between the highly complex and the elementary and the naive; in the placement of a tart, cacophonous harmony against a trite little melody; in the use of simple everyday harmonies in unusual progressions. Those who have come to know Prokofiev through some of his more popular works are familiar with this method. The saucy little march from the opera, *The Love for Three Oranges,* which for so many years identified the American radio program, "The F.B.I. in Peace and War"; the charming *Peter and the Wolf,* about which we shall speak in a later chapter, are examples of this method. But this style appears even in his most ambitious sonatas and symphonies.

Soon after Revolution erupted in Russia in 1917, Prokofiev left his native land. He set up home in Paris where he lived for more than a decade, and from which he set off on numerous world tours as pianist and conductor in presentations of his major works. Among his most significant creations during this Parisian decade were a ballet, *The Age of Steel;* the *Fifth Piano Concerto;* and the *Fourth Symphony.* The last was written on a commission from the Boston Symphony to help commemorate its fiftieth anniversary.

Then in 1933 Prokofiev decided to go back to the land of his birth. He was welcomed back as a hero. Forthwith he occupied a dominant place in the cultural life of the Soviet Union. Both as a man and as a composer Prokofiev became a member of the proletariat. As a spokesman in music for the new social order in Russia he entered upon an entirely new creative phase which will subsequently be discussed.

III

What may very well be considered the ultimate in Primitivism was achieved in 1948 by Olivier Messiaen (1908–   ) in *Turangalila,* a symphony. Though usually inspired by religious subjects and mysticism, as in *Les Offrandes oubliées, L'Ascension,* and *Les Visions de l'amen,* Messiaen digressed in *Turangalila* to produce a mammoth ten-movement symphony which was an apotheosis of rhythm. From beginning to end the symphony is a most complex and, at times, abstruse exercise in rhythmic virtuosity for which not only are the more usual percussion enlisted, but such rarer ones as temple blocks, wood blocks, Chinese cymbals, and tam-tams.

In opera, Primitivism probably went as far as it could go—but in a direction completely opposite to that of *Turangalîla*—in the remarkable trilogy, *Trionfi*, by Carl Orff. Orff is a German composer born in 1895 who, in 1935, discarded everything he had thus far written for completely new avenues of thought, form, and expression. Believing that music, in the long-accepted classical or romantic tradition had outlived its usefulness, Orff ventured into a primitive operatic world in which everything was reduced to barest essentials. He made no effort to describe the scenery, costuming, or staging he required, leaving these matters entirely to the discretion of producers. And his score was concerned primarily with rhythm; his lyric line was a declamation made up of rapidly repeated notes often without any accompaniment whatsoever. His music had the most rudimentary harmony and melody, and no counterpoint or thematic development to speak of. In such an ascetic and austere vein he completed between 1937 and 1951 the three operas of his trilogy, respectively entitled *Carmina Burana, Catulli Carmina,* and *Trionfi di Afrodite.* The first was based on thirteenth-century medieval poems of unknown authorship (discovered in a Bavarian monastery); the second, was based on poems of Catullus and had a classic-Latin text; the third, with a text alternately in Latin and Greek, came from a Latin poem of Catullus and Greek poems by Sappho and Euripides. "Orff," says Henry Pleasants, "has retreated to the Middle Ages and even to the Greeks, turning his back on the entire fund of harmonic, polyphonic, rhythmic and instrumental resources inherited by the contemporary composer."

141

CHAPTER 7

The Neo-Classicists

IN his return to classic simplicity, Carl Orff reverted to the Greeks. The Neo-Classicists, in their search for simplicity and condensation, and in their desire to eliminate non-essentials, went back to the sixteenth and seventeenth centuries. The Neo-Classicists wrote concerti grossi, ricercari, passacaglias, or fugues, but brought to these earlier forms atonality, discords, polyrhythms, and other present-day idioms.

The man most often credited with being the father of Neo-Classicism is Ferruccio Busoni (1866–1924) an Italian-born but German-trained musician. The same restless and inquisitive intelligence that made Busoni a classical scholar, a poet, a painter, and an essayist— and at the same time an outstanding composer and one of the foremost concert pianists of his time—compelled him to seek out new horizons for music. He devised new scales, worked out a new system of musical notation, and experimented with new harmonies and with quarter-tones. He was continually formulating new theories and putting them into practice. If any single prejudice dominated his musical thinking it was against Romanticism and Wagnerism—the bombastic kind of music that liked to sprawl across vast structures and give lip service to philosophic or theosophic concepts. Mozart was his ideal. In his own com-

positions—in the *Comedy Overture,* the *Rondo arlec-
chino,* or the opera *Doktor Faustus,* for example—Busoni aimed at Mozartean clarity, lucidity, economy; he
also used all the modern resources at his command.
"What he sought to achieve was a Neo-Classicism in
which form and expression may find their perfect balance," explains Professor Edward J. Dent, professor of
music at Cambridge. Busoni progressed so far along
this path that to Ernst Křenek, "the concept of Neo-
Classicism originated with Busoni."

Igor Stravinsky was the first Neo-Classicist to become world-famous, and by the same token, the first
to become a world influence. When Stravinsky established a new permanent home in Paris in 1919 and
became a French citizen, he did more than just re-
nounce the land of his birth. He was also forsaking
the Primitive style and materials with which he had
achieved world fame. After 1919, he became more partial to a purer and more objective kind of musical expression; an abstract rather than a pictorial art whose
principal interest lay in musical values. Now as a reaction against his former Primitivism, he wrote compositions that were lean and spare in texture, concise,
lyrical, contrapuntal rather than rhythmic in technique, classical in structure, and calling for comparatively modest forces. He went back to such old classical
forms as the concerto grosso, the concerto, the symphony, the oratorio, the Mass, opera buffa, and the
highly stylized serious opera of the eighteenth century.
From eighteenth-century music he expropriated its
logic, its symmetry and most important of all, its purity
of expression.

There were several important steps that led Stravinsky from Primitivism to Neo-Classicism, from pictorial

representation of Russian subjects and legends to a pure and absolute musical expression. First, in 1918, came the ballet *L'Histoire du soldat* (*The Soldier's Tale*) which required only three characters and a narrator, and an orchestra of only seven instruments. In 1919, came the ballet *Pulcinella,* in which the eighteenth-century melodies of Pergolesi were dressed in twentieth-century orchestral garb. In 1920, the *Symphonies for Wind Instruments* represented an even more advanced stage of Neo-Classicism, particularly the coda, with its classical balance and objectivity. *Mavra,* in 1922, was a conscious attempt to return to the opera buffa of the eighteenth century. The cantata, *Les Noces* (*The Wedding*), in 1923, employed an orchestra consisting merely of four pianos and a battery of percussion.

Stravinsky's Neo-Classic style became completely crystallized with the *Octet,* introduced in Paris on October 18, 1923. Aaron Copland, who was in the audience, has attested to the "general feeling of mystification" that characterized the reaction to this work. The audience had come expecting a Neo-Primitive work like those with which Stravinsky had previously made his mark. They heard something entirely different, something not readily identifiable; a work of classical structure and contrapuntal texture completely divorced from any Russian association whatsoever.

The Neo-Classic period lasted about forty years as far as Stravinsky himself was concerned. Meanwhile, soon after World War II broke out, Stravinsky once again made a radical change of home and nationality. This time he became an American citizen, and set up home in Beverly Hills, California. For a while he continued his Neo-Classical tendencies, and in this vein he completed in

144

1950 his first full-length opera, *The Rake's Progress,*
libretto by W. H. Auden and Chester Kallman based on
eight engravings by Hogarth. Here, the Neo-Classicist succeeded in writing a twentieth-century opera modeled after
Handel, Gluck, and mostly Mozart.

The Rake's Progress was Stravinsky's last work in the
Neo-Classic style. Now, once again, Stravinsky broke new
ground for himself—this time by adopting serialism (see
Chapter 15). The shock that had greeted Stravinsky's conversion from Primitivism to Neo-Classicism was just a faint
flutter compared to the reaction of his fellow musicians to
Stravinsky's new trend. For Stravinsky had always held the
twelve-tone technique (out of which serialism developed)
and Schoenberg in more or less disdain as long as Schoenberg was alive. Then, five years after Schoenberg's death,
Stravinsky—aged seventy-four—found a new musical gospel
to propound though through Webern rather than Schoenberg. Stravinsky's first work in a strict serial technique was
the *Canticum sacrum* in 1956. He remained faithful to
serialism in all his later works, the most significant of
which were the ballet *Agon (*1957), *Threni,* based on the
Lamentations of Jeremiah for solo voices, chorus and
orchestra (1958), and in his subsequent works on religious subjects as well as in his *Variations,* for orchestra
(1965).

II

The escape from complexity to simplicity, from
modernity to the past, which characterizes Neo-Classicism, can be found with Prokofiev in one of his most
frequently performed and best-liked masterworks for
orchestra, the *Classical Symphony.* Written in 1917,
and first heard in Leningrad about a year after that,
the *Classical Symphony* is one of the earliest successful

attempts *à la Busoni* to return to the structures and instrumentation of Classicism. The third movement, as a matter of fact, is in the seventeenth-century dance form of the gavotte. As Prokofiev himself explained his aim was "to catch the spirit of Mozart and put down that which, if he were living now, Mozart might put into his scores." Thus Prokofiev is not merely imitating the old masters. His form may be Classical, but the Prokofiev style as previously identified was evident throughout. Terse, pellucid, of an old-world grace, the *Classical Symphony* is nevertheless aglow with Prokofiev wit and whimsy, often generously spiced with tart Prokofiev harmonies and capricious Prokofiev-like melodic inflections. Despite the *Classical Symphony,* and its pronounced artistic success, Prokofiev never did become an avowed Neo-Classicist the way Stravinsky did. He refused to graze permanently in these fields. But many other composers were ineluctably drawn to the Neo-Classical style and remained true to it for many years, producing in this vein a great number of outstanding compositions. The most significant of these composers is Paul Hindemith.

III

Counterpoint is a basic element in the works with which Hindemith first gained world fame. But with Hindemith this essentially sixteenth- and seventeenth-century technique is skilfully combined with the most modern resources and devices to achieve a new kind of idiom—linear writing. In linear writing the voices acquire relative freedom to move independently of all harmonic relationships.

Hindemith's Neo-Classicism was first developed in seven works completed between 1922 and 1930 for

ARNOLD SCHOENBERG   *Courtesy of* Musical America

SERGE PROKOFIEV
Courtesy of Boosey and Hawkes

RALPH VAUGHAN WILLIAMS   *Courtesy of Boosey and Hawkes*

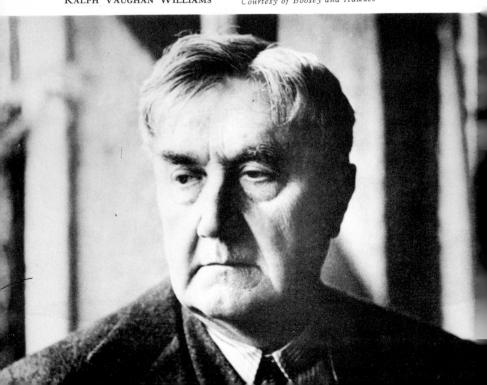

SAMUEL BARBER   *Courtesy of G. Schirmer, Inc.*

BENJAMIN BRITTEN
Courtesy of Boosey and Hawkes

BÉLA BARTÓK
Courtesy of Boosey and Hawkes

AARON COPLAND
Photo by Paul Moor,
Courtesy of Boosey and Hawkes

GIAN CARLO MENOTTI
Courtesy of G. Schirmer, Inc.

FRANCIS POULENC

DIMITRI SHOSTAKOVICH   *Courtesy of* Musical America

JOHN CAGE
Courtesy of
Musical America

HEITOR VILLA-LOBOS
Courtesy of
Musical America

JAN SIBELIUS   *Courtesy of the Finnish National Travel Office*

LEONARD BERNSTEIN and IGOR STRAVINSKY   *Courtesy of CBS Television*

chamber orchestra or for solo instrument and chamber orchestra. These received the general designation of *Kammermusik (Chamber Music)*. Here we find Hindemith making his first efforts to marry the old and the new: the contrapuntal style of the past with modern rhythmic, melodic and tonal idioms. This was Bach, but in terms of the twentieth century—or, as one German put it facetiously, "the *Brandenburg Concertos*—upside down." No less successful in realizing a modern counterpoint was the opera *Cardillac*. The operatic structure may here be more or less formal—arias, recitatives, duets, ensemble numbers—but the style is primarily polyphonic. Hindemith originally completed this opera in 1926, but a quarter of a century later he subjected it to drastic revision.

Hindemith was born in Hanau, Germany, on November 16, 1895. The compulsion to make music proved so powerful and irresistible that, since his parents opposed his studying music, he ran away from home when he was eleven. He supported himself while attending the Frankfort Conservatory by playing the violin in theater and café-house orchestras. After completing his studies, and winning the Mendelssohn Prize for his *First String Quartet,* Hindemith joined the Frankfort Opera orchestra, and later for eight years served as its concertmaster. During this period he began developing himself as a violist of the first order. From 1921 to 1929 he was violist of the Amar String Quartet (which he had helped to organize), a group devoted mainly to the performance of new music. It was for this quartet that Hindemith wrote his first significant chamber music. His *Second String Quartet,* was introduced by the Amar Quartet at the Donaueschingen Festival in 1921, and was so enthusiastically

147

received that it had to be repeated at this same festival a year later; other of his works were also heard here with marked success, including the *Kammermusik No. 1* and the song cycle *Die junge Magd*. Still more of his chamber music was given at the Salzburg Festival and in Venice. His opera, *Cardillac*, introduced in Dresden on November 9, 1926, solidified his position as one of the most brilliant and inventive new composers to appear in Germany since World War I.

It was at about this time that Hindemith began doing those functional pieces for which the term *Gebrauchsmusik* was devised, as well as specimens of popular "contemporary art" (*Zeitkunst*) with which he reached out to the masses. But Hindemith was much too trenchant a musical intellect, too profound a creative artist, and too complex a technician to find permanent asylum in such areas. By the late 1920's he was through with *Gebrauchsmusik* and *Zeitkunst*. He preferred concentrating on a contrapuntal technique, on developing his "linear" style into a subtle and highly expressive medium.

By the time the Nazis rose to power in Germany in 1933, Hindemith was second only to Richard Strauss as that country's most highly esteemed musician. As a composer, as a professor of composition at the Berlin Hochschule, as a violist, as a chamber-music performer, and as a theorist he dominated German music in virtually all its facets. His prominence and significance were both officially recognized when he was made a member of the renowned German Academy.

Then the Nazis set out to establish a new order in German music as well as in German society and politics. All Jews had to be purged from Germany's musical life; all avant-garde art had to be considered

148

degenerate. Music, like every other facet of human endeavor, had to be a spokesman for, and the glorification of, the new ideals of the Third Reich. The Nazi Chamber of Culture (*Kulturkammer*) set the rules while the Gestapo saw to it that these rules were rigidly followed.

In such a scheme of things, a man of Hindemith's high principles could find no resting place. He was not a Jew, but he refused to disavow his Jewish friends and colleagues, and insisted upon performing with eminent Jewish musicians. Besides, Hindemith's wife was Jewish. Finally, Hindemith was the composer of complex and cerebral music that was most distasteful to Nazi tastes. The high officials of the party insisted that Hindemith had committed "the foulest perversion of German music" by creating his "degenerate" works.

One composition above all others brought Hindemith into immediate conflict with the powers—his opera, *Mathis der Maler*, which many critics regard as one of his finest achievements. The text had for its central character the German religious painter of the sixteenth century, Mathias Grünewald; its plot revolved around his leadership in the peasants' uprising against the tyranny of nobility and church. Once Grünewald becomes embroiled in the struggle he is disenchanted by the oppressive measures employed by men in his own ranks, and by their display of bigotry. He deserts the world around him to return to the sanctuary of his own art which, as Hindemith explains, is "henceforth rooted in the talent bestowed upon him by God and in his attachment to his native soil."

The *Kulturkammer* had never liked Hindemith to begin with, and it liked his new opera (completed in

1934) even less. For one thing, the *Kulturkammer* was disturbed by Hindemith's advanced style and technique which, it insisted, did not reflect the spirit of the times. ("Technical mastery," bellowed Dr. Goebbels, Minister of Propaganda, "is not an excuse but an obligation. To misuse it for meaningless musical trifles is to besmirch true genius! Opportunity creates not only thieves but also atonal musicians who in order to make a sensation . . . befoul their works with the most atrocious dissonances of musical impotence.") But what disturbed the *Kulturkammer* most about *Mathis der Maler* was the way in which it treated the defeat of German liberalism during the Peasants' War. Such a theme was too delicate for discussion in the Third Reich. Consequently, *Die Musik* considered Hindemith's opera "unbearable." Richard Strauss—then still in harmony with the new order—insisted that the opera be kept from the boards. All the leading Nazi musical societies joined in boycotting all of Hindemith's music.

One voice rose loud and clear in this wilderness to defend Hindemith. This voice belonged to Germany's most eminent conductor, Wilhelm Furtwaengler, head of the Leipzig Gewandhaus Orchestra, the Berlin Philharmonic, the Berlin State Opera, and the Bayreuth Festival. In some ways he, too, was a Nazi. In the all-important post of Deputy President of the Third Reich Chamber he did little to oppose the destructive musical policies of the *Kulturkammer*. But in 1934, and only because of *Mathis der Maler*, he put himself squarely in opposition to the Nazi ruling powers. For one thing, he regarded the opera as a masterwork and was eager to be the one to introduce it to the world; for another, he had only the highest regard for Hinde-

150

mith's genius. Consequently, he insisted upon performing the opera's première. But personal pride also had a good share in his courageous decision to defy his superiors. As the foremost musical figure in Germany he felt that both his position and integrity had been seriously jeopardized by the *Kulturkammer* in their efforts to dictate artistic policy.

In 1934, without consulting the *Kulturkammer*, he placed on one of the programs of the Berlin Philharmonic a "symphony" which the composer had adapted from the opera score. This consisted of three eloquent orchestral episodes, now a staple in the repertory of contemporary symphonic music. When no wave of reaction swept in upon him from the ruling powers, Furtwaengler was emboldened to take an even stronger position. He firmly announced that he planned to conduct the world première of *Mathis der Maler* at the Berlin State Opera. At the same time he despatched a fiery letter to Marshal Goering insisting that as the music director of the Berlin State Opera Furtwaengler, and Furtwaengler alone, was in authority. Furtwaengler also published an open communication in a prominent German newspaper in defense of Hindemith and his new opera. Furtwaengler seemed sure of his ground. He was confident his great position in German music would protect him. To his astonishment, he discovered he had miscalculated. The Nazi authorities relieved him of all his official posts in Germany, and sent him into a six-month period of "retirement." When he was finally restored to his former posts, and to the government's good graces, Furtwaengler proved much more docile to the demands and wishes of his Nazi bosses.

Hindemith, too, had to leave Germany. He first

went to Turkey where that government had asked him to help modernize its music-educational system and its concert activities. After that, in 1937, he came to the United States, where he established permanent residence and applied for citizenship. During the next quarter of a century he was on the music faculty of Yale University. He also gave occasional lectures and seminars at Harvard University and the Berkshire Music Center in Tanglewood.

Ever an extraordinarily prolific composer, Hindemith proved even more fertile in America than he had previously been in Europe. He completed numerous symphonies, concertos, ballets, chamber music, songs and choral and orchestral compositions of all sorts. He also completed a new opera, *Die Harmonie der Welt*. These of his works were of particular significance: *Noblissima visione,* both a ballet and an orchestral suite; the *Symphony in E-flat* and *Symphonia serena; Theme and Variations According to the Four Temperaments; Symphonic Metamorphosis on Themes by Carl Maria von Weber;* the *Fifth String Quartet.* During this same period he wrote *Ludus Tonalis,* a monumental work for piano comprising twelve fugues in as many keys of the chromatic scale—a twentieth-century equivalent of Bach's *Well-Tempered Clavier.*

In these scores, Hindemith's linear writing grew ever more subtle, and the train of his musical thought ever more complex. But in later efforts, beginning in the middle 1930's, Hindemith revealed a new bent for expressive lyricism and a more studied effort to achieve clarity and precision. There were times when a kind of spiritual radiance hovered over his writing, as in *Noblissima visione;* occasionally, he demonstrated his gamut of emotion to be unusually wide, as in *Symphonic Metamorphosis;* and in his American requiem, *When Lilacs Last in the Dooryard Bloom'd,* he reached a profound emotional depth rarely encountered in his earlier works.

As one of the world's greatest composers—and certainly the foremost German composer after Richard Strauss's death—Hindemith was given a hero's welcome when he paid a return visit to his native land in 1949, following a fifteen-year absence. Honors and tributes were heaped upon him by leading German musicians and journals; a street was named after him. But every attempt to get him to stay in Germany fell on deaf ears.

When in 1953 Hindemith returned to Europe for good, he settled in Zurich, Switzerland, where he joined the faculty of its University. One year later he received the Sibelius Award of $35,000 for outstanding creative achievement in music. Hindemith died in Frankfurt, Germany, on December 28, 1963.

IV

The Neo-Classical movement even touched and influenced many composers whose greatest talent lay in music of a radically different character. Ottorino Respighi is most widely represented on concert programs by his picturesque programmatic impressions of Rome—*The Fountains of Rome, The Pines of Rome,* and *Festivals of Rome.* But Neo-Classicism lured him into the writing of many compositions in that vein. Gustav Holst wandered into the Neo-Classical camp after a lifetime of successful exploitation of other idioms, with his very last two works. Alfredo Casella,

Jean Françaix, Albert Roussel, Manuel de Falla were several others who, at certain periods, turned temporarily to Neo-Classicism.

One of the by-products of the Neo-Classic movement was the revitalization of old forms, long since in discard. The concerto grosso, for example, had passed from general usage once the solo concerto was developed. But in the twentieth century the concerto grosso acquired a new lease on life with some major creations by Ernest Bloch, Bohuslav Martinu (1890–1959), Sir Edward Elgar, Jacques Ibert (1890–1962), and Ildebrando Pizzetti (1880–1968). Other earlier forms were suddenly lifted out of their century-old neglect to become the media for some distinguished twentieth-century music. Alexander Tansman (1897–   ) and Norman Dello Joio (1913–   ) wrote ricercari; Vaughan Williams, Alfredo Casella (1883–1947) and Sir William Walton, partitas; Roy Harris, passacaglias, and preludes and fugues.

CHAPTER 8

The Nationalists

O F the many currents and cross-currents of
twentieth-century music, one in particular
has caught and swept composers of many lands to artistic fulfillment: nationalism. This is a significant
carryover from the nineteenth century when the tides
of nationalism, political upheaval and emancipation
swept over and inundated Europe and Scandinavia.
Composers there became increasingly conscious of
their national heritage and sought the inspiration for
their music in the cultural and historical backgrounds
of their native lands.

When Chopin wrote Mazurkas and Polonaises, when
Liszt wrote his *Hungarian Rhapsodies,* and when
Glinka wrote operas like *Russlan and Ludmilla* and
A Life for the Czar, musical nationalism was beginning to take root. But it did not come to full flower
until late in the nineteenth century when a national
school came into being in Russia. Identified in the
history book as "The Five"—and comprising Mussorgsky, Balakirev, Borodin, Cui, and Rimsky-Korsakov—
this group set for itself the mission of producing an
authentic Russian musical art based on Russian folk
songs, dances, and church music. These composers
sought out Russian subjects for operas and programmatic symphonic music, and paid tribute to Russian
history, religion, and culture. All this represented

155

a complete divorce from the Germanic traditions so long governing musical creation in all parts of the civilized world. This new movement also represented a reaction against Wagnerism, whose impact had been strongly felt in Russia.

The success of "The Five" in realizing a native Russian musical art inevitably inspired imitation in other countries. Dvořák and Smetana, for example, wrote Bohemian music; Grieg, Norwegian music; Felipe Pedrell and Isaac Albéniz, Spanish music.

This goal to produce a national expression in music is probably pursued more eagerly in the twentieth century than ever before. There is hardly a country anywhere today that has not found a musical spokesman for its national pride and aspiration.

Folk music, to be sure, is the music of the people handed down from one generation to the next. By its very nature, and by virtue of its origin, it is usually simple in structure and direct in emotional appeal. Though the contemporary composer may often lapse into complexity through the employment of modern techniques, he has often succeeded in capturing the fresh, spontaneous and unsophisticated spirit of his country's folk music in large and ambitious concert works of a national identity. He has successfully blended the simple and homey material of the native folk song and dance with the advanced idioms with which this material is handled. Some composers have used actual folk songs and dance tunes for symphonic treatment. Many others wrote nationalistic music using only their own thoughts and materials, but thoughts and materials which had skilfully assimilated many of the more obvious idioms, traits, and mannerisms of their country's folk music.

of nationalists   Side 9
                                      10/23/72

II

In the latter group we find one of the giants of twentieth-century music—Jean Sibelius. He forged no new trails the way Stravinsky and Schoenberg did. His music was a natural outgrowth of the German Romanticism of the late nineteenth century, and to the end of his creative days he stayed an avowed Romanticist. His writing never betrayed the influence of the newer ideas that were changing the face and body of music. For the most part he was a traditionalist. Yet, he was one of the most original composers of his generation—a composer whose identity is readily in evidence in any one of his masterworks. And that identity is Finland.

He was not only Finland's greatest composer; he was Finland in music. His tone poems and symphonies were directly or indirectly stimulated by Finnish legends, literature (particularly the monumental epic, the *Kalevala*), history and landscapes, and are all unmistakably Finnish in spirit and mood. In Sibelius' music we recognize the turbulence and the passion of old Finnish sagas contrasted with the tranquillity and pastoral beauty of the Finnish countryside. To his writing there clings the bleakness and loneliness of a Finnish landscape under a gray sky. His rugged rhythms and occasional piercing sonorities suggest Finland's repeated struggles for independence, just as in his stately and angular melodies there can be found something of the fierce pride of a people determined to stay free.

No cultural figure in Finland has done more to propagandize the country's ideals and aspirations to the outside world than Sibelius. No cultural figure was more greatly honored in Finland than he. Sibelius was a national hero, an "uncrowned king," as some of his compatriots spoke of him. He was the first living composer in Finland honored with a postage stamp bearing his picture; and, if he had not vigorously opposed the project in 1940, he also would have been the first living composer to have a statue in a Finnish public square. Finnish children in the streets not only recognized him, but even hummed his melodies—paying him the same kind of adulation children elsewhere usually reserve for a renowned athlete. His seventy-fifth, eightieth, eighty-fifth and ninetieth birthdays were celebrated throughout the country as national holidays; and his death sent the whole country into public mourning.

He was born in Tavastehus on December 8, 1865. He received his first music instruction on the violin. His first piece of music, written when he was ten, was a descriptive duet for violin and piano, *Drops of Water*. After leaving high school, he attended the Helsingfors University where he studied law. At the same time his music study was continued at the Musical Academy. After a single year at the University he knew with finality that it was music he wanted as a life's career, and not law. He abandoned academic study for good to concentrate on music. Under such distinguished teachers as Ferruccio Busoni (then in Helsingfors) and Martin Wegelius he made impressive progress. In 1889 a scholarship brought him to Germany where he studied composition with Albert Becker. After additional study in Vienna with Karl Goldmark and Robert Fuchs, Sibelius returned to his native land in 1891.

Absence from Finland had not only stirred his nostalgia for home but also fed his love of his country.

These feelings became crystallized in Berlin at a concert in which a Finnish symphony, *Aino*, by one of his compatriots, Robert Kajanus was being performed. For the first time, while listening to this music, Sibelius caught a glimmer of what his own destiny as composer should be. Until now he had imitated either Brahms or Tchaikovsky, his writing aglow with the ardor and passion of a Romanticist. Though he would never desert his Romantic tendencies, he now became dissatisfied with compositions distilled from the German or Russian schools. The need for a more personal form of self-expression became pressing.

Back in Finland, he earned his living teaching theory at the Musical Academy and the Philharmonic Society School, and playing the violin in a string quartet. At the same time he was thrown into the vortex of his country's struggle against the ruthless despotism of its Russian rulers. Underground movements in Finland spread the gospel of freedom to patriots, and set off the sparks of a nationalist movement soon to erupt into an uncontrolled conflagration. Sibelius was profoundly affected by this political movement. He now started to write Finnish compositions which paid tribute to his country, his people and his culture. He gave voice to the proud determination of a courageous people to free itself of foreign tyranny.

Sibelius' first national composition was a five-movement tone poem, *Kullervo,* based on the Finnish national epic, the *Kalevala.* It was a tremendous success when introduced in Helsingfors under the composer's direction in 1892. This was followed by several other remarkable Finnish works: in 1893, the tone poem *En Saga,* still one of Sibelius' best-loved symphonic creations, and the *Karelia Suite;* the *Four Legends* for orchestra, in

1894, once again inspired by the *Kalevala*, one of whose movements is the exquisitely sensitive tone portrait, "The Swan of Tuonela"; and most famous of all, in 1899, *Finlandia*, surely the work above all others which through the years has been the instrument to promulgate Finnish national ideals to the rest of the world. The robust chords with which this tone poem opens seem to direct a closed fist against oppressors. The poignant subject for the woodwinds that follows is like a prayer for peace and deliverance. And its most celebrated melody, an exalted subject for the woodwind, speaks with unforgettable accents of a world where liberty, truth and tolerance prevail at last, and where the people are free to pursue a good life with dignity and self-respect. Then the work surges to a conclusion with a thunderous climax—an exultant paean to ultimate, inevitable deliverance. So thoroughly Finnish in mood and feeling and texture are these and other themes in *Finlandia* that for many years the belief was in general circulation that Sibelius was here quoting actual Finnish folk melodies. But this is not the case. All the thematic material in *Finlandia* is Sibelius' own.

Sibelius wrote *Finlandia* primarily as a way of protesting a wave of censorship and repression then imposed on the little country by Russia. It was first performed in 1899 under the title of *Finland Awakes,* and as the last movement of a suite. One year after that, the composer divorced the composition from the other movements, revised it drastically, and gave it the title of *Suomi* ("Suomi" is the name Finns use for their country). In France, however, it was performed under the name of *La Patrie,* in Germany under *Vaterland.* Recognizing the emotional impact this fiery patriotic music had upon an inflammable people, the Russian authorities banned it in Finland, and allowed performances elsewhere in the Empire only if some such undescriptive generic title as *Impromptu* were used for it. At least this is the story that was long believed as gospel, since it was the one that Sibelius told his biographer Karl Ekman, who duly reported it. But after Sibelius' death programs were discovered proving conclusively that *Finlandia* had never been censored; and that, when performed, it bore that title. Nevertheless, it is true that until Finland won independence, *Finlandia* was the country's eloquent battle cry of freedom. Some have said that this single piece of music did more to help bring about Finland's liberation than all the fiery speeches and pamphlets combined. Outside Finland, no single piece of music—not even the Finnish national anthem—served so effectively to speak of this country's national purpose. When, during the era of World War II, Finland was overrun by the Soviet army and once again was victimized by oppressors, *Finlandia* was heard throughout the free world to speak once again of the hope of liberation that stirred so restlessly in every Finnish heart.

Among Sibelius' later national compositions the most significant was *Tapiola* in 1926. *Tapiola* is one of several names by which Finland is often identified—Tapio being the country's ancient forest god. This deeply brooding and sober music is a picture of the Finnish forests, and the gnomes and sprites reputed by legend to inhabit them.

But Sibelius' creative significance rests even more solidly on his symphonies than on his national tone poems. He is, perhaps, the most significant symphonist of the twentieth century, and the most frequently performed since Tchaikovsky. Sibelius' first two symphonies—written in 1899 and 1902—are still the legitimate offspring of the late nineteenth-century Romantic movement, even though Sibelius had successfully freed himself from this influence in his national tone poems. In their partiality for dramatic or grandiloquent statements, in their emotional outbursts, in their intensity and passion these two early symphonies bear the recognizable fingerprints of Tchaikovsky and Brahms.

In the five symphonies that followed between 1907 and 1924, Sibelius achieved a highly individual, a distinctly Finnish, personality through broad and spacious melodies touched elegiacally by subdued harmonies, pastoral moods, and expressive sonorities. He also arrived at a personal concept of the symphonic structure. In place of the traditional contrasting themes of sonata form, subject to development and recapitulation, Sibelius shaped a flexible mold of his own and filled it with terse, concentrated ideas progressing towards a climactic point with a great surge of power and, at times, a grandeur of utterance.

Sibelius was already recognized in his own country as Finland's foremost composer when in 1897 the first annual grant ever bestowed on a Finnish musician was given him. This endowment enabled Sibelius to give up teaching chores and to take more time for composition and undertake tours as composer-conductor. He paid only a single visit to the United States, in late spring of 1914 to direct a concert of his works at Norfolk, Connecticut. After World War I he made several tours of Europe. But after 1924 he lived more or less in retirement in his villa in Järvenpää, a small town near Helsingfors. His main contact with the outside world was through the newspaper, the radio, and an endless stream of visitors who stopped off at his town to pay him tribute. He was not personally molested when the Red Army overran Finland. The food raised on his grounds was enough to feed him and his family adequately; and the imported cigars, so basic to his well-being, kept coming as gifts from his American admirers.

After World War II he withdrew more than ever. Now he did not even stop off to visit the local tavern to gossip and drink wine with his neighbors the way he used to do frequently before the war. He even discouraged foreign visitors from calling on him. There were continual rumors that he was working on an eighth symphony, but these were without any foundation whatsoever. In fact, Sibelius' last published work—*Esquisses* for piano—had come out as far back as 1929. After that he wrote virtually nothing. He died in his villa on September 20, 1957, at the patriarchal age of ninety-two.

III

Another twentieth-century giant of music to dominate the nationalist school was Béla Bartók. He was born in Hungary, in the town of Nagyszentmiklós in Transylvania, on March 25, 1881. As a boy he received some piano instruction from his mother and at the age of ten made his public debut as pianist. Subsequently he studied the piano with Laszlo Erkel in Pressburg, and from 1899 and 1903 was a pupil of Thomán and Koessler at the Liszt Academy in Budapest. Under the stimulus of Academy life, Bartók, who had been writing music since he was nine years old, intensified his creative efforts. He completed a symphony, *Kossuth,* performed in 1903 by the Hallé Orchestra in Manchester, England. After Bartók left the Academy in 1903, he earned a precarious living by teaching, playing the piano, and making musical

163

transcriptions. Some financial relief came in 1907 with an appointment as professor of the piano at the Academy.

One day in 1905 he overheard a servant girl singing a song with strange progressions and a most unusual melody. Upon being pressed to identify the piece, the servant could only reveal that she had learned it from her mother, who knew many other such tunes. This was the first clue for Bartók that there existed a storehouse of Hungarian folk music about which little or nothing was known outside the regions in which it was heard. With the excitement of a detective tracking down a criminal, Bartók set forth on a journey through many far-flung towns and villages of Hungary to search for these songs and dance tunes. What he found exceeded his wildest expectations. Here, indeed, was a treasury of the most original, unusual, and haunting folk melodies. Bartók now set for himself the goal of uncovering as much of this unfamiliar music as possible. For about eight years—often in collaboration with his friend and colleague, Zoltán Kodály, who was also to achieve note as a nationalist composer—he traveled into the remotest regions of Hungary. Everywhere he took down on paper and through a recording apparatus the melodies that were sung to him. Thus he discovered about six thousand Hungarian folk songs and dances which he edited and had published. The world of music found to its amazement that this folk art was completely different from the sentimental, meretricious gypsy melodies which for so many years had been regarded as Hungarian folk music, and long since exploited by such masters as Brahms and Liszt as authentic native material The exotic character of the music discovered by Bartók was a result of the frequent deployment of church modes. In

164

place of sensuality and sentimentality, this music had vigor and brute force in the severity of its melodic line (which often followed the inflections of the Hungarian tongue) and irregular rhythms.

This folk material, as Bartók himself once said, was "destined to serve as the foundation for a renaissance of Hungarian art music." In the vanguard of this renaissance stood Bartók himself, whose music now assimilated the traits and idiosyncrasies of the Hungarian folk art he had helped to discover. As he once wrote: "The appropriate use of folk-song material is . . . a matter of absorbing the means of music expression hidden in the treasury of folk tunes. . . . It is necessary for the composer to command this language so completely that it becomes the natural expression of his own musical ideas." Bartók's melodic line, like that of the Hungarian folk song, had a declamatory character; his use of free tonalities (which almost had the semblance of atonality) and modal harmonies endowed his writing with an esoteric character. His music had a savage thrust in its abrupt and shifting accents and intricate rhythms. Yet his compositions were as subtle in their thought as they were complex in technique.

A key to Bartók's modern style in general and his nationalist style in particular is provided by a remarkable suite of 153 pieces for the piano assembled in six books and collectively entitled *Mikrokosmos*—a word that can be translated as "little world." Bartók completed this mammoth work between 1926 and 1927 for the functional purpose of teaching children such modern idioms as polytonality, polyrhythm, the five-tone scale, dissonance, and so forth. In the first four volumes we get pieces, each planned as an exercise for a particular modern technical problem designated in the title. In the

165

next two books, children are given the opportunity of learning something about Bartók's national idiom through examples of various types of folk music from the Balkan countries. The six books also contain many delightful descriptive pieces in some of which extra-musical sounds are suggested, as in "Buzzing" and "Clashing Sounds."

For a more adult audience, Bartók created a library of piano pieces that included the early *Allegro barbaro* and *Bear Dance,* both highly discordant. His six string quartets, written between 1908 and 1939, are perhaps the greatest single contemporary contribution to chamber-music literature. Other important works are the *Second Piano Concerto* in 1931, the distinguished *Music for Strings, Percussion and Celesta* in 1936, and the *Violin Concerto* in 1938. Discriminating critics and musicians recognized all these as works of first importance; but for the general music public they were too intricate for pleasurable consumption. When Bartók paid his first visit to the United States in 1927—in performances of his major works—he received little more than a polite welcome. And when once again he came to the United States, this time during World War II to make America his permanent home, he still found very little general interest in and understanding of his life work. His music was a comparative stranger in American concert halls at that time.

The last years of Bartók's life, all of them in America, were for the most part unhappy. He was sick from the ravages of leukemia. The loss of his homeland made him lonely, and the failure of his music to get frequent hearings left him frustrated. Besides, he was in such a bad way financially that he had to be supported by a special fund created for him by the American Society of Composers, Authors, and Publishers. But all this notwithstanding, he kept on producing masterworks: the *Concerto for Orchestra* in 1943, now his most celebrated symphonic work; the *Third Piano Concerto;* a *Viola Concerto* which he did not live to complete.

Bartók knew he was dying as he worked on the *Third Piano Concerto,* which he had planned as a last touching testament to his beloved wife. On the last bar of his sketches he wrote the Hungarian word *vege* meaning "the end"—something he had never before done—as an indication that his creative life and the piano concerto had both come to a simultaneous conclusion. He died just before he put his last pen strokes on this concerto: the last seventeen bars, for which he had left instructions, had to be written in and scored by one of his friends.

In the works of these last years, and most particularly in the *Concerto for Orchestra,* Bartók had not only simplified his methods and means but also introduced into his writing a humanity and emotion never encountered in his earlier austere works. And it is these last works that finally brought about the full recognition of Bartók's formidable stature. Just before his death, the première of his *Concerto for Orchestra*—in Boston on December 1, 1944—actually inspired an ovation. But it was really only after Bartók had died, in New York on September 26, 1945, that he came fully into his own in American concert halls. Within a few months there took place almost fifty performances of his major works, including the world premières of his *Third Piano Concerto* and the unfinished *Viola Concerto.* After that came all-Bartók concerts—even cycles of Bartók concerts—in several American cities, together with recordings of his most significant orchestral works and all the six string quartets. Today, of course, Bartók is no stranger to American concert audiences. Music so long elusive to the general public is now readily accepted by it as one of the most vital contributions made by any single composer to the music of our times.

IV

The career of England's foremost nationalistic composer, Ralph Vaughan Williams, parallels that of Bartók in one significant respect: Vaughan Williams did not realize his creative potential until he had discovered his country's folk music and had absorbed its elements into his own style. Born in Down Ampney, England, on October 12, 1872, Vaughan Williams received a thorough training in music: first at the Royal College of Music; then privately with the composer, Max Bruch in Berlin; after that at Cambridge from which he received his doctorate. Upon completing these studies he entered professional ranks by becoming the organist of the St. Barnabas Church in London where for three years he gave recitals, trained and directed a choral group, and participated in church services. By the time he was thirty-two, the sum total of his creative achievements consisted of some minor church hymns, a few unimpressive works for orchestra, and the editing of an English hymnal. He gave little evidence, then, that he was destined for greatness.

Then a "new planet" swam into his ken—the English folk music of the Tudor period. So absorbed did he become with these remarkable examples of early English vocal and polyphonic music that, in 1904, he joined the Folk-Song Society, a group which did research in this field. Several years of digging into England's distant musical past followed. In that time he helped to resurrect a wealth of forgotten folklore, including such gems as

168

"The Turtle Dove," "We've Been Awhile A-wandering" and "Down in Yon Forest" which he introduced to his contemporaries through his skilful adaptations and harmonizations.

The reverberations of this old music were soon apparent in his own creative thinking. Between 1905 and 1907, he wrote three *Norfolk Rhapsodies* for orchestra, their melodic material derived from melodies from the King's Lynn district of Norfolk. Vaughan Williams planned the three compositions as the movements of a folk symphony, but he abandoned this project upon recognizing the inferior quality of the second and third rhapsodies. After scrapping those two works, he issued the first—in the key of E minor—a masterful orchestral fabric utilizing the colorful thread of such songs from Norfolk as "The Captain's Apprentice," "A Bold Young Sailor," and "The Basket of Eggs." The *Rhapsody* was introduced at a Promenade concert in London on August 23, 1906, and was well received.

Feeling the need of strengthening his technical resources, Vaughan Williams went to Paris in 1908. For a while he studied with Maurice Ravel, from whom he learned how to make effective use of nuance, color, and subtle effects. This training period over, Vaughan Williams proceeded to create his first masterwork in 1909: the *Fantasia on a Theme by Thomas Tallis*, for double orchestra. Tallis was a sixteenth-century English church composer. In the *Fantasia* one of his tunes is quoted by Vaughan Williams before being subjected to considerable enlargement and transformation. As the melody grows, changes, expands, as it appears now antiphonally, now contrapuntally, now in passing statements by solo instruments, a mood of tranquillity is created which is never permitted to lapse. First heard at the Three Choirs

Festival in Gloucester, on September 6, 1910, this work placed its composer as the foremost musical nationalist of his country and one of its significant creative figures in music. The *Fantasia* has always remained a strong favorite in the symphonic repertory.

What was particularly important about the *Fantasia,* as far as Vaughan Williams' development as a composer was concerned, was that here he had learned that folk music could not be an end in itself as had been the case with his *Norfolk Rhapsody.* He knew now that folk music was only the beginning. Henceforth, he realized, he might occasionally quote an English folk song or a popular song to achieve a certain local or native flavor; he would do so in his *London Symphony,* in his beautiful *Fantasia on Greensleeves,* and sundry other works. But for the most part he must use folk music merely to stir his own creative processes. When he would fail to use actual folk material—and this proved most frequently the case with his later works—his compositions nonetheless often had the same kind of modal writing, contrapuntal texture, and serenity of mood associated with so many English folk songs and madrigals.

Thus, like Bartók, he arrived at his personal idiom, in which he created nine symphonies, numerous concertos, many shorter orchestral works, incidental music to plays, chamber and choral music, the masque *Job,* and the operas *The Shepherds of the Delectable Mountains* and *The Pilgrim's Progress.* As he grew older his style became bolder and more original. There were times when he introduced a note of introspection into his music; at times a mystical quality was evident in his works. On several occasions he had recourse to the most modern approaches of harmony, tonality, and rhythm. But the

170

essentially English character of his style was never altogether obscured.

After Elgar's death in 1934, Vaughan Williams usurped the first place in English music. He was not only England's foremost composer, but also one of its most notable teachers: for over thirty years he was professor of composition at the Royal College of Music. A grateful country honored him with the Order of Merit in 1935. Two decades later he was presented with the Albert medal by the Royal Society of Arts. His eightieth birthday, in 1952, was celebrated throughout England with commemorative concerts of his major works.

He remained productive and at the height of his creative powers to the very end. His last symphony, the ninth, was completed only a year and a half before his death. This work had been planned by him as a kind of summation of all the artistic principles, all the articles of faith by which he had been governed. But as it turned out, the symphony became a document of despair and frustration, rather than an affirmation. After the last bar, the composer scribbled the word *niente* or "nothing" —almost as if he had by now been completely overwhelmed by futility. He died in London on August 26, 1958, at the age of eighty-six.

V

Manuel de Falla was Spain's foremost twentieth-century composer. He, too, was a dedicated musical nationalist. Born in Cádiz, in southern Spain, on November 23, 1876, Falla was a highly musical child. He received instruction in piano as well as in harmony from his mother and local teachers. As a child he joined his mother in performing a four-hand arrangement of Haydn's *The*

171

Last Words of Christ in one of Cádiz' churches; and he was still only a child when he started to write music of his own. Later on he attended the Madrid Conservatory where he won several prizes in piano playing, and where his teacher, José Tragó, tried to develop him into a virtuoso. But the Conservatory faculty included another professor whose influence on the young student was more profound and lasting. That professor was Felipe Pedrell, one of Spain's most distinguished music scholars. Pedrell had done a considerable amount of research in Spanish folk and church music and had become convinced that the destiny of Spanish composers lay in drawing their inspiration and material from these sources. In Falla, Pedrell found a willing disciple. Before long, Falla rejected all thoughts of the concert stage and directed his energies into creative channels; at the same time he became Pedrell's ally in the promotion of national music. In 1905, Falla completed a Spanish national opera, *La Vida breve,* which won first prize in a competition conducted by the Academy of Fine Arts in Madrid. Two delightful Spanish dances from this opera are still popular.

To gain still further mastery of the tools of his trade, Falla came to Paris in 1907 and stayed there seven years. Plunging into the maelstrom of its musical life, and coming into contact with its leading musicians, proved an important factor in Falla's artistic development. Debussy was a revelation, not only for his Impressionist style and theories—some of which Falla now tried to absorb into his own writing—but also for his Spanish compositions in which he had succeeded in catching the spirit and essence of Spanish life and backgrounds. Largely as a result of the examples he found in that French master, Falla now veered toward a new direction as a nationalist composer. Henceforth the mere exploitation of Spanish folk songs and dances would not be enough. He became a mystic seeking out the soul of his country and his people, not just a literal tone painter interpreting specific programs. His musical style would, to be sure, remain unmistakably Spanish in the sinuous line of his flamenco-like melodies, in the old-world modalities of old Spanish church music, and the electrifying and varied rhythms of Spanish dances. But perfecting and refining an essentially Spanish style of composition would not be an end in itself. It could only be the means by which to carry over into music the essence of the Spanish people, the culture, and the geography. The Spaniards had a word for this essence— *Evocación*. Falla's music became a vibrant *evocación* of Spain, rather than a picture of the land. As he himself said: "You must go *really* deep, so as not to make any sort of caricature. . . . You must go to the natural living sources, study the sounds, the rhythms, use their essence, not just their externals."

While he was busily engaged in Paris absorbing musical experiences, he composed several Spanish songs and a number of Spanish pieces for the piano. He also worked upon the sketches of a large Spanish work for piano and orchestra. Some of his music was performed. The *Pièces espagnoles* for piano were given at a concert of the Société Nationale in Paris in 1908. In 1913, *La Vida breve* finally received its world première at the Casino in Nice. It proved so successful that soon after that the Opéra-Comique in Paris accepted it for its repertory.

Just before World War I, Falla returned to his native land where he wrote the score for the ballet, *El Amor Brujo*, the first of his masterworks to win world acclaim. The scenario, based on an old Andalusian legend, tells

173

of the love affair of Candela and Carmelo—an affair soon complicated by the fact that the ghost of Candela's husband insists upon haunting them. Carmelo finally erases this annoyance by getting an enticing little gypsy girl to engage the time and interests of the ghost. Falla completed his score in 1914, and the ballet was first produced in Madrid on April 15, 1915. It was an outstanding success. The orchestral suite which Falla adapted from his score, comprising twelve sections, is one of the crowning works of the twentieth-century symphonic repertory. This is languid and sensual music, as haunting and as deep-throated in its lyricism as gypsy songs, as passionate and abandoned as Andalusian folk dances. A climactic point comes with the "Ritual Fire Dance," now familiar not only in its original orchestral version but also in all kinds of transcriptions, including an electrifying one for the piano which has long been a tour de force at concerts by Artur Rubinstein and other virtuosos.

After *El Amor Brujo,* in 1915, Falla completed *Nights in the Gardens of Spain,* the ambitious work for piano and orchestra which he had sketched in Paris. It was introduced in Madrid a year later. This composition is made up of three sensitive and occasionally Impressionist symphonic pictures of Spain. The first evokes the celebrated Generaliffe gardens near the Alhambra in Granada; the second recreates a native Spanish dance; the third describes the gardens of the Sierra at Córdoba. The basic style is the same that characterizes Andalusian folk songs and dances. Falla's orchestration, at times, even imitated the effects produced by native Spanish instruments. But this music is not imitative but evocative. The three impressions are the work not of a realist but of a poet and mystic who makes us catch a glimpse of the soul of Spain through his own eyes.

174

In 1922 Falla went to Granada where he lived for the next seventeen years, leading a completely withdrawn life consecrated to creative work. He was never a prolific or facile composer; each composition entailed many years of the most fastidious and exacting effort. After 1922, his principal works were the ballet, *The Three-Cornered Hat*, popularized by its exciting Spanish dances, which Diaghilev's Ballet Russe introduced in London in 1919; a remarkable Neo-Classic concerto for harpsichord, flute, oboe, clarinet and 'cello in 1925; a little marionette opera based on episodes from *Don Quixote*, *El Retablo de Maese Pedro*, in 1922.

A profoundly religious man, Falla regarded the Spanish uprising of 1937, headed by Generalissimo Franco, as a crusade. Falla became one of Franco's most ardent supporters and, by reciprocity, Franco made him president of the Institute of Spain. But Franco's iron-rule dictatorship over the Spanish people soon disillusioned Falla completely. Though weak and sick, Falla voluntarily expatriated himself in 1939 and found a new home in Argentina. There, living practically like a hermit, he worked passionately on his last, and what he hoped would be his greatest work—*La Atlantida*, for chorus, soloists and orchestra. He did not live to complete it, dying in Alta Gracía, Argentina, on November 14, 1946.

VI

Other countries besides Finland, Hungary, England and Spain had their musical nationalists. Georges Enesco (1881–1955) wrote two brilliant *Roumanian Rhapsodies* between 1901 and 1902, the first of these now an established classic. Filled with the most exciting contrasts of rhythm, color, and feeling, the music of the *First Rhapsody* is at turns languorous, sensual, melan-

175

choly, introspective and uninhibited in its frenetic outbursts.

Jaromir Weinberger (1896–1967) and Bohuslav Martinu (1890–1959) created a national musical idiom for modern-day Czechoslovakia—but deeply rooted in the rich soil of Dvořák and Smetana. Weinberger is the composer of a remarkable Bohemian folk opera, *Schwanda, the Bagpipeplayer*, introduced in Prague on April 27, 1927. The hero, Schwanda—though married—tries to win the heart of Queen Ice-Heart. When she learns he is married, she orders his execution. But Schwanda's magic music-making saves him from this fate. He gets into trouble again when a rash oath sends him into Hell. Once again he manages to extricate himself, and is now happy to become reconciled with his wife. From this colorful score, the modern symphonic repertory has plucked the charming Polka and Fugue.

Martinu's Bohemian nationalism belongs to a comparatively early phase of his career. In the early 1920's he wrote the ballet *Istar* and the *Czech Rhapsody* for orchestra in a Bohemian style and idiom. Both Weinberger and Martinu came to live in the United States where their writing took directions remote from Bohemian nationalism; Martinu became a Neo-Classicist, while Weinberger experimented in several different veins, one of which brought him to a strongly American idiom based on popular or folk American melodies.

Moravia is a part of Czechoslovakia, and the foremost composer of its national music was Leoš Janáček (1854–1928), among whose works will be found *Moravian Dances, National Dances of Moravia, The Ballad of Blaník* for orchestra. Janáček's most celebrated work is the opera *Jenufa*, which some regard as the most successful Bohemian folk opera since Smetana's *The Bartered*

176

Bride. It took Janáček seven years to write *Jenufa*, which was produced in Brünn in 1904. Jenufa is a peasant girl who bears a child to her stepbrother, Stewa. When Stewa's brother, Laca, discovers that Stewa no longer loves Jenufa, he (Laca) stands ready to marry her and accept the child as his own. But Laca's mother, to thwart the marriage, murders the child, buries it hastily, then tells Jenufa the baby died of natural causes. During the marriage ceremony of Jenufa and Laca, the dead body of the child is found. The mother now openly confesses her crime and is arrested. *Jenufa* is a grimly realistic opera of great dramatic power in which the recitatives are shaped from the patterns of Bohemian speech (Janáček referred to these patterns as "melodies of the language"), and the lyrical passages are based on Moravian peasant music.

Musical nationalism emerged in Italy in compositions like the *Italia* of Alfredo Casella (1883–1947), a rhapsody depicting Sicilian and Neapolitan life which quotes such popular Italian tunes as *Funiculi, Funicula* and *Amarechiare.* In Sweden, Hugo Alfven (1872–1960) wrote several Swedish rhapsodies, of which the most notable is *Midsummer Vigil,* depicting a revel celebrated during the St. John's Eve Festival, and based on native folk songs and dances. One of Poland's most significant twentieth-century nationalists was Karol Szymanowski (1882–1937). His national identity is most clearly recognized in *Stabat Mater,* a large choral work rooted in old Polish religious music, and in the ballet *Harnasie,* many of whose melodies are adaptations of peasant music of the Carpathian Mountains.

CHAPTER 9

The American Nationalists

Oᴺᴇ of Europe's most significant Romantic composers gave the first boost to American nationalism in music. He was Antonin Dvořák, whose *Slavonic Dances* and other compositions in a Bohemian style placed him in the vanguard of Europe's musical nationalists. In 1892, Dvořák came to New York to assume the post of director of the National Conservatory. He stayed three years. In 1893, he paid a visit to the town of Spillville, Iowa, which boasted a large Bohemian colony. At that time three Iroquois Indians visited him and played some of their tribal songs. This experience led Dvořák to write several major works imitating some of the thematic ideas and rhythms of the American Indian: the *American Quartet;* the *String Quintet in E-flat major*; and the *Violin Sonatina in G major,* whose plangent slow movement was transcribed by Fritz Kreisler and renamed *Indian Lament.* In all these works Dvořák used his own thematic material exclusively. He took special pains to explain that while this material embodied "the peculiarities of Indian music," it nevertheless was developed with "all the resources of modern rhythm, harmony, counterpoint, and orchestral color."

In New York, at about the same time, Dvořák was also initiated into the world of the Negro Spiritual. This folk music moved him so profoundly that tears would come to his eyes as he listened to it. "They are the folk

178

songs of America," he said of these melodies, "and your composers must turn to them. In the Negro melodies of America I discovered all that is needed for a great and noble school of music." Perhaps with the hope of pointing the way to this goal, he himself produced two masterworks in which the Negro idiom was prominent. One was the *'Cello Concerto in B minor,* where the second theme of the first movement (first heard in the orchestral introduction in solo horn against strings) is in the style and spirit of a Negro Spiritual. The other was his famous *Symphony from the New World,* his fifth, in the key of E minor. Here the second theme of the first movement bears a striking family resemblance to the Spiritual, "Swing Low, Sweet Chariot." And the main elegiac melody for English horn, in the slow movement, sounds so much like a Spiritual that many have long held the erroneous belief that it actually was one. This beautiful melody has since been adapted into a Spiritual-like song, with lyrics by William Arms Fisher—"Goin' Home."

Up until the 1890's, and for some years after that, most serious composers in America copied the Romantic style of Europe in general, and Germany in particular. What they produced was unmistakably foreign. But several composers soon started to experiment with a native art involving the musical idioms of either the American Indian or the American Negro. Edward MacDowell (1861–1908), perhaps America's foremost composer of the late nineteenth century, wrote an *Indian Suite,* for orchestra; Charles Wakefield Cadman (1881–1946), one of America's most successful composers at the beginning of the twentieth century, became popular with the *Thunderbird Suite* for orchestra, the opera *Shanewis,* and especially with his concert song, "From the Land of the Sky-Blue Water." Victor Herbert (1859–1924), essentially a composer for the popular musical theater, also completed a serious opera about the American Indian, *Natoma*.

Other composers went to the Negro melodies for materials and stimulation. Rubin Goldmark (1872–1936) wrote the *Negro Rhapsody,* for orchestra; John Powell (1882–   ), the *Rapsodie nègre,* for piano and orchestra; Henry F. Gilbert (1868–1928), the *Comedy Overture on Negro Themes.*

Extensive research throughout the United States in the 1910's and 1920's revealed that the area of folk music was far greater, and far more fertile, than the limited grounds offered by Negro and Indian music. Through the field work of musicologists, through publications and recordings, a rich harvest of American folk songs was reaped. There were songs with which the lumberjacks (or shantyboys) brought down the timber in the West; the chanteys with which American sailors lightened the oppressive burdens of their shipboard duties; the songs born, and developed during the American migration West which continued throughout the nineteenth century, the "white Spirituals," fiddle tunes, and the music for square dances and play parties. There were the songs on the lips of the Forty-niners en route to California to find gold. There were the bleak, lonesome tunes of the Western cowboy as he drove his herd across the Texan plains to a shipping point in Dodge City, Kansas. There were the varied work songs that sprouted among steel-workers, railroad-workers and Negro chain gangs. And, finally, there was a vast repertory of English ballads that were preserved for generations in the Appalachian and Cumberland mountains.

Aaron Copland, the dean of American composers, is best known for his work with folk music.

Copland was born in Brooklyn, New York on November 14, 1900. He started studying the piano when he was fourteen, then entered Rubin Goldmark's class in harmony. Hearing about the opening of a new music school for Americans in Fontainebleau, France, he applied for admission and discovered he was the first student to be accepted. He went through its curriculum with more assiduity than enthusiasm. One day he sat in on the harmony class of Nadia Boulanger. "I immediately suspected," he later said, "that I had found my teacher." That fall he became a private pupil of Boulanger in Paris, and the years he spent with her fashioned him into a trained musician. Under her guidance he wrote a ballet, *Grohg,* together with some choral music and piano pieces. His teacher also commissioned him to write a large symphony with organ which she hoped to introduce in the United States during her American tour as an organist.

Copland came back to America in the summer of 1924. That fall his symphony was introduced by the New York Symphony Society, with Walter Damrosch as conductor, and Nadia Boulanger as organ soloist. This music was so discordant, so unpalatable to the ear, that during one of the rehearsals Damrosch remarked acidly: "A man who can write this kind of music can commit murder."

Copland first attracted general interest with two large works employing a jazz idiom. The first was *Music for the Theater,* commissioned by Serge Koussevitzky, who led its première performances in New York and Boston. Copland had no specific play in mind, but tried to convey the idea that his music had some of the dramatic qualities of the theater. The second and fourth movements (respectively a "Dance" and "Burlesque") of *Music for the Theater* were exciting examples of jazz within a symphonic structure.

Music for the Theater was immediately followed by Copland's *Piano Concerto*, first given in Boston by the Boston Symphony under Koussevitzky with the composer playing the piano. Jazz rhythms and blues melodies predominate in this work which has considerable vitality and bounce, and is consistently pleasurable listening.

But Copland soon grew weary of jazz, soon became convinced he had exhausted its artistic possibilities. He now embraced an avant-garde style, complex in harmonic and rhythmic structure, austere and esoteric in style. The *Dance Symphony* (based on material from his earlier ballet, *Grohg*) received a prize of $5,000 in a contest sponsored by RCA Victor. His *Symphonic Ode* introduced by the Boston Symphony was commissioned to help commemorate the fiftieth anniversary of the orchestra. After that came *Statements,* for orchestra, and the complicated *Piano Variations.*

In the early 1930's Copland began to feel that by becoming so cerebral and complicated he had lost contact with his audiences. He sensed the need for greater simplicity of technique and a wider mass-appeal of materials. He put it this way: "I felt that it was worth the effort to see if I couldn't say what I had to say in the simplest possible terms."

During a visit to Mexico in 1932, he dropped into a Mexican dance hall where he became intrigued with some of the popular Mexican dance tunes played there. The idea suddenly came to him to write a symphonic work in which these popular Mexican tunes were used and developed. He completed that work in 1935, and called it *El Salón México,* that being the name of the dance hall he had visited. One of the tunes he heard there, *El Mosco,* was quoted directly in this work, while other Mexican tunes were suggested rather than realized. "My purpose," Copland explained, "was not merely to quote these tunes literally but to heighten them without in any way falsifying their natural simplicity. . . . I adopted a form which is a kind of modified potpourri in which Mexican themes, and their extensions, are sometimes inextricably mixed for the sake of conciseness and coherence."

Without "writing down" in the least—for *El Salón México* is a work of extraordinary skill, effect, and of the highest integrity—Copland had here succeeded in producing a rhythmically and melodically exciting native Mexican work which had completely captured the spirit of the Mexican dance hall. Audiences loved it, and for the first time Copland managed to win over the general public completely and decisively.

From a successful exploitation of Mexican popular melodies, it was just a step to the employment of American folk music. Copland took that step and with it achieved greatness. It is with his works in an American folk style and works stimulated by American folk backgrounds and idioms that Copland finally achieved his creative identity.

In 1938 he wrote the music for a ballet, *Billy the Kid.* Its chief character was the notorious frontier-town outlaw who effects legendary escapes from justice but in the end meets his doom at the hands of a posse. For this score, Copland made copious use of cowboy songs, including "Git Along Little Dogie," "The Old Chisholm Trail," "Goodbye, Old Paint" and "O, Bury Me Not." *Rodeo,* a ballet in 1942—described as "a love story of the American Southwest"—was another highly successful attempt to exploit cowboy songs.

With the ballet *Appalachian Spring*, introduced in Washington, D.C. in 1944 by Martha Graham and her dancers, Copland achieved his greatest artistic and public success up to that time. The music received the Pulitzer Prize and the New York Music Critics Award; the symphonic suite adapted from the ballet score became a staple in the contemporary American orchestral repertory. The ballet setting is the Pennsylvania hills; the main characters, Pennsylvania pioneer folk. The action is built around a celebration attending the completion of a newly built farm house, the future home of a farmer and his bride. Square dances, fiddle tunes, revivalist hymns, and an actual Shaker melody ("Simple Gifts," which is quoted literally, then subjected to five variations) form the warp and woof of Copland's remarkable musical fabric.

Though Copland's *Third Symphony*, one of his masterworks, does not quote a single American folk melody or rhythm, its folk personality is so unmistakable that one Boston critic described its composer as "the Shostakovich of the Appalachians." The symphony was introduced by the Boston Symphony under Koussevitzky in 1946, and it was the recipient of the Boston Symphony Award of Merit and the New York Music Critics Circle Award. This is a work in a monumental design, so compelling in emotion and so personal in speech that Koussevitzky was tempted to call it "the greatest American symphony," a work that "goes from the heart to the heart."

No less deeply rooted in American nationalism is Copland's opera, *The Tender Land* (libretto by Horace

Everett), introduced by the New York City Opera in 1954. Above and beyond his compositions of an obviously national identity, Copland has written a good deal of music for the screen, theater, radio and public-school performances. Other major concert works include a *Piano Sonata*, a *Clarinet Concerto*, and a *Clarinet Quintet*. Every work that leaves Copland's hands reveals a mastery of technique and a musical articulateness that never fail to command respect.

III

Of the many different strains that course through the works of Roy Harris, that of American nationalism is both the most prominent and the most significant. Occasionally, Harris has leaned upon structures and contrapuntal procedures of the sixteenth century; sometimes his thematic material springs from Celtic folk-song sources or Protestant hymns; he has employed archaic modality and asymmetrical rhythms time and time again. But whatever the methods or means, whatever the artistic purpose, Harris has never failed to create music with an unmistakable American identity. His music, as Aaron Copland once remarked, "is American in rhythm, especially in the fast parts, with a jerky, nervous quality that is peculiarly our own. It is crude and unabashed at times, with occasional blobs and yawps of sound that Whitman would have approved of. . . . American, too, is his melodic gift. . . . His music comes nearest to a distinctively native *melos* of anything yet done, at least in the ambitious forms."

While sometimes he bases his melodies directly on American folk music, on other occasions he allows his musical thinking to be governed, as John Krueger, a noted authority on Roy Harris, has written "by the same emotional natures that caused our ancestors to sing as they did. If he uses a folk song for a theme, he generally does not quote it literally. . . . At times the folk song is almost unrecognizable, but the essence of it is still present."

Harris came from pioneer American stock. His grandfather drove a pony express between Chicago and points west. His father traveled by ox-cart during the Cimarron rush to Oklahoma, staked a claim, and built a log cabin in Lincoln County. It was there, on Lincoln's birthday in 1898, that Roy Harris was born and lived for the first five years of his life. After two of his brothers had succumbed to malaria, the family sought a new home in Gabriel Valley, California. Thus Harris spent his childhood and boyhood on a farm in pioneer country. While attending public school in Covina, he took music lessons from a local teacher, and learned to play the organ and clarinet by himself. He also did a good deal of reading—practically everything in print that invaded his home. By the time he finished high school, his intellectual world embraced not only music and literature, but also philosophy and poetry.

When Harris was eighteen he acquired a farm of his own which he cultivated for two years while continuing his cultural pursuits during leisure hours. Service in the Armed Forces during World War I was a hiatus separating Harris the farmer from Harris the musician. Once out of uniform he knew where he wanted to go. He entered the University of California, where he took courses in harmony. After that he studied composition with Arthur Farwell, piano with Fanny Charles Dillon, and orchestration with Modest Altschuler. "I am convinced," Farwell said of him, "that he will one day challenge the world."

He gave the first unmistakable sign of creative talent

with an Andante, for string orchestra, introduced in Rochester in 1926, and soon thereafter performed at the Lewisohn Stadium in New York and the Hollywood Bowl in California. A few patrons, impressed by this music, financed a trip to Europe for Harris. As a pupil in Paris of Nadia Boulanger, Harris completed his first major work—the *Concerto for String Quartet, Piano and Clarinet,* introduced in Paris in 1927. This was performed in the United States on the concert stage, over the radio, and even recorded, and was largely responsible for bringing Harris the Guggenheim Fellowship in 1927.

An accident in Paris in 1928 turned out to be a blessing in disguise. An injury to his back confined Harris to a plaster cast. After a while he had to return to the United States for a serious operation on his spine. For several months he was a prisoner in a hospital bed. To escape boredom, he soon had to go back to composition. Whereas up to now he had done his writing at the piano, he was now compelled by his confinement to work away from the instrument, to set down his thoughts on paper without previous experimentation at the keyboard. This he says, freed him from his former subservience to harmonic thought. His ideas now took wing and expressed themselves in broad, sweeping melodic lines and in counterpoint.

Thus he began evolving his own idiom, and used it to create the first compositions which made him one of the most highly regarded and widely performed American composers of his time. A piano trio, the *String Sextet* and the *Second String Quartet* were among his early works in this new style. His *Symphony* written in 1933, was outstandingly successful when introduced by the Boston Symphony under Koussevitzky in 1934. In

1935 a poll among radio audiences of the New York Philharmonic placed Harris as the most popular living American composer; he was returned to this position two years later by still another poll, this time one conducted by *Scribner's Magazine*.

In 1938, Harris completed the *Third Symphony,* his greatest work up to then, and still one of the most impressive symphonic works by an American. Koussevitzky, who introduced it in Boston early in 1939, called it the "greatest orchestral work yet written by an American." Said *Modern Music* at the time: "For significance of material, breadth of treatment, and depth of meaning; for tragic implication, dramatic intensity, concentration; for moving beauty, glowing sound, it can find no peer in the musical art of America." Before long practically every important American orchestra played it; it became the first American symphony conducted by Toscanini; and it sold exceptionally well on records.

The *Third Symphony* was still, for the most part, contrapuntal and modal. But in succeeding works Harris stressed American nationalism with compelling effect: in two works inspired by Walt Whitman, *Song for Occupations* and *Symphony for Voices;* in the *Folk-Song Symphony* consisting of five choral movements in which the thematic material consists mainly of American popular and folk songs, including cowboy, Negro and mountain tunes, fiddle dance melodies and ballads of the Civil War; in a symphony inspired by Lincoln's Gettysburg Address.

IV

The career of Elie Siegmeister parallels that of Copland. He was born in Brooklyn, New York (on January 15, 1909); studied in Paris with Nadia Boulanger;

and first realized his full potential as a composer with works grounded in American folk music.

Siegmeister had literally absorbed the style and spirit of American folk music before he assimilated these into his own work. For many years he was conductor of the American Ballad Singers, which gave concerts of folk music throughout the United States; with Olin Downes he was editor of *A Treasury of American Folk Music;* he wrote the folk-music score for *Sing Out Sweet Land,* produced by the Theater Guild in New York in 1944, starring Burl Ives; and he has done a considerable amount of basic research work in different parts of the country digging up native folk songs. The effect that all this study and activity in folk music had upon his own creative thinking became evident in large orchestral compositions like *Ozark Set, Wilderness Road, Prairie Legend,* and *Western Suite.*

There were many other composers who found that our folk music could be the starting point from which to set forth on creative journeys. Morton Gould used cowboy songs in the *Cowboy Rhapsody.* In *Spirituals,* for string choir and orchestra, he imitated the style of "black" and "white" Spirituals. Negro Spirituals also played an important role in Louis Gruenberg's (1884–1964) fine opera *The Emperor Jones,* based on Eugene O'Neill's famous play; "Standin' in the Need of Prayer" is used with overpowering effect in the second act as Jones falls on his knees and begs God to forgive him for his sins. Spirituals and hillbilly music are simulated in Gruenberg's *Violin Concerto.* Fiddle tunes of the West and Negro Spirituals are quoted in Douglas Moore's (1893–) delightful orchestral suite, *The Pageant of P. T. Barnum,* with which he achieved his first success in 1924. Cajun folk tunes are the source of Virgil Thomson's (1896–

) *Louisiana Story,* a score originating as background music for a documentary film. Later it became sufficiently famous as a symphonic suite to earn the Pulitzer Prize in music.

Kurt Weill, apostle of "contemporary art" in Germany, and a leading composer of Broadway musicals in America, wrote an excellent folk opera at the dusk of his career—*Down in the Valley,* first heard at Indiana University in 1948. Arnold Sundgaard's libretto related the tale of Brack Weaver, sentenced to die for the murder of Bouche. Brack escapes in order to visit his beloved Jenny a last time. He reviews with her the circumstances that led him to kill Bouche in a brawl after Bouche had obnoxiously forced his attentions upon Jenny. Strengthened in the knowledge that Jenny still loves him, Brack gives himself up to a posse. Within the framework of Weill's thoroughly American score can be found five folk songs: "The Lonesome Dove," "The Little Black Train," "Hop Up," "My Ladies," and "Sourwood Mountain."

There are many outstanding American concert works in which either folk tunes or old hymn tunes are quoted or imitated. In Charles Ives's remarkable *Third Symphony,* the old church hymn "O for a Thousand Tongues" is treated fugally in the first movement and "Just as I Am," another hymn, is quoted in the finale. Henry Cowell (1897–1965), first famous (or notorious) as the creator of discordant "tone clusters," became mellow enough later in life to produce conventional music whose ideas came from American hymnology and American folk songs. In or about 1941, Cowell encountered an old collection of hymns, *Southern Harmony,* which revived in him memories of songs heard in boyhood among the Primitive Baptists in Kansas and Oklahoma. "Cowell be-

190

gan to wonder," explains his wife, "what the result would have been if our musical culture had not cut itself off from its living roots as it did during the last century. . . . Suppose the musical elements which formed the style of the shaped-note hymns had been allowed to develop and to penetrate our art music, what might they have become in the modern symphonic fabric?" Cowell answered this self-questioning by producing a series of compositions for various instrumental combinations, all of them entitled *Hymn and Fuguing Tune*. The most celebrated is the second, introduced in 1944—a work exalted in mood, classic in its purity, and contrapuntal in style.

Fuguing tunes had been the invention of America's first composer, William Billings, who lived during the Revolutionary War and was an outstanding creator of psalms and hymn tunes. The contemporary American composer, William Schuman, took some of Billings' church melodies as the point of departure for the *New England Triptych* for symphony orchestra, in 1956. Among the Billings hymns and anthems elaborated upon here were "Be Glad America," "When Jesus Wept" and "Chester." The last of these, incidentally, appeared soon after the outbreak of the Revolutionary War. With new martial lyrics it became the *Marseillaise* of the American Revolution.

V

The two greatest Latin-American composers are nationalists: Heitor Villa-Lobos of Brazil, and Carlos Chávez of Mexico.

Villa-Lobos was probably the most prolific composer of the twentieth century, if not of all time. Nobody can say for sure how many works he wrote; Villa-Lobos himself could never approximate the number. A fair estimate would be about two thousand, in every shape, manner, and form, including musical comedy. He used to pile his manuscripts all over his study in Rio de Janeiro; when one of them was lifted by a visitor as a souvenir he never seemed to care, knowing there were more where that came from. The inevitable result of such formidable creative fertility is an unevenness of quality. Few top-flight composers wrote so much actually bad music as did Villa-Lobos. But he also created many works of singular imagination and power, and these were invariably stimulated by both the folklore and the popular art forms of his native land, Brazil. So deep were the national ties of Villa-Lobos to Brazil that on one occasion, when an interviewer asked him what Brazilian folklore was, he replied: "*I* am Brazilian folklore."

Villa-Lobos devised two new musical forms, and into these molds he poured some of his finest inventions. One new form was the "Bachiana Brasileira." This was a suite combining Bach's contrapuntal style with some of the traits of Brazilian folk music. Villa-Lobos completed nine such works, of which the second and fifth are especially popular. The second, in 1930, contains a delightful descriptive movement entitled "The Little Train of Caipira," a toccata that closes the suite and portrays the course of a little train as it puffs its way along the Brazilian countryside. The fifth *Bachiana Brasileira* has two movements. The first movement, "Aria," completed in 1938, has become outstandingly successful. This is a three-part song for voice and an orchestra of 'cellos in which the outer parts consist of a passionate folk melody utilizing no words but just the syllable "ah."

The other form invented by Villa-Lobos was the *Chô-ros*. The *Chôros* is a popular Brazilian dance performed by a street band. The composer borrowed this term to designate popular Brazilian music in which the different modalities of Brazilian, Indian, and popular music are embodied. Villa-Lobos' various *chôroses* (fifteen in all) are for many different combinations of instruments: piano solo; winds and male chorus; horns and trombones; flute and clarinet; violin and 'cello; chamber orchestra; orchestra and chorus; two orchestras and band; and large orchestra, military band, and mixed chorus. One of the best is the fifth, *Alma Brasileira,* for piano solo—a three-part composition with the middle lyrical section in the style of a Brazilian folk song and the flanking parts in the restless rhythmic movement of a Brazilian popular dance. The sixth and the tenth are also frequently heard. The former is scored for orchestra, guitar and native percussion instruments, and is a polyphonic treatment of several Brazilian folk and popular tunes. The latter, for chorus and orchestra, was described by the composer as "music . . . full of nostalgia and of love" reflecting "the reaction of a civilized man to stark nature."

Villa-Lobos was born in Rio de Janeiro on March 5, 1887. He is unique among contemporary composers in that he received virtually no formal instruction in music. As a child he did get a few lessons on the 'cello from his father, while later on in life he made a brief and unsuccessful attempt to attend a conservatory. But this represents about all the musical training he ever received. He hated lessons, exercises, school discipline; he would have no traffic with any of them. He preferred picking up his musical knowledge haphazardly, by experiments, by trial and error. He learned to play the violin in a vertical position on his knee (like a 'cello) because he

193

just did not know that the violin was to be played any other way. He taught himself to play several wind instruments and picked up the elements of piano playing.

His real conservatory was Brazilian popular music to which he listened endlessly, and which he tried to recreate on any musical instrument he happened to have on hand. When his normal academic schooling ended with the death of his father—Villa-Lobos was then just eleven—the boy made his living playing in popular theater and restaurant orchestras. Later on he came to know well Brazilian folk songs and dances, which held for him an even greater fascination than did popular music. By 1909 he had completed a major work based on Brazilian folk music—an orchestral suite. In 1912 he made the first of several expeditions into the interior of Brazil to acquaint himself not only with its indigenous music, but also with its ceremonies and rituals.

Slowly he developed his own style of composition assimilating the more recognizable features of Brazilian popular and folk music. His writing, like that of his country's songs and dances, tended towards improvisations, vital rhythms and syncopations, dramatic alternations of moods, vivid harmonizations and orchestrations. He also made frequent use of native instruments.

With such means he produced a fabulous library of symphonies, concertos of all sorts, shorter works for orchestra, chamber music for many different combinations of instruments, piano works, songs, operas, choral music, and operettas. In 1915, a concert of his works, given in Rio de Janeiro, did little to attract attention to his pronounced gifts. When interest in him was finally aroused, it came through the efforts of Artur Rubinstein, the world-famous piano virtuoso. While touring Brazil in 1919, Rubinstein happened to hear a Villa-Lobos composition in a movie theater. This impressed him so strongly that he paid a personal call on the composer. A few days later, Villa-Lobos returned the visit, by bringing to Rubinstein's hotel suite a small orchestra. The whole day was spent in a performance of Villa-Lobos's music. Now made aware of the extent and nature of Villa-Lobos's creative gift, Rubinstein used his influence to get for the young composer an annual stipend from the Brazilian government. A few years later, in 1926, Villa-Lobos expressed his gratitude to Rubinstein by writing a remarkable piece (originally for piano, but later orchestrated) entitled *Rudepoema.* The title means "savage poem," and the music was intended as a tonal portrait of Rubinstein.

The government stipend made it possible for Villa-Lobos to go to Europe in 1923, and live for three years in Paris. After a brief journey to Brazil in 1926, Villa-Lobos returned to Paris for three more years. But though he loved the French capital dearly and was delighted with his personal contacts with the foremost French musicians of the time, French music had little effect upon him. By now he knew where his creative strength lay, that first and foremost he was a Brazilian composer. He had no intention of being deflected by the startling new works he was continually hearing in Paris. His aim was to spread propaganda in Paris for Brazilian music in general, and his own in particular. As he told a French interviewer one day: "Did you think I came here to absorb your ideas? I came here to show you what I've done. If you don't like what I do, I'm going away."

Back in his native land in 1930, Villa-Lobos was appointed Director of Musical Education, an office in which he revolutionized the methods and techniques of teaching music to children. From now on he achieved recognition in and out of Brazil as that country's foremost musician. Consequently, when he paid his first visit to the United States in 1944–5, the occasion was celebrated throughout the country with a "Villa-Lobos Week," and performances of some of his major orchestral works by leading American symphonic organizations.

In the last years of his life, Villa-Lobos spent a good deal of his time in the United States, a country he came to regard as his second homeland. Though seriously ill most of the time, Villa-Lobos did not relax his prodigious creative activity. Up to his last days he continued to produce one work after another. He died in Rio de Janeiro on November 17, 1959.

In the music of Carlos Chávez we find many of the attributes of Mexican-Indian folk music: the simple, austere, bleak melodic line; the hard percussive sounds; the elemental rhythmic power; the occasional archaic idiom. He often uses native Mexican instruments, as in *Xochipili-Macuilxochitl* which is scored entirely for a Mexican orchestra, or the *Toccata for Percussion Instruments* which requires Yaqui drums, hardwood sound sticks, rattles, and small Indian drums. Sometimes he has had recourse to actual thematic quotation, as was the case with one of his most popular works, *Sinfonia India,* in which actual Mexican-Indian tunes are heard. Most often, however, the material is his own, but given shape and design by the folk music of his native land.

Chávez was born in Mexico City on June 13, 1899. Like Villa-Lobos, he was virtually self-taught in music. He often has said that his complete creative independence, and his daring to try the new and the unusual, came from the fact that he had never been hampered by a conservatory training. Though he began composing seri-

196

ously when he was eighteen, he did not find himself creatively until a few years later when he happened to come upon some examples of Mexican-Indian music. He then went to live with several tribes, steeping himself in their art and customs, learning to play their instruments. He also made several arduous trips into the mountain regions in search of rare examples of native songs and dances.

The first significant music in which the impact of this research is felt can be found in two ballets: *New Fire* in 1921 and *H.P.* in 1926–7. Both are Mexican in subject matter; the scores for both derive their strong fiber, linear style, and abounding contrasts of mood from Mexican-Indian music. In his later works—symphonies, operas, concertos, string quartets, sonatas, and various shorter pieces—Chávez combines these and other native Mexican elements skilfully with the most advanced techniques of modern music.

After a considerable amount of travel in Europe and America in the middle 1920's, Chávez settled down in his native country to become its foremost composer and its most influential musician. He founded, and for many years led, the National Symphony; he founded and directed the National Conservatory; he became head of the Department of Fine Arts. He was Mexico's musical spokesman to the rest of the world. In his many visits as guest conductor in Europe and the United States, as well as through his many compositions, he has passionately espoused the cause of native Mexican music.

CHAPTER 10

The Hebraists

IN 1927, the Swiss-born American composer, Ernest Bloch, completed *America*, an epic rhapsody that won first prize of $3,000 in a contest sponsored by the journal *Musical America*. Written in three sections, this rhapsody is a tonal representation of three periods in American history: 1620, when the Pilgrims landed on soil previously inhabited by the Indians; the period of the Civil War; and finally, the year of 1926, with a prognostication of the future. In the first movement, Bloch quoted the famous old American hymn, "Old Hundredth," and used other melodies in the style of American-Indian songs and dances. In the second movement, we find quotations of American patriotic and war songs, Creole folk songs, and Negro Spirituals. And in the finale we are reminded again of "Old Hundredth," of several Negro tunes, and of "Yankee Doodle."

America is the only work by Bloch in a distinctly national character. Bloch's roots reach not into a national soil but a racial one. Often consciously, but at times even unconsciously, Bloch set out to write Hebrew music that mirrored "the Jewish soul . . . the complex agitated soul that I feel vibrating through the Bible." As he himself once explained, "the freshness and naïveté of the Patriarchs; the violence of the prophetic Books; the Jew's

198

savage love of justice; the despair of the Ecclesiastes; the sorrow and the immensity of the Book of Job; the sensuality of the Song of Songs. . . . It is all this that I endeavor to hear in myself, and to translate in my music; the sacred emotions of the race that slumber far down in our soul."

Of course, Bloch was not the first composer stimulated by Hebrew music. In Russia, in 1908, there was founded by Joel Engel (1868–1927) the Society for Jewish Folk Music. The Society spent a decade doing scholarly researches into old Hebrew religious music and Jewish folk songs, adapting them to modern harmonizations, and gathering them into significant publications. The Society arranged thousands of concerts of Jewish music throughout Europe. It also encouraged Russian-Jewish composers to write racial music in ambitious forms for concert performance.

But Bloch was the first serious composer whose Hebraic concert works achieved international recognition. He devoted himself to composition—and for a number of years specifically to Hebrew music—with an almost religious consecration. When he was a child he made a vow he would devote his life to music, writing that oath down on paper. He placed the paper under a mound of rocks over which he built a ritual fire. He remained true to that vow, just as he remained ever true to the highest ideals of his calling.

The son of a shopkeeper, he was born in Geneva, Switzerland, on July 24, 1880. Music study began early; at fourteen he studied the violin with L. Rey, and composition with Émile Jaques-Dalcroze, the creator of "eurhythmics." After that Bloch's musical education was continued in Brussels and Germany with such eminent masters as Eugène Ysaÿe, Ivan Knorr, and Ludwig Thuille. Bloch's first mature work, the *Symphony in C-sharp minor,* was completed when he was twenty-two.

His father's business reverses compelled him to go to work in the Geneva shop. But he did not forget his vow. All his spare hours, sometimes deep into the night, were devoted to creative work which he pursued with undiminished intensity. Thus, he completed several important works—*Poèmes d'automne* for voice and orchestra; *Hiver-Printemps,* two symphonic sketches for orchestra; an opera, *Macbeth.*

Macbeth was his first work to get an important performance. This took place at the Opéra-Comique in Paris on November 30, 1910. Romain Rolland, France's eminent musicologist, was so moved by the opera that he made a trip to Geneva to persuade Bloch to give up his work as shopkeeper and concentrate on music. Rolland's faith in Bloch was further strengthened when, at long last, the early *Symphony in C-sharp minor* received its world première, in Geneva in 1915. "Your symphony," Rolland wrote the composer, "is one of the most important works of the modern school. . . . Continue expressing yourself in the same way, freely and fully; I will answer for your becoming one of the masters of our time."

Bloch's early works were a mixture of Romanticism and Impressionism. But soon after he had left commerce to become a full-time composer, Bloch found his personal style in Hebrew music. This period began in 1912 with *Three Jewish Poems.* It reached its summit within the next few years with *Schelomo,* for orchestra with 'cello obbligato, and the *Israel Symphony.*

As a composer of Hebrew music Bloch made no effort to quote synagogue chants or Jewish folk songs, or to adapt them. But he did imitate some of the stylistic at-

200

tributes of this music—the intervals, rhythmic patterns, and the progressions found in authentic Jewish music. The broad rhapsodic feeling, the spirituality and mysticism, by which so much of Hebrew music is identified also are apparent in his compositions.

Schelomo, completed in 1915, is a rhapsody for 'cello and orchestra glorifying the Biblical Jew, King Solomon. The solo 'cello represents the king, and as Guido M. Gatti once wrote, it "lends itself to a reincarnation of Solomon in all his glory." *Israel Symphony,* which absorbed Bloch from 1912 to 1916, was inspired by the Day of Atonement, the holiest day in the Jewish calendar, when the pious Jew seeks mercy for his year's sins through grief and repentance. The conclusion of this one-movement work is a poignant prayer for chorus: "Adonoi, my Elohim, O my Elohim! Alleluia, O My Elohim! Hear my voice my Elohim, Hear my prayer!" And it is on such a note of humility that the symphony ends.

In 1916 Ernest Bloch came to the United States as the conductor of the Maud Allen dance troupe then touring the country. He did not stay long with this organization since it soon went into bankruptcy. All-Bloch concerts were now given in Boston, Philadelphia and New York by such eminent conductors as Karl Muck, Leopold Stokowski and Artur Bodanzky. Further attention was directed to Bloch when, in 1919, he received the Elizabeth Sprague Coolidge Prize of $1,000 for his *Suite for Viola and Piano.*

From 1920 through 1925 Bloch was the director of the Cleveland Institute of Music. This period saw the creation of one more significant Hebraic work, the *Baal Shem Suite,* for violin and piano; its inspiration and subject were the late eighteenth-century Hebrew seer and founder of a sect known as Hasidism. But Bloch also wrote many non-Hebraic works. The *Concerto Grosso* for piano and string orchestra in 1923, was one of Bloch's rare excursions into Neo-Classicism. He wrote it to prove to his pupils that "modern" music could be created within a strictly classical structure and with traditional means. But the *First Piano Quintet,* also in 1923, while never intended as a Hebraic work, is steeped in religious and spiritual feelings. Its rhapsodic style, brooding mysticism, and occasional exaltation, place it unmistakably with Bloch's Hebrew compositions.

In 1927, Bloch transferred his teaching and directorial activities to San Francisco. There he completed the already described *America* rhapsody, which was introduced simultaneously by several major American orchestras. Bloch stayed in San Francisco until 1931. A generous endowment from a patron then enabled him to spend several years in Switzerland and concentrate on the writing of a major religious work, the *Sacred Service,* to a text derived from the Sabbath morning liturgy. He completed it in 1933, and it was introduced the following year in Turin. A work of rare eloquence and power, and imbued with religious fervor, the *Sacred Service*—while intended for the synagogue—was nonetheless a testament to all mankind and to all faiths. "It symbolizes," said Bloch, "a philosophy acceptable to all men."

After returning to the United States, Bloch made his home in Agate Beach, Oregon, overlooking the Pacific Ocean. He lived there for the rest of his life. Though often seriously ill, he did not interrupt his creative activity. On the contrary, he proved more productive than ever! Symphonies, concertos, quartets, and various other orchestral and chamber music left his industrious pen in abundance. In 1942, the American Academy of Arts and

Letters presented him with a gold medal. Five years later, the New York Music Critics Circle gave him its annual award for his *Second String Quartet;* and in 1954 Bloch became the first composer ever to receive in a single year from that Circle an award in two different categories, in chamber music for his *Third String Quartet,* and in orchestral music for his *Second Concerto Grosso.*

Occasionally, in his later works, Bloch returned to the Hebraic fold, as in the *Suite hebraïque,* for viola and orchestra, in 1952. But most of the time neither by title nor by program notes did he identify his works as Hebraic, though in style, intensity of feeling, and little mannerisms they remained racial. Bloch died in Portland, Oregon, on July 15, 1959.

II

Bloch's *Sacred Service,* on the one hand, and his *Israel Symphony* and *Schelomo,* on the other, represent two directions a Hebraic composer can take. One is to bring his invention and techniques to Hebrew liturgy, and set actual prayers to music for service in synagogues. The other is to use Hebrew subjects, and the identifying fingerprints of Hebrew music, for concert-hall music. Many important composers in writing Hebrew music have successfully worked in both areas. Darius Milhaud wrote an excellent *Sacred Service* for the Sabbath morning services; Mario Castelnuovo-Tedesco (1895–   ) and Paul Dessau (1894–1968) have set to music the Friday evening services. These and others have also written music for individual prayers rather than complete services: Arnold Schoenberg with the *Kol Nidrei* for speaker, choir, and orchestra, a free adaptation of the famous Yom Kippur chant; Castelnuovo-Tedesco with *Lecho dodi,* which he wrote for a synagogue in Amsterdam, Holland; Leonard Bernstein, with *Hashkivenu* for four-part mixed chorus, cantor, and organ; Jan Meyerowitz with *Shir Hadash L'Shabbat.*

More plentiful still are the concert works in a Hebraic style and idiom. In such a vein Castelnuovo-Tedesco wrote the Hebrew rhapsody for orchestra, *Le Danze del re David,* and the *Violin Concerto,* "The Prophets"; Milhaud wrote *Poèms juifs,* the *Chants populaires hebraïques,* and the opera, *David;* Jan Meyerowitz (1913–   ) wrote the oratorio, *Esther;* and the American composer, Henry Brant (1913–   ), wrote the symphony, "The Promised Land."

One of the most successful of these Hebraic concert works is Leonard Bernstein's "Jeremiah" *Symphony.* The wonder-boy of American music—famous as conductor, pianist, teacher, musical commentator, author, composer of musical comedies, and composer of serious music—Leonard Bernstein made his bow as a composer for orchestra with this "Jeremiah" *Symphony* in 1944. It was forthwith played by most of America's leading orchestras; was recorded in its entirety by Victor; and was the recipient of the New York Music Critics Circle Award. In writing "Jeremiah," Bernstein was more than passingly influenced by Bloch. "Jeremiah" has much of the rhapsodic sweep, the rich emotional content, the sensuality, and the burning intensity of *Schelomo.* Sometimes Bernstein makes use of quotation. The first theme of his second movement is based on a phrase used for the reading of the *Haftorah* on Sabbath morning; the opening phrase of the vocal section in the finale comes from a liturgical cadence heard in the synagogue during the holiday of Tisha B'Av. But most of Bernstein's music, while genuinely Hebraic in style, feeling and texture, is of his own invention. As he himself explained: "Other resemblances to Hebrew liturgical music are a matter of emotional quality rather than of the notes themselves. The first movement aims to parallel in feeling the intensity of the prophet Jeremiah's pleas with his people; and the Scherzo, to give the general sense of destruction and chaos brought up by the pagan corruption within the priesthood and the people. The third movement being a setting of a poetic text (from the Book of Lamentations) is naturally a more literary conception. It is the cry of Jeremiah as he mourns his beloved Jerusalem, ruined, pillaged, and dishonored after his desperate efforts to save it."

On several notable occasions, the exotic nature of Hebrew music appealed strongly to non-Jewish composers. There is a Jewish Song in Ravel's *Chants populaires* of 1910; in 1914 he wrote *Deux mélodies hebraïques* which includes the memorable "Kaddish." It is mainly on the strength of these works that Ravel was for a long time erroneously identified as a Jew. Prokofiev wrote an *Overture on Jewish Themes,* for clarinet, string quartet, and piano in 1919. In 1936, the American composer, Harl McDonald (1899–1955), wrote *Three Hebrew Poems* for orchestra, based partly on Aramaic, and partly on Hebrew folk music (including a quotation from the very popular Jewish melody, "Eili, Eili").

In Palestine, and subsequently in the State of Israel, the boundaries of Hebrew music were considerably extended through researches undertaken in that country not only in old Hebrew and Jewish music, but also in the music of the Persian, Yemenite and Bukharian Jews. One of the earliest pioneers in seeking out native folk songs and dances indigenous to Palestine was Joel Engel (1868–1927), the same man who had founded the Society for Jewish Folk Music in Russia in 1908. Engel came to Palestine in 1924 where he lived for the three years that still remained to him. In that time he collected numerous examples of Palestinian folk music, some of which was published after his death.

Jewish composers from both Eastern and Central Europe, in Palestine to find a new homeland, discovered there a rich Jewish-Oriental folk vein to tap. Paul Ben-Haim, who was born in Germany in 1897, and emigrated to Palestine in 1933 wrote a symphony (his second, completed in 1945) in which a climax is reached with an exciting hora. He used a native Palestinian folk song for a set of variations for piano trio, and old Hebraic and Chassidic themes for his *Liturgical Cantata*. Marc Lavry (1903–   ) from Riga, also used a hora with impressive effect in *Emek*, an eloquent paean to his new land. Among his other works are *Country Dances of Israel*, an oratorio, *Shir Hashirim* (The Song of Songs), and an opera, *Dan Hashomer*. Oedoen Partos (1907–   ), from Budapest, completed in Palestine a *Fantasy on a Yemenite Theme*, *Yizkor* (Memorial Service), and a symphonic fantasy, *Ein Gev*.

Ben-Haim, Lavry, and Partos represent the older generation of Hebrew-music composers. Since the birth of Israel, new young men have arisen not only in Tel-Aviv, Haifa, and Jerusalem but also in the *kibbutzim* to enrich further the literature of Hebrew music produced for the synagogue, opera house, and concert hall.

CHAPTER 11

The Popularists

"THE Six" in France, and Villa-Lobos and Chávez in Latin America, were not the only ones to use popular tunes with serious intent. Many American composers wrote ambitious concert works based on familiar melodies. Roy Harris wrote an excellent concert overture on "When Johnny Comes Marching Home," a Civil War song by Patrick S. Gilmore. Stephen Foster's beloved ballads have been adapted into symphonic compositions by Mario Castelnuovo-Tedesco in *Humoresques on Foster's Themes;* by Werner Janssen in the *Foster Suite;* by Lucien Caillet in *Fantasia and Fugue on Oh, Susanna;* and by Morton Gould in *Foster Gallery.* Jaromir Weinberger wrote the *Prelude and Fugue on Dixie*—"Dixie," of course being the minstrel-show tune by Dan Emmett which became a classic of the Civil War.

The one branch of popular music that has proved the most fertile area for exploitation by American composers is jazz. The embryo of jazz was fertilized in West Africa. To jazz the native songs and dances of Africa contributed their complex rhythms, accentuations and syncopations, the blues tonality, and such structural devices as the "break" and the "call and response." But jazz for all that is an essentially American product, an outgrowth of the religious, work, and play songs with which the American Negro sought escape from his grim world of slavery and oppression. The word "jazz" is believed to have come out of Chicago in or about 1914. It may possibly be a corruption of the name of some famous Negro musician ("Charles" into "Chas" or "Jas"); or it may be a contraction of a term long popular in minstrel shows—jasbo. But as a style of popular music, jazz appeared long before 1914 and far from Chicago.

Jazz was born in the honky-tonks of New Orleans in the closing years of the nineteenth century. Since New Orleans was a wide open and tolerant city, it welcomed Negro musicians and readily found employment for them in its many night spots. Most of these musicians could not read a note of music; consequently they were compelled to depend mainly on improvisation for their music-making. Most of these musicians never had any sort of formal training and so were not inhibited by textbooks or teachers; they experimented freely with the most unusual and unorthodox sounds produced in the most unconventional ways.

And so jazz sprang up in New Orleans, more as a style of performance than a style of composition. At first nobody put jazz down on paper. Improvisation became a basic element in all good jazz, sometimes occurring in a solo passage by an individual performer, and at other times produced by several members of an ensemble in a remarkable network of rhythm and melody. Two important idioms distinguished these improvisations and henceforth characterized real jazz. One was "ragtime." The term came from Negro clog dancing referred to by the Negro as "ragging." Ragtime consisted of syncopation in the treble against an even, inflexible rhythm in the bass. The other idiom was the "blues," an offshoot of the sorrowful songs in which Negroes lamented their sad lot in a world they never made. The blues introduced the flatted third and seventh notes into the diatonic scale, from this point on identified as "blues notes." Out of the blues also came the dissonant harmonies in the accompaniment when the blues note was absent, and the interpolation of "breaks" in the melody to allow for such exclamations as "Oh, Lawdy" and "Oh, Baby." Later on "breaks" were used to permit a jazz musician to indulge in some spontaneous improvisation. Add to ragtime and the blues the distinct colorations of saxophones, muted trumpets, squealing clarinets, and novel percussion effects, and you get the basic physiognomy of New Orleans jazz.

II

Long before Americans started writing symphonic works in a jazz style, significant European composers were tentatively using now one element, now another of American popular music. Debussy used the cakewalk rhythm in "Golliwog's Cakewalk" from the *Children's Corner* in 1908, and syncopation and ragtime in *Minstrels* from the first book of *Preludes* in 1910. In 1917, Erik Satie interpolated jazz rhythms into his score for the ballet *Parade*. Stravinsky introduced a ragtime tune in *A Soldier's Tale* in 1918. He also wrote two compositions entitled *Ragtime,* one for eleven instruments in 1918, and another for orchestra in 1920. Milhaud used jazz with uncommon effect in his remarkable ballet *La Création du monde* in 1923.

But it was an American whose extensive utilization of jazz melodies and rhythms with serious artistic purpose firmly established jazz as an idiom deserving concert treatment. That man, of course, was George Gershwin.

From boyhood on, Gershwin seemed to know his musical mission: To bring to American popular songs the resources of serious music, and to bring to serious music the vitality and personal idiosyncrasies of jazz. Later on in his career, he had this to say about his purpose: "I regard jazz as an American folk music, a very powerful one which is probably in the blood of the American people more than any other style of music. I believe that it can be made the basis of serious symphonic works of lasting value." He also wrote with prophetic insight: "Jazz has contributed an enduring value to America in the sense that it has expressed ourselves. It is an original American achievement that will endure, not as jazz perhaps, but which will leave its mark on future music in one way or another."

Even as a boy he held these convictions strongly. Time and again he argued with his teacher, Charles Hambitzer, that there was artistic validity and importance to a song like Irving Berlin's "Alexander's Ragtime Band"; that a serious composer would do well to work within the framework of the popular song; that an American composer could achieve a national identity by affiliating himself with American popular idioms. "The boy is a genius without doubt," Hambitzer wrote to his sister. "He wants to go in for this modern stuff, jazz and what not. But I'm not going to let him for a while. I'll see that he gets a firm foundation in the standard music first."

Gershwin was born in Brooklyn, New York, on September 26, 1898, but spent most of his boyhood in New York's East Side. His was a normal American boyhood. He liked to play with his friends the games of the streets; he was a baseball fan; he hated anything that smacked of culture. In the East Side, any boy who took lessons on a musical instrument or showed any interest in music, was derisively referred to as a "Maggie." For a while Gershwin had no intention of being called that. Never-

210

theless, in spite of himself, several musical experiences *did* stir him profoundly: Rubinstein's *Melody in F,* which he heard in a penny arcade; the sound of jazz drifting from the window of a Harlem night club; a violin performance in the public-school assembly by one of his fellow students, Maxie Rosenzweig. (Maxie, who became a famous violinist, later changed his name to Max Rosen). When Gershwin came upon a piano in the home of one of his friends, he enjoyed playing around at the keyboard. Sometimes he would try to reproduce a favorite popular song, but most of the time he would create little melodies of his own. One day he played something of his own for Maxie. The young violinist said firmly: "You'd better forget about music, George. You haven't the talent to be a composer."

He was twelve years old when a piano entered his own home. From then on he monopolized the instrument, spending tireless hours working out tunes. He also started taking piano lessons with local teachers, and in 1912 he sought out Charles Hambitzer for advanced instruction. A remarkable musician, Charles Hambitzer proved a powerful influence in Gershwin's musical development and was the greatest single factor in transforming an ebullient amateur into a sound musician. Because of Hambitzer, Gershwin not only started going to concerts but began the study of theory, harmony and counterpoint with Edward Kilenyi.

Determined to make his way in popular music, and equally determined to learn as much as he could about it, Gershwin, aged fifteen, found a job in Tin Pan Alley as song plugger and staff pianist. He was writing popular songs all the time. The first to get published was "When You Want 'Em You Can't Get 'Em"; the first to be heard on the Broadway stage was "The Making of a Girl" in

211

the *Passing Show*. This was in 1916. Three years later came *La La Lucille*—Gershwin's first Broadway musical comedy—and "Swanee," his first hit song.

Between 1920 and 1924, Gershwin wrote the complete scores for the annual *George White Scandals*. In songs like "I'll Build a Stairway to Paradise" and "Somebody Loves Me" he revealed an uncanny skill in rhythm and meter, and an uncommon freshness of lyricism. Beryl Rubinstein, a concert pianist and renowned teacher, was so impressed by Gershwin's songs that he told an interviewer that Gershwin had "the spark of musical genius." Then he added: "When we speak of American composers, George Gershwin's name will be prominent on our list." Another eminent musician who was impressed by Gershwin was the concert singer Eva Gauthier who presented some Gershwin songs in a recital at Aeolian Hall, with Gershwin as her accompanist.

Gershwin's artistic horizon began to expand. For the *Scandals of 1922*, he wrote a one-act Negro opera to a libretto by Buddy De Sylva. Originally called *Blue Monday* it received only a single performance—on opening night. George White considered it too somber for a revue and had it deleted from the program. But Paul Whiteman, the orchestra leader who was one of the stars of the *Scandals* that year, was convinced of the importance of this little opera. (Later on he gave it several times in Carnegie Hall and elsewhere under its new title of *135th Street*.) When, late in 1923, Whiteman planned an all-American music concert of popular music at Aeolian Hall, New York, he asked Gershwin to write an extended concert work for him.

That work was the *Rhapsody in Blue* for piano and orchestra, introduced by Paul Whiteman and his orchestra, with the composer at the piano, on February 12, 1924.

212

From the opening trill of the clarinet followed by its seventeen-note ascent toward the first jaunty theme through the broad and rhapsodic song for strings (probably the most celebrated single melody in all contemporary American music), the *Rhapsody* sounded a new voice both for jazz and for music. This was American music and music of the 1920's in its brashness, vulgarity, muscular energy, and emotional abandon. The vocabulary of jazz—the blues, ragtime, jazz instrumental colors—were here assembled for a new kind of music, pulsing with vitality, and as fresh as youth. Some of the critics, failing to see the forest for the trees, were disturbed by the occasional awkward technique, diffuse form, and lapses in inspiration. But others knew that something important in contemporary music was happening that afternoon in Aeolian Hall. "Mr. Gershwin," said Gilbert W. Gabriel, the noted drama critic, "has an irrepressible pack of talents." Deems Taylor reported that the *Rhapsody* "revealed a genuine melodic gift and a piquant and individual harmonic sense to lend significance to its rhythmic ingenuity. Moreover it is genuine jazz music. . . . Mr. Gershwin will bear watching; he may yet bring jazz out of the kitchen." In an outburst of what is surely excessive excitement, H. O. Osgood regarded the *Rhapsody* as "greater than Stravinsky's *The Rite of Spring*"; and Henry T. Finck proclaimed it with equally excessive enthusiasm to be "far superior to Schoenberg, Milhaud, and the rest of the futuristic fellows."

The *Rhapsody in Blue* first became known to the nation at large through a Victor recording by Paul Whiteman and his orchestra that sold a million discs. But this was just an echo of a gathering storm. Before long, the *Rhapsody* was heard in the concert hall, over the radio, on the stage, on screen, and in the ballet theater, achiev-

213

ing a popularity equalled by few serious works of modern music before or since. Royalties mounted to over a quarter of a million dollars in a decade. But the *Rhapsody* not only made Gershwin a wealthy man; it also spread his fame around the globe, and gave him, for the first time, status as a serious American composer.

The *Rhapsody* has never lost its popularity. It is perhaps the most frequently performed composition in the entire contemporary American concert repertory. It would be impossible to estimate the number of millions of records sold of this work; there are no less than two dozen different versions on the active list in the present-day catalogue. Its title was used for Gershwin's screen biography in 1946, and its main melody has been used through the years as Paul Whiteman's signature over radio and television.

With a remarkable capacity to grow both in his technique and in his inspiration, Gershwin went on from the *Rhapsody* to produce a handful of other remarkable works with which jazz became fully emancipated. For one thing, though the *Rhapsody* had been orchestrated by Ferde Grofé, Gershwin himself orchestrated all his later symphonic works. Gershwin continually demonstrated a greater self-assurance in his use of form, of thematic development, of subtlety of expression. A year and a half after the *Rhapsody* came the *Concerto in F,* for piano and orchestra, introduced by the composer with the New York Symphony conducted by Walter Damrosch. In 1926 Gershwin wrote the *Three Preludes* for piano solo; that in C-sharp minor, a poignant three-part blues melody, is particularly famous. The orchestral tone poem, *An American in Paris,* was first heard in 1928 in a performance by the New York Philharmonic under Damrosch. This was a vivid programmatic work describing an Amer-

214

ican's emotional responses both to Paris and to home as he saunters along the boulevards. To simulate the sounds of the Paris streets, Gershwin interpolated into his orchestration actual Parisian taxi horns. The *Second Rhapsody* followed, its première performance taking place in Boston with Koussevitzky conducting. After that came the *Cuban Overture*, in which effective use is made of some native Cuban percussion instruments. Gershwin's last work for the concert hall was a set of variations for piano and orchestra on "I Got Rhythm." This was the song that Ethel Merman had introduced in the musical-comedy *Girl Crazy* when she made her Broadway debut.

Gershwin was so completely wrapped up in his music—writing it, playing it, talking about it—that he was often accused of being egocentric. He was a man of many interests and diversions; he was also a man who through the years loved many women. But his music always came first. One day he was deeply absorbed in revising his music for a forthcoming Broadway show when he received a telephone call from one of his girl friends, whom he had been planning to marry. She told him she was tired of waiting and was marrying somebody else. "You know," he told his brother Ira, when he returned to the piano, "I would be heartbroken—if only I weren't so terribly busy." This incident is revealing. Perhaps the reason Gershwin never married was because he refused to let anyone usurp even a small part of the place music held in his life. He worked at his music all the time with complete dedication. Time and again he sacrificed a fortune in contracts to spend weeks, sometimes even months, on a serious piece of music from which he could only earn a pittance.

That he was not egocentric was perhaps proved by the fact that he never stopped studying. After studying with Hambitzer and Kilenyi, he entered the harmony class of

Rubin Goldmark. Later on, he studied counterpoint with Henry Cowell, and after that, the Schillinger method with its creator. Until the end of his life, Gershwin sought guidance and instruction in a ceaseless effort to strengthen his technique and to enrich his fund of musical knowledge. He was continually studying the scores of modern composers—Berg's *Wozzeck,* for example, or Schoenberg's string quartets. He worked painstakingly over textbooks on orchestration, harmony, and theory. He never hesitated to "pick the brains" of every famous musician with whom he came into contact, questioning them about their own work and seeking from them valuable advice and criticism about his own. Here, there, everywhere, he picked up little stylistic tricks, methods, approaches, effects which he forthwith fixed into his own equipment. "What I don't know about music," he once told an interviewer when he was at the height of his success, "is enough to keep me occupied for the rest of a normally long life." It was this unquenchable thirst for musical information, this restless search for answers to his creative problems, that made it possible for him to grow all the time.

Gershwin's last work in a serious vein was his folk opera, *Porgy and Bess,* first introduced in Boston on September 30, 1935, then given in New York on October 10. At first a box-office failure—and treated with no little condescension and lack of appreciation by the critics—*Porgy and Bess* went into temporary discard, and seemed destined for the oblivion that seemed to await most contemporary operas. But in 1942, more than four years after Gershwin's death, the opera was revived in New York to unqualified critical and public acclaim. Virgil Thomson, originally quite harsh in his estimate of the opera, now described it as "a beautiful piece of music and a deeply moving play for the lyric theater." Olin Downes, who had also found a good deal to condemn in it when he reviewed it for the first time, now said that "Gershwin has taken a substantial step, and advanced the cause of native opera." The New York Music Critics Circle singled it out as the most significant musical revival of the year. The audience response was so enthusiastic that its run of eight months proved the longest of any revival up to that time in the history of the Broadway stage. After it closed on Broadway, it went on an extended tour of twenty-six cities, establishing box-office records in several of them.

Then, between 1952 and 1956, an American-Negro company, under the auspices of the State Department, made a monumental tour with *Porgy and Bess*, achieving an artistic triumph of the first magnitude in Europe, the Near East, the Soviet Union, countries behind the Iron Curtain and Latin America. In Vienna, *Porgy and Bess* was hailed as "an unqualified masterwork"; in Yugoslavia, reported a cable to *The New York Times*, "the Communist officials, the man in the street, the students, all are singing the songs of George Gershwin and the praises of the cast of the folk opera"; in Israel it was described as "an artistic event of first-class importance." It became the first opera by an American-born composer given in the historic La Scala in Milan; this was also the first time that a single opera held the La Scala stage for an entire week. In the Soviet Union it was rapturously hailed not only by the general public but by most of the leading Soviet composers.

Today we know that *Porgy and Bess* is an enduring classic, the only American opera that is continually being revived in different parts of the country; the first Ameri-

217

can opera made into a motion picture; one of the few American operas recorded in its entirety, with its principal excerpts found in more than twenty-five recordings in the present-day catalogue. *Porgy and Bess* finds Gershwin at the peak of his career as a composer bringing artistic significance to the styles and idioms of American popular music.

Though *Porgy and Bess* makes extensive use of Negro folk material, the melodic invention is entirely Gershwin's. He models his chants, choral numbers and songs on Spirituals, Shouts (chants improvised during the actual religious service by the congregation) and work songs. His recitatives are given shape by the inflections of Negro speech. He interpolates street cries simulating some of those heard in Charleston. The ease and authenticity with which Gershwin brought the style of Negro music into his writing was one indication of his expanding creative power. Other indications came from his capacity to portray through music many different moods, backgrounds, and incidents. This new power is evident in the subtle way he kept the action moving by using vocal glissandi, alternation of chords, and ostinato rhythmic patterns. The use of spoken dialogue for the white people (the only time that dialogue replaces recitatives) to provide a contrast between the races, the distinguished tone-speech, the powerful antiphonal choruses, expressive dissonances and chromaticisms, the skillful counterpoint—all showed Gershwin as a serious musician at the height of his technical and creative powers.

In *Porgy and Bess* there are also overtones of Tin Pan Alley—popular styles and methods employed with the most consummate skill and artistic effect. Tin Pan Alley echoes and re-echoes in songs like "It Ain't Necessarily So," "There's a Boat That's Leavin' Soon for New York,"

218

and in the blues-melody, "A Red-Headed Woman Makes a Choochoo Jump Its Track." In this juxtaposition of the serious and the popular, in this merger of the Metropolitan Opera with Tin Pan Alley, there is never a feeling of incongruity. Popular tunes and ditties are basic to Gershwin's artistic purpose and have their specific function in the overall design.

Of course, while developing himself as a serious composer Gershwin did not desert his more popular endeavors. He wrote scores for many outstanding Broadway musicals and Hollywood motion pictures, filling them with some of the most remarkable popular songs written during this period. The peak of his career on Broadway was reached in 1931 with *Of Thee I Sing!*, the political satire which became the first musical comedy in Broadway history to receive the Pulitzer Prize.

Gershwin died in Los Angeles on July 11, 1937 after an unsuccessful operation on the brain. He was thirty-nine.

III

Gershwin's success in utilizing American popular idioms in classical music had profound worldwide repercussions. There is little doubt that it was Gershwin's example which led many important composers to emulate him. Maurice Ravel openly conceded the impact Gershwin had had upon him when he wrote a "blues" sonata for violin and piano and injected jazz in his last two piano concertos. Other composers were perhaps more hesitant in expressing their indebtedness, but consciously or unconsciously they were affected and given direction by Gershwin.

In America, Gershwin's impact was felt by a good many composers. Ferde Grofé (1892–   ), who had orchestrated *Rhapsody in Blue* for the Paul Whiteman Orchestra followed Gershwin's lead by writing *Broadway at Night,* his first symphonic composition in a jazz style, late in 1924. In 1925 he wrote the *Mississippi Suite,* his first successful work in this new vein, and in 1931, he completed his greatest work, *Grand Canyon Suite.* Aaron Copland produced his two major jazz works (his *Piano Concerto* and *Music for the Theater*) immediately after the success of the *Rhapsody in Blue* and the Gershwin *Piano Concerto.* Among other American composers to enter the symphonic-jazz world were the following: John Alden Carpenter (1876–1951) with *Krazy Kat* and a remarkable jazz ballet, *Skyscrapers;* Robert Russell Bennett (1894–) with the *Charleston Rhapsody* and the *Concerto Grosso* for jazz band and orchestra; Louis Gruenberg (1884–1964) with *Daniel Jazz* and the *Jazz Suite* for orchestra; Edward Burlingame Hill (1872–1960) with the *Jazz Studies.*

Many European composers besides Ravel found jazz a rewarding medium for serious creations: Georges Auric (1899–) in a fox trot for piano, *Adieu New York;* Alexander Tansman (1897–) in his *Triptych;* Ernst Křenek (1900–), Hindemith and Kurt Weill in their operas, *Jonny spielt auf!, Neues vom Tage,* and *The Rise and Fall of the City Mahagonny;* Constant Lambert (1905–1951) in *Rio Grande;* William Walton in *Façade.*

Perhaps the most significant and the most successful American popularist besides Gershwin is Morton Gould. He was born in New York City on December 10, 1913, and received his musical training at the Institute of Musical Art, New York University, and privately with Abby Whiteside. He made several successful appearances on the concert stage as a prodigy pianist. After his studies were completed, he earned his livelihood playing the piano in motion-picture theaters and on the vaudeville circuit. In his eighteenth year he found a job as staff pianist at the Radio City Music Hall. Three years later he received his first important radio assignment to conduct an orchestra. Meanwhile he had begun to tap the resources of jazz for serious compositions by producing the *Chorale and Fugue in Jazz* (introduced in 1931 by the Philadelphia Orchestra under Stokowski), the *Boogie-Woogie Etude* for piano (extensively performed by José Iturbi at his recitals), and a *Swing Sinfonietta*.

Gould acquired national fame as a conductor of radio orchestras for many important programs. His fresh and invigorating arrangements of popular classics, in which new instrumental effects were continually exploited, made him a successful radio feature for many years, as well as a highly successful recording artist. But his greatest significance in American music came from his abundant compositions for the concert stage, in many of which he made astute and artistically rewarding use of either American folk or American popular styles. The blues can be found in his *Third Symphony* and in *Interplay*. The latter is a composition for piano and orchestra first entitled *American Concertette,* and later used by Jerome Robbins as background music for an original modern ballet. The old-fashioned and sentimental waltzes reverberate in the *Philharmonic Waltzes* for symphony orchestra. There are times when Gould manages to combine the old classical forms with popular modern American styles with unique effect as in *Interplay,* whose second movement is a gavotte; or as in *American Symphonette No. 2,* one of whose movements is a pavane. There are other times when he gives a scintillating modern orchestral dress to our popular songs, as was the case with *Foster Gallery* (based on several beloved melodies of Stephen Foster), *Yankee Doodle Went to Town* ("Yankee Doodle" in modern symphonic dress) and in his symphonic adaptations of "When Johnny Comes Marching Home" and Gershwin's song, "I Got Rhythm."

An altogether new direction in symphonic jazz was taken by a young American composer, Gunther Schuller, born in New York in 1925. Schuller is the creator of a new style which he has identified as the "third stream of music." It is not jazz, nor classical music, but a combination of jazz and serial music. This new kind of symphonic jazz is found in works like the *Variations on a Theme of Thelonius Monk*, *Abstraction No. 1*, and *Concertino for Jazz Quartet and Orchestra*. When an entire program of Schuller's music was given in New York on May 16, 1960, John S. Wilson reported in *The New York Times:* "Mr. Schuller's compositions reveal a highly provocative mind at work, for he composes not only with a sense of adventure but also with an extremely sensitive feeling for proportion and balance. At this stage in the use of techniques from both jazz and classical music, both of these qualities are all important."

Schuller's most important composition in the "third stream" technique is his opera *The Visitation,* which created a sensation when it was given its world premiere by the Hamburg Opera in Germany on October 12, 1966. This is an opera based on Franz Kafka's *The Trial,* but with an American setting, and its theme the racial problem in the South.

222

CHAPTER 12

The Proletariat

AFTER the Revolution in Russia on November 6, 1917, musical nationalism in that country was directed into an altogether new channel. Music now became an instrument of government propaganda. It had to promote the ideals of the state and glorify the achievements and the heroes of the Revolution. It had to pay tribute to the common man. It had to speak out loud and clear for the economic and social reforms of the new regime. It had to seek out the grandeur of labor, the factory, the collectivist farm, the five-year plan. Most important of all, perhaps, it had to be addressed to the masses and, by the same token, had to be simple, tuneful, rooted in Russian folk and military music.

In 1924, the Association for Proletarian Musicians was formed to "cross the t's and dot the i's" of what constituted good music in the proletarian sense. One of their manifestoes read: "In their creative work, composers, members of the Association of Proletarian Musicians, strive above all to reflect the rich, full-blooded psychology of the proletariat, as historically the most advanced, and dialectically the most sensitive and understood class. . . . New musical forms are created and will be created by the proletariat. Proletarian music must 'penetrate into the innermost masses of workmen and peasants, unite the thought and the will of these masses and raise them'

223

for further struggle and construction, organizing their class consciousness in the direction of the ultimate victory of the proletariat as builder of Communist society."

And so, Soviet composers trimmed their sails to the prevailing winds. They wrote work after work in praise of Lenin, Stalin, and other revolutionary leaders. They wrote ballets and operas about the ideals and problems of the working class. They paid tribute to each and every important economic or social policy promulgated by the government. Sometimes a composer might feel the impulse to wander off in his own direction, driven by the urgency to express himself rather than his government. But he would soon be steered by government order or threats of reprisal to the proper course. The changing political currents might carry the Soviet composer now in one direction, now in another, but always he steered his course by the Northern star of government edicts.

II

Dimitri Shostakovich was a child of the Revolution. He grew up to become its foremost musical voice. Born in Leningrad on September 25, 1906, he was only eleven when the Revolution erupted. The new regime and the young musician, consequently, went through their growing pains together. As a child, Shostakovich proved his exceptional musical gifts by continually associating images with musical sounds; by being perpetually at the piano; and by trying to compose music before he could even read or write. He wrote his first large work very early in his boyhood, while he was attending the Glasser Music School; it was a *Theme and Variations,* for piano. After the Revolution, he became a student at the Leningrad Conservatory, where his phenomenal musical ability was remarked and frequently commented upon by his teachers Nikolaev and Maximilian Steinberg. During his initial year at the Conservatory he completed a remarkable set of eight piano preludes; he also saw his first publication, *Three Fantastic Dances,* for the piano. Alexander Glazunov, director of the Conservatory, compared him to Mozart. A fellow pupil, Simon Barere—later world-famous as a piano virtuoso—referred to him at the time as "a musician who deeply feels and understands his art. Shostakovich's compositions . . . are fine examples of serious musical thought."

Upon being graduated from the Conservatory in 1925, Shostakovich completed his *First Symphony.* It was introduced in Leningrad on May 12, 1926, after which it was heard in Moscow, in Berlin under Bruno Walter's direction, and in the United States conducted by Leopold Stokowski. A work of extraordinary vitality and exuberance filled with the most exciting musical ideas and constructed with a master's hand, this symphony helped make Shostakovich world-famous by the time he passed his twenty-second birthday. And it lifted him to the top rank of Soviet composers.

There was nothing in this symphony to suggest proletarian music. Here Shostakovich had no political or social program to propound, no dogma to promote, no dictated formula to follow. He merely had to give voice to his inmost emotional urges and express them with honesty and conviction. For this reason, this work, written when the composer was only nineteen, is still one of his best, and the one that is most popular today.

But it was not long before Shostakovich made the transition to proletarian music. During 1926 he wrote nothing, while evaluating himself and his mission as a Soviet musician. When, in 1927, he returned to his work,

225

it was with a new purpose and direction. "I cannot conceive," he now said, "of my future creative program outside of our socialist enterprise, and the aim which I assign to my work is that of helping every way to enlighten our remarkable country." He also said: "There can be no music without an ideology. . . . Lenin himself said that 'music is a means of unifying broad masses of people'. . . . Even the symphonic form . . . can be said to have a bearing on politics. . . . Good music . . . is no longer an end in itself but a vital weapon in the struggle."

And so he completed the *Second Symphony* to commemorate the tenth anniversary of the October Revolution; and the *Third Symphony*, honoring May Day, which concluded with a choral movement. He wrote an opera, *The Nose*, satirizing government officialdom, his first work to be subjected to severe criticism by the authorities who regarded his tentative experiments with atonal devices as "bourgeois decadence." He wrote three ballets with strongly political overtones. The first, *The Age of Gold*, mocked capitalism, Fascism and "bourgeois psychology." (Still popular from this score are the "Polka" and "Russian Dance." The first satirized the Geneva Peace Conference.) His second ballet, *The Bolt*, tried to expose the pettiness of bourgeois living. In the third, *The Limpid Stream*, he treated the subject of collective farming frivolously. He also produced a good deal of background music for Soviet plays and motion pictures.

The two symphonies were complete failures. The ballets were moderately successful. But in all instances Shostakovich proved himself a composer with an engaging bent for lyricism and dynamic rhythmic forces;

226

a composer with a remarkable flair for wit, burlesque, and satire.

The first time Shostakovich's position in Soviet music and culture was severely threatened was in 1936. Two years before this, his opera, *Lady Macbeth of Mzensk*, had been introduced in Leningrad to tremendous public and critical acclaim; during the next two years it was performed throughout the length and breadth of the Soviet Union. It was also given in Cleveland and New York in 1935. Then, without much warning, the government bludgeon descended on the opera and its composer. Suddenly *Pravda* described *Lady Macbeth* as "pandemonium, instead of music," as "crude, primitive, vulgar." *Pravda* concluded: "The composer apparently does not set himself the task of listening to the desires and expectations of the Soviet public. He scrambles sounds to make them interesting to formalist-aesthetes, who have lost all good taste." Apparently this brisk rap on Shostakovich's knuckles had come not only because some Soviet officials regarded several scenes in the opera as pornographic, but also because they felt that by employing modern techniques and styles Shostakovich was losing contact with the Soviet masses. A similar point of view was expressed about *The Limpid Stream*. "The composer," said *Pravda* editorially, "apparently has only contempt for our national songs."

For over a year Shostakovich was more or less *persona non grata* in Soviet musical circles. If the critics mentioned him at all it was only to denounce him; leading Soviet musicians avoided him socially; performances of his compositions were reduced to a trickle. It seemed that to all intents and purposes he was "through." But then, as several times later, Shostakovich proved his remarkable resiliency and bounced back into government and public favor. The première of his *Fifth Symphony* on November 21, 1937—given during the celebration of the twentieth anniversary of the Soviet Republic —was a triumph. One of the leading Soviet critics spoke of it as a "work of great depth, with emotional wealth and content," and considered it "of great importance as a milestone in the composer's development." The work is, indeed, an unqualified masterwork, with a breadth of structure, a maturity of expression, and a dramatic sweep and surge previously not often encountered in Shostakovich.

After that, by rapid degrees, Shostakovich not only returned to his former high position in Soviet music but even mounted a few notches higher: He became a national hero. In 1940 he received the Stalin Prize for the *Piano Quintet*. Soon after that, the Soviet Union was invaded by the Nazis during World War II. He completed a new monumental symphony (his seventh), entitled "Leningrad," and dedicated "to our struggle against Fascism, to our future victory, to my native city Leningrad." The symphony was first heard with the war in the Soviet Union at its height; the performance took place in Kuibyshev, the temporary capital set up by the government on the Volga when Moscow seemed in danger of falling. The highest officials of the army and government joined the leading representatives of foreign military and diplomatic corps to attend the première, which excited unprecedented enthusiasm. It brought Shostakovich the Stalin Prize for the second time. After that, his *Seventh Symphony* traveled around the free world, a vibrant testament of the times, a dramatic expression of the will to victory. In 1942 virtually every

228

important American orchestra played it; as *Life* wryly remarked it almost became treasonable not to be enthusiastic about it. Stirring in its martial moods, and ending with a mighty paean to victory, this is music that does not achieve effect either through subtlety or understatement. It wears its heart on its sleeve. As a result, the symphony remained popular only so long as the war fever infected the world. Since the war's end, it has been rarely given.

In a totalitarian state a hero one day can become the goat the next. This is what happened once again to Shostakovich after the war. His *Ninth Symphony*, in 1945, was found to contain "ideological weakness," to be a distorted reflection of the life in and ideals of the Soviet Union. This indictment was just a straw in the wind. When the wind came, it turned out to be a typhoon.

On February 10, 1948, the Central Committee of the Communist Party announced a new policy for music. No one can say for certain why this policy was suddenly invoked. The general opinion is that when Stalin attended the première of a new Soviet opera (Muradeli's *Great Friendship*), he expressed his dislike of composers who go to such great lengths to be noisy, modernistic, complicated. This was enough to set off a wave reaction which affected Soviet music for many years. A new set of standards was established for Soviet musicians. All avant-garde music was to be avoided and a studied attempt was to be made to write music easily comprehended by the masses. The ideal toward which Soviet composers were now to reach was a melodious music, simple in structure, straightforward in appeal and grounded in the country's folk songs and dances. "Decadent formalism," "bourgeois decadence," "cerebral-ism" were some of the official words and phrases used to describe "modern music"—a music which "negated the basic principles of classical music" and preached a "sermon for atonality, dissonance, and disharmony."

This blanket indictment covered virtually every major Soviet composer, Shostakovich included. Forthwith, each composer made a public demonstration of beating his breast in repentance, of confessing the error of his artistic ways, of promising to make amends. Here is what Shostakovich said in an opportunistic effort to rehabilitate his sadly shaken position and prestige:

"As we look back on the road traversed by our art, it becomes quite clear to us that every time the Party corrects errors of a creative artist and points out the deviation in his work, or else severely condemns a certain tendency in Soviet art, it invariably brings beneficial results for Soviet art and for individual artists. . . . I now can clearly see that I overestimated the thoroughness of my artistic reconstruction; certain negative characteristics peculiar to my musical thought prevented me from making the turn that seemed to be indicated in a number of my works of recent years. I again deviated in the direction of formalism, and began to speak a language incomprehensible to the people. Now, when the Party and our entire nation, speaking through the Resolution of the Central Committee . . . condemn this tendency in my music, I know that the Party is right. . . . The absence in my works of the interpretation of folk art, that great spirit by which our people lives, has been with utmost clarity and definiteness pointed out by the Central Committee. . . . On the basis of the principles clearly given in the Resolution . . . I shall try again and again to create symphonic works close to the spirit of the people from the standpoint of ideological subject matter, musical language, and form."

Hewing closer to the official line forcefully set down by the Central Committee, Shostakovich proceeded to create works with one eye on his political bosses, and the other on the public. His *Tenth Symphony,* an oratorio glorifying Stalin's reforestation plan ("Song of the Forest"), incidental music for a movie (*Fall of Berlin*) and sundry other functional pieces, helped to restore him to the good graces of the Soviet authorities. In 1949 he was selected as one of seven to represent the Soviet Union at the Cultural and Scientific Conference for World Peace in New York. This was his first visit to the United States. In 1950 he was once again the recipient of the Stalin Prize and in 1956 he was also awarded the Order of Lenin.

When the dictum of the Central Committee against "decadent formalism" was officially revoked after Stalin's death, Shostakovich profited from this laissez-faire policy. He revised his opera *Lady Macbeth of Mzensk,* renamed it *Katherina Ismailova,* and saw it become successful both on the stage and the screen. He kept producing major orchestral and chamber-music works progressive in style and thinking. On his sixtieth birthday he became the first musician to receive the highest honor the Soviet Union could bestow, the title of Hero of Socialist Labor.

III

Long before Prokofiev returned to his native land for good following his self-imposed exile, he had produced important proletarian music: the ballet, *The Age of*

231

Steel, completed in 1925, introduced by the Diaghilev Ballet in Paris on June 8, 1927. Its scenario was a glorification of the growth of industrialization in the Soviet Union. The music was strident with factory noises, and the rhythms of machines and engines in motion were so realistically produced by musical instruments that one unidentified critic described the score as "an apotheosis of machinery."

When Prokofiev had once again become a Soviet citizen in 1933, he identified himself completely and unequivocally with the goals of Soviet music. Much of what he produced was functional, but even in this area he was able to complete several works of lasting value. The background music to two Soviet motion pictures (*Lieutenant Kije* and *Alexander Nevsky*) were adapted by the composer into a pair of his most famous symphonic works.

Lieutenant Kije was a satire on Czarist stupidity. Kije is a mythical character who comes into existence when the Czar misreads a military report. The Czar's aides, unable to tell him he has erred, are compelled to invent Kije and from time to time to fabricate for him all sorts of heroic exploits. But when the Czar insists that the Lieutenant be brought to him, the aides are forced to create the fiction that the Lieutenant died a hero's death in battle. This merry satire gave the composer ample opportunity to release his remarkable gifts at irony and grotesquerie. A fanfare of cornets, a roll of the drums, and a mocking tune for fifes caricatures our hero. A mock sentimental tune tells us about his love affair, and a section full of pseudo pomp and ceremony describes his marriage. After that the music depicts no less vividly and amusingly the Lieutenant regaling himself in a tavern

232

and after that his death in battle. The score ends with trumpet tones evaporating in air, even as did the life of the mythical Kije.

Alexander Nevsky was of more serious intent and of far greater sobriety. Directed by Sergei Eisenstein and Vasilev, the motion picture told of the defense of Novgorod in 1242 under the leadership of Prince Nevsky against the invading Knights of the Teutonic Order. Prokofiev shaped his motion-picture score into a stirring choral cantata made up of seven tonal pictures beginning with a bleak description of desolate Russia in the grips of invasion. A chorus then lifts a song of praise to the hero Nevsky. We then catch a glimpse of the Teutonic knights masquerading as religious crusaders. The Russian people are urged to rise as one against the enemy. Now is depicted a realistic picture of a savage battle on the frozen waters of Lake Chud, after which a young girl voices grief for the dead in a poignant lament. The cantata ends with a mighty hymn of triumph, by chorus and orchestra, to celebrate Nevsky's victory and hail his arrival into the city of Pskov.

A composition intended for school children has also become one of Prokofiev's most popular works for orchestra: the fairy tale, *Peter and the Wolf,* for narrator and orchestra. It was meant to teach children the instruments of the orchestra, and was first given at a children's concert in Moscow in 1936. The story tells about Peter, a boy who defies the warning of his grandfather, and goes out into the meadow. There he comes face to face with a wolf, who has just frightened the life out of a cat, bird, and duck. But Peter is not afraid. He captures the wolf, ties him up with a stout rope, and proudly leads him off to the zoo.

Each character in this tale is represented by a different musical instrument: the bird by a flute; the duck by an oboe; the grandfather by a bassoon; the wolf by French horns; Peter by the string quartet. Each character is also represented by his own *Leitmotiv*. Thus with an equal measure of wit and technical skill Prokofiev weaves the different melodies for the various instruments—continually varying them to meet the demands of his story—into an integrated work combining the spoken word with musical sound.

The grim events of World War II greatly changed the quality and texture of Prokofiev's music. This was no time for comedy; the satire, grotesquerie, and whimsy had to be curbed. Music now had to be either an instrument for war propaganda or a mirror reflecting the epic struggle. Prokofiev produced a goodly amount of military marches and anti-fascist songs. He also completed several works of major dimension. In 1942 he wrote a monumental piano sonata, his seventh, now known as the "Stalingrad" because its stirring and strong-fibered music spoke of the heroism of the Red Army at that beleaguered city. For this sonata, Prokofiev received the Stalin Prize. Equally significant artistically, and equally effective in echoing the overtones of those turbulent years, was the *Fifth Symphony,* perhaps the greatest of the seven works by the composer within the symphonic frame. Here we get first a picture of the tragedy and destruction of war, and after that we hear the proud affirmation of faith and hope. Throughout the symphony we hear a tremendous sweep of melody, an intensity of expression, and an overpowering strength of rhythm which places this symphony with the greatest of the twentieth century. In and out of the Soviet Union the

Fifth Symphony has enjoyed successes of formidable dimensions.

Perhaps the most significant of all of Prokofiev's war compositions was an epical opera that took him over a decade to write. It was based on Tolstoy's epic, *War and Peace*. Napoleon's invasion of Russia was used by Myra Mendelssohn (Prokofiev's librettist and wife) as a historic counterpart to the Nazi invasion of the Soviet Union. Thus, while the opera was set in the past, the theme and message were vibrantly immediate. In a vast work of five acts, which required two evenings for full performance (and called for sixty characters), the composer tried to depict, as he once explained "the Russian people's struggle, their sufferings, wrath, courage, and victory over the invaders. In this part, the people themselves constitute the hero of the opera in the person of the peasants, of the popular militia, the regular Russian army, the Cossacks and guerillas." Big choral episodes are combined with descriptive orchestral tone poems to depict a mighty drama of war and its havoc. *War and Peace* was first heard in Leningrad in 1946. But after that, Prokofiev kept on revising the opera, virtually up to the time of his death; the last and definitive version was introduced in Leningrad in 1955.

Not even a giant creative figure like Prokofiev was able to escape censure when the Central Committee decided in 1948 to frown upon all forms of modernism in music. All of Prokofiev's major works had used the fullest resources of dissonances and modern techniques. "Prokofiev's creative style"—this was the way the official indictment read—"was formed to a considerable extent during his years in the West, where the external novelty of his manner pleased the narrow, bourgeois circle of aesthetes, for whom he wrote his music. . . . For that reason, Prokofiev was unable to reflect the greatness of our people. The unfeeling essence of his music is alien to our reality."

Prokofiev might grumble to his fellow musicians at a Moscow meeting that *"they* should stick to politics and leave music to musicians." But, like Shostakovich, he had no intention of defying the all-powerful State. He forthwith despatched a humble apology to the head of the General Assembly of Soviet composers. "Elements of formalism were peculiar to my music as long as fifteen or twenty years ago," he confessed, repeating almost by rote what was expected of him. "Apparently the infection was caught from contact with Western ideas." Then he swore to make amends. "Lucid melody, and as far as possible a simple harmonic language, are elements which I intend to use."

And so, as atonement for his past sins, Prokofiev wrote *Winter-Bonfire,* a vocal symphonic suite which was in a pleasing lyric style but completely unoriginal and without a suggestion of vitality; he also wrote an oratorio, *On Guard for Peace,* one of the few of his works to suggest a hack, contrived for the purpose of condemning "Western warmongers" and at the same time of singing the praises of the "Soviet international peace movement." These two works did the trick. In 1951 they received the Stalin Prize, and restored him to his exalted station in Soviet music. In that same year his sixtieth birthday was celebrated throughout the Soviet Union, highlighted by a concert of his works broadcast throughout the country. And when Prokofiev died of a cerebral hemorrhage in Moscow on March 5, 1953, his passing occasioned nationwide mourning.

IV

Shostakovich and Prokofiev are the leaders of Soviet proletarian music. But this movement had followers as well as leaders. These other composers were of lesser stature, perhaps, but nevertheless achieved widespread recognition in and out of the Soviet Union.

Aram Khatchaturian, born in Tiflis, Armenia on June 6, 1903, combined his Soviet proletarian tendencies with Armenian folk songs and dances. Until his twentieth year, the folk songs of Armenia were the only kind of music he knew. Then, at twenty, he started music study for the first time, at the Gniesen School of Music in Moscow; after that he attended the Moscow Conservatory. His success came between 1935 and 1937 with two significant works: his *First Symphony,* and a piano concerto, the latter a rousing *tour de force* that became a favorite with many piano virtuosos. In 1939, Khatchaturian received the Order of Lenin for his contributions in developing Armenian music. After that he won the Stalin Prize three times: for his *Violin Concerto* in 1941; the ballet, *Gayane,* in 1942; and his *Second Symphony* in 1946.

Into his music, Khatchaturian carried the intonations, Oriental mannerisms, rhythmic peculiarities, striking contrasts of mood and tempo, and the improvisational character of melody which abound in Armenian folk music. Khatchaturian can be effective both in his lyricism and in his dramatic moods; his music, falling easily on ear and heart, has an immediate impact.

Gayane, in 1942, was one of his most characteristic scores. It was introduced in Molotov, the Soviet Union, in 1942. Described as a "patriotic folk ballet," *Gayane* carries us into a collective farm where Giko, a traitor

237

to his country, joins up with a group of smugglers, sets fire to his farm, and tries to murder his wife, Gayane, and their daughter. The farm, Gayane, and her daughter are all saved by the hero, Kazakov. After Giko has been brought to trial and sentenced to death, Gayane and Kazakov, who are very much in love, are married.

The score—from which come two delightful and frequently played orchestral suites—is rich with songs and dances of an unmistakable Armenian character. One of the most poignant in its lyricism is the "Lullaby," a good example of the composer's pronounced gift at producing a soaring melody. A dramatic and exciting page, irresistible in its rhythmic force, is the "Saber Dance." This has been heard so often in this country that there is perhaps no single piece of Soviet music better known to the average concertgoer. It has been repeatedly played at concerts (both in its original orchestral version and in a dynamic transcription for piano), has been heard over radio and records, has even been adapted for a jazz ensemble, and was featured in the motion picture, *One, Two, Three.*

Another extraordinarily successful Soviet ballet came from the pen of Reinhold Glière (1875–1956): *The Red Poppy* written in 1927. As a matter of fact, this was the first important Soviet ballet to use a revolutionary theme as text. The setting is a Chinese port where the arrival of a Soviet ship has a far-reaching influence on the lives of the exploited coolies. Beautiful Tai-Hao falls in love with the Soviet captain, and is inspired by him to fight for the freedom of the Chinese masses. When she meets death at the hands of the port commander, she hands over to some Chinese children a red poppy, symbol of liberty. With her dying breath she exhorts them to die for their freedom. The first act rises to a climax with a series of dances for sailors of various nationalities. Here we find the thrice-familiar orchestral excerpt, "Russian Sailors Dance" which has found a secure place in the orchestral repertory.

In 1911 Glière wrote a remarkable programmatic symphony—*Ilia Mourmetz*. Here the protagonist is an ancient Russian hero of the twelfth century who achieved fabulous exploits in war and peace. The principal melodic theme in this symphony is a chorale subject in free meter with which the work opens and which recurs throughout the work with variations; at the conclusion of the symphony this subject is built with overwhelming effect. Two other basic melodies describe two different facets of Ilia's personality: One is heard in strings and bassoons in the low register and has a moody character; the other, more virile, is sounded by the trombones.

Dmitri Kabalevsky, born in St. Petersburg on December 30, 1904, has paid tribute to the political and social ideologies as well as to the historic and cultural past of the Russian people in several symphonies, concertos, and chamber-music works. His *Second Symphony* has enjoyed particular success. Introduced in 1934, it tells of man's salvation through the building of a new society. The symphony was followed by several equally impressive compositions: the *Second Piano Concerto,* in 1935, one of the composer's most frequently played works; the opera *Colas Breugnon,* in 1938, whose sprightly overture is a perennial favorite in our concert halls; and the *Violin Concerto,* in 1948, dedicated to the "Soviet youth," for which the composer received the Stalin Prize.

Nikolai Miaskovsky (1881–1950) was one of the most prolific symphonists in twentieth-century music. He wrote twenty-seven works in that form, many stimulated by the accomplishments of the Soviet regime. His *Sixth Symphony* was inspired by French revolutionary songs; his twelfth, by a collective farm. His greatest symphony is the twenty-first in F-sharp minor, written in 1940. More abstract than most of Miaskovsky's other symphonies, it is a short single-movement composition that opens in a contemplative vein but soon rises to great emotional peaks before reverting to the introspective character of the first measures. This symphony earned the Stalin Prize for its composer, an award he received several times later: for his *Ninth String Quartet;* his *Cello Concerto;* his *Twenty-Seventh Symphony;* and his *Thirteenth String Quartet.*

CHAPTER 13

The Traditionalists

O<small>N</small> and off through the preceding pages we have talked a good deal about composers who have broken with the past to create new sounds, new systems, new techniques. But not all modern music is "modern." Much of it is traditional. A good many composers still prefer to use the established forms, and to follow accepted procedures. Their aim, like that of composers before them, is to create beauty and to express emotion.

"Music, I have always felt, should be the expression of a composer's complex personality; it should not be arrived at cerebrally, tailor-made to fit certain specifications. A composer's music should express the country of his birth, his love affairs, his religion, the books that have influenced him, the pictures he loves. It should be the product of the sum total of a composer's experience. . . . I try to make my music speak simply and directly that which is in my heart at the time I am composing. If there is love there, or bitterness, or sadness, or religion, these moods become a part of my music and it becomes either beautiful or sad or religious. For composing music is as much a part of my living as breathing and eating. I compose music because I must give utterance to my feelings, just as I talk because I must give utterance to my thoughts."

Words such as these might have been the credo of a nineteenth-century Romanticist. Actually they were spoken by a twentieth-century composer, perhaps the most significant of the traditionalists: Serge Rachmaninoff. Rachmaninoff wrote symphonies, concertos and many shorter pieces for the piano. He evolved no new forms; he did not experiment with new chords, scales, intervals, or tonal combinations. He respected innovation in others, but as far as he himself was concerned he would have none of it. Instead, he leaned heavily upon Tchaikovsky, whom he admired extremely. He followed Tchaikovsky's lead in creating a lyricism that was filled with sentiment and at times melancholy, and that was Russian in personality. Tchaikovsky discovered no new worlds of sound, and neither did Rachmaninoff after him. But both opened new vistas of beauty for the musical art.

Rachmaninoff was born in Onega, in the district of Novgorod, Russia, on April 1, 1873. The Rachmaninoffs were prosperous landowners, until their estates went into bankruptcy in 1882. At that time, the family moved to St. Petersburg. There Serge entered the Conservatory. But he was indolent, indifferent to classwork, lackadaisical about doing his lessons, often playing truant. In spite of all this, he still managed to reveal a brilliant musical intelligence. His grandmother wisely decided that a change of scene might be beneficial. She brought him to Moscow and placed him under the strict musical tutelage of Nikolai Zverev, who prepared the boy for the Moscow Conservatory. The young Rachmaninoff still continued more or less on his shiftless and irresponsible ways, which, fortunately for him, were partially negated by his natural gifts. In spite of himself, he outstripped his friends in class and became the recipient of honors. At one ex-

242

amination, playing one of his own piano pieces for a jury that included Tchaikovsky, that master gave him the highest possible rating. Soon afterward, in 1892, Rachmaninoff received the gold medal for piano playing, and his name was inscribed on the school's Honor Roll.

While still at the Conservatory as a student of composition, Rachmaninoff completed a piano piece that carried his name throughout the civilized world: The *Prelude in C-sharp minor*, one of a set of five piano works published in 1892. Siloti performed it in London and set into motion a wave of popularity that gave more performances to the piece, and a greater sheet-music sale, than any single twentieth-century composition. Rachmaninoff, however, never profited from this success, since he had failed to copyright the *Prelude*.

Compositions in more ambitious forms and with greater scope included *Aleko*, a one-act opera performed at the Bolshoi Theater in 1893, and his *First Symphony*, introduced in St. Petersburg in 1897. The opera was a success; the symphony, a disastrous failure. Always hypersensitive, extremely delicate in nervous makeup, Rachmaninoff broke under the impact of the hammer blows leveled on him by the critics. He suffered a nervous breakdown which left him permanently scarred. From this time on he was a composer who continually questioned his own ability, and a man who was perpetually overwhelmed by melancholia.

It was some time before he found the courage to continue composing. In this he was helped by Dr. Dahl, a Moscow physician and a pioneer in the use of autosuggestion. Dr. Dahl subjected Rachmaninoff to psychotherapeutic treatment. Each day, for three months, he kept repeating to his patient: "You will compose again. You will write your concerto. You will work with great facility. The concerto will be of excellent quality." The treatment seemed to fill Rachmaninoff with the necessary courage to return to work. He completed a new piano concerto, his second. When he himself introduced it with the Moscow Philharmonic in 1901, it was a triumph. As it turned out, this is Rachmaninoff's most celebrated composition; possibly it is the best loved concerto written in the twentieth century. Dramatic in its force, passionate in its speech, and highly emotional, this lyrical music never fails to affect audiences favorably. (One of its most beautiful melodies was made into the American popular song, "Full Moon and Empty Arms.")

After the success of the *Second Piano Concerto*, Rachmaninoff followed three careers in music. He became one of the world's foremost piano virtuosos—in some respects second to none—and in this capacity he toured the world many times. From 1904 to 1906 he was the principal conductor of the Bolshoi Theater in Moscow; after that he made many guest appearances with major orchestras in and out of Russia in performances of his symphonic works. And, of course, he kept on producing major works. Two major works for orchestra came in 1907: the *Second Symphony*, the most famous of Rachmaninoff's three works in that form; and a sensitive and at times Impressionist tone poem, *The Isle of the Dead*, inspired by a painting by Arnold Böcklin.

The first of his many tours of the United States took place in 1909—10. On this occasion he gave the world première of the *Third Piano Concerto* which he had written expressly for this American visit.

Completely unsympathetic to the "anarchistic upheaval" in his country, and revolted by the death and destruction he saw everywhere in Russia, Rachmaninoff decided in 1917 to leave the land of his birth forever.

For a year he lived in Scandinavia, and in 1918 he established his permanent winter home in the United States. Summers were spent in a villa near Paris, and after 1932, in a beautiful home on the edge of Lake Lucerne in Switzerland. He continued to tour as concert pianist, and he never stopped making music. Among the works he now completed were his *Third Symphony,* his *Fourth Piano Concerto,* and a large work for piano and orchestra, *Rhapsody on a Theme of Paganini.*

But his heart was heavy. He missed Russia. Honored though he was everywhere, he felt he was a stranger without roots. He also knew he would not live to see Russia again.

Toward the end of his life, Rachmaninoff made his home in Beverly Hills, California. "This," he said when he entered his new abode, "is my last home on earth. Here I will die." He was embarking on a new extended tour of the United States when he collapsed in New Orleans. Brought back to California, he died there on March 28, 1943.

II

There is a good deal of Brahms' respect for Classical form combined with strong Romantic tendencies in the music of Sir Edward Elgar. He is often described as England's greatest composer since the seventeenth-century composer Henry Purcell. Elgar lived to see three decades of the twentieth century, but musically speaking he never left the nineteenth century. We hear in his music the echoes of Brahms, Delibes, and Wagner. He was the musical spokesman of the Edwardian era. He wrote with an excess of emotion that sometimes touched the sentimental, and with a passion and ardor we associate with the last century. But Elgar's music also

245

had dignity, a nobility of style, an elevation of thought, and an infectious charm. For these reasons his greatest compositions enjoy high rank even though they may seem to lack a strong personal identity.

He was born in the town of Broadheath, near Worcester, England, on June 2, 1857. He was the son of an excellent musician. Father Elgar played the organ in the Worcester Cathedral; was a violinist in a local orchestra; and was the proprietor of the town music shop. Inevitably, the boy Elgar became music-conscious early in life. He learned to love the organ works of Bach while sitting at his father's feet in the Cathedral organ loft. He became acquainted with symphonies and operas by reading the scores in his father's shop; he learned musical theory by memorizing textbooks.

His father wanted him to be a lawyer, and with this aim in view he was sent to London. But his passion for music soon made him abandon law and return home. There he was indefatigable making music: playing the violin in an orchestra; becoming a member of a wind quintet; giving violin recitals in small auditoriums; sometimes even playing the organ for Cathedral services. For a brief period he returned to London to study the violin with Adolf Pollitzer.

He was without direction or purpose in his music until 1889 when he married Caroline Alice Roberts. His wife convinced him not to scatter his energies so recklessly and to concentrate his enormous drive and industry on composition. Elgar and his wife left Worcester and for a time lived in London. After that they settled in Malvern, where Elgar completed several choral works that were performed at English festivals.

Two major works written between 1899 and 1900 made him famous. One was the *Variations on an Original*

Theme for orchestra, better known as the *Enigma Variations*. It was introduced in London under Hans Richter's direction, on June 19, 1899. Elgar later revised this composition extensively and directed the new version at the Worcester Festival. From the beginning, the *Enigma Variations* was popular with audiences; it was, in fact, the first symphonic work by an Englishman to acquire permanency in the symphonic repertory. Elgar intended it as a tonal portrait of fourteen friends and relatives, each variation a character sketch to which he appended either initials or nicknames for identification. The identity of each of these personalities is one of the reasons why Elgar referred to this work as an "enigma." Another, often cited in program notes, is that Elgar used a "hidden theme," never actually played, but frequently suggested; it serves as a "silent accompaniment" to each variation. (Some suggest that this silent theme is "Auld Lang Syne," others that it is a motif from Wagner's *Parsifal*.) Whatever the enigma, the work as a whole is stately music in which a highly expressive melody (presented by the strings in the opening measures) undergoes fourteen variations. The work rises to a peak of eloquence in Elgar's portraits of his wife and his friend August Jaeger, and in the self-portrait with which the work concludes.

Successful though the composition was from its inception, it was eventually outdistanced in public esteem by *The Dream of Gerontius,* an oratorio based on the poem by Cardinal Newman. The work was first given at the Birmingham Festival on October 3, 1900. English audiences had been partial to oratorios since the time of Handel, and they embraced *The Dream of Gerontius* with the ardor they had previously reserved only for Handel's *Messiah* and Mendelssohn's *Elijah*. Almost

Wagnerian in idiom, *The Dream* is suffused with the poetic and touched with the mystic. Richard Strauss did not hesitate to proclaim it a "masterpiece" when he first heard it at the Lower Rhine Festival in 1901. Repeated hearings on the concert stage and in recordings have fully confirmed Strauss' lofty estimate.

In the *Enigma Variations* and *The Dream of Gerontius,* Elgar was the unashamed Romanticist, drawing his material from the depths of his heart. He remained the nineteenth-century Romanticist in subsequent works, of which the most significant are a violin concerto, two symphonies, a 'cello concerto, and several delightful shorter orchestral compositions including the *Cockaigne Overture, In the South,* and the *Introduction and Allegro* for string quartet and orchestra.

But Elgar was an Englishman as well as a Romantic. As Basil Maine, the biographer of Elgar, has written: "In a broad sense, the *First Symphony* can be regarded as a salute to national heritage and attainment, the *Second Symphony* as a last exulting in the glories of an epoch which has already closed, and the *Violoncello Concerto* as a lament for the irrevocable years. They are respectively a paean, an epic, and an elegy."

But his national pride is felt even more strongly in many of the functional pieces he created for State occasions; and it is felt most strongly of all in his set of five marches, *Pomp and Circumstance,* written between 1901 and 1930 to prove that march music could be written with the most serious artistic intent. The second of these marches, in A minor, is the most famous. Its majestic main melody for strings—later used as music for Laurence Houseman's patriotic poem, *Land of Hope and Glory*—is almost as celebrated an English patriotic hymn as "God Save the King."

248

As England's foremost twentieth-century composer, a distinction disputed by few, Elgar was the recipient of many high honors. He was knighted in 1904, was made Master of the King's Music in 1924, and in 1931 became a baronet. He died in Worcester, England, on February 23, 1934.

III

Among the American composers preferring to travel a traditional route is Howard Hanson. Probably nobody has done more through the years to promote every facet of modern musical expression, or to encourage the avant-garde tendencies of the younger men, than Hanson as conductor and the director of the Eastman School. Yet in the privacy of his own study, while setting down on paper his own musical thoughts, he has been faithful to Romantic language within a Classical structure. Thus, one of his most popular works is his *Second Symphony,* the "Romantic," written in 1930 on a commission from the Boston Symphony to help celebrate its fiftieth anniversary. This is music of a highly emotional character, its emphasis placed on pleasant sounding melodies and harmonies. But Hanson's pronounced Romanticism is also combined with a strong Nordic strain which makes its presence felt in exotic melodies of modal character and the subdued colorations of some of his harmonic writing. Thus, too, another of his symphonies—his first, completed in Rome in 1923—is subtitled "Nordic." Similarly Nordic in color and style are some of his early tone poems (including *North and West*) and choral music (such as *Hymn for Pioneers*), all of which earned for their composer the sobriquet, "the American Sibelius." Yet whether he is Romantic or Nordic, or both, his works are unmistakably American. It is music, as Hanson himself once said, "of the plains rather than of the city" reflecting "something of the broad prairies of my native Nebraska."

He was born in Wahoo on October 28, 1896, and received his early academic and musical education at the Luther School of Music in Wahoo, and Wahoo High School. Later he studied at the Institute of Musical Art in New York and at Northwestern University. When he was twenty he was appointed professor of theory and composition at the College of the Pacific in San José, California; from 1918 to 1920 he was Dean of its Conservatory of Fine Arts. In 1920, Hanson was the first American to get a fellowship in the then recently instituted American Academy of Rome. He spent three years in Italy—years of study and creation. During this period he completed a tone poem *Lux Aeterna* and his *First Symphony,* both introduced in Rome.

When he returned to the United States in 1924, he conducted the American première of his *First Symphony* in Rochester, N.Y. Soon after that he received an appointment as director of the Eastman School of Music which he has held with pre-eminent distinction. Since 1925, Hanson has also led an annual festival of American music in Rochester: It has been estimated that over a thousand works by more than seven-hundred and fifty composers were heard at these concerts.

Hanson's *Third Symphony,* completed between 1936 and 1937, pays tribute to the valiant pioneers who settled the first Swedish community on the Delaware in 1638. The *Fourth Symphony,* in 1944, earned for Hanson the Pulitzer Prize in music. This is a deeply emotional work with strong religious overtones inspired by the death of the composer's father. For its four movements the Latin titles of the Requiem Mass are utilized. The *Fifth*

250

Symphony, in 1954, is even more strongly religious both in subject and character. Entitled *Sinfonia sacra* it relates the story of the first Easter as described in The Gospel According to St. John. The composer's aim, in his own words, was "to invoke some of the atmosphere of tragedy and triumph, mysticism and affirmation of this story which is the essential symbol of the Christian faith."

Among Hanson's many other works is the American opera, *Merry Mount*, whose first stage performance was given by the Metropolitan Opera in New York on February 10, 1934. Based on a poem by Richard Stokes, which in turn derived its subject from Nathaniel Hawthorne's story *The Maypole of Merry Mount*, *Merry Mount* was a highly melodic work with a strong bent for old-style lyricism, and with an occasional excursion into the kind of modal writing that prevailed in old American Puritan hymns.

IV

While Samuel Barber has never disdained to use modern harmonies, rhythms and other advanced contemporary idioms, he may well be placed in the American traditionalist camp by virtue of his respect for Classical structure, his use of lyricism, and his strong Romantic bent. The nephew of Louise Homer, the celebrated contralto of the Metropolitan Opera during its "golden age," Barber was born in West Chester, Pennsylvania, on March 9, 1910. Precocious in music, he began composition when he was seven; at twelve he played the organ at church services. In 1924 he entered the then recently founded Curtis Institute of Music in Philadelphia where he studied composition with Rosario Scalero and piano with Isabella Vengerova. Winning the Bearns Award for a violin sonata in 1928 provided some testimony to his

251

creative talent. Even stronger evidence came from two excellent orchestral works: the *Overture to the School for Scandal,* introduced in Philadelphia in 1933, and *Music for a Scene from Shelley,* first heard at a concert of the New York Philharmonic Orchestra in 1935. Between 1935 and 1937, Barber traveled in Europe by virtue of two Pulitzer Traveling Scholarships and the American Prix de Rome. While in Italy he completed his *First Symphony,* introduced in Rome under Molinari's direction in 1936. This one-movement work became the first composition by an American composer given at the world-famous Salzburg Festival, a performance that took place in the summer of 1937, Artur Rodzinski conducting. Barber's reputation achieved an even more solid foundation when, in 1938, Toscanini introduced two of his orchestral pieces with the NBC Symphony. One was the beautiful *Adagio for Strings,* transcribed by the composer for string orchestra from one of the movements of an early string quartet. Here a serene melody, sounded by the first violins, and commented upon by the other strings, is treated canonically, and then built up to a powerful climax. The other work was the *Essay No. 1.* This work was an attempt by the composer to carry over into music the literary form of the essay by enlarging upon some reflective subjects in an improvisational manner. The *Adagio* and this first *Essay* are still Barber's most frequently played compositions.

Between 1939 and 1942, Barber was a faculty member of the Curtis Institute in the department of orchestration. He left Curtis to join the Army Air Force. While serving in the Air Force he wrote a most unusual work, the *Second Symphony,* in which sights and sounds familiar to air pilots are reproduced. In the second movement Barber recreated the staccato sounds of a radio

252

beam on a special electronic instrument. In the third movement, a rapid figure for strings depicts a plane descending to the ground. The style of this symphony is discordant and rhythmic, in sharp contrast to Barber's earlier lyrical and Romantic compositions. In 1947 Barber revised this symphony to eliminate some of the more realistic passages.

After leaving the Air Force, Barber settled in Mt. Kisco, New York, in a house which he shared with the opera composer, Gian Carlo Menotti. Honor after honor helped to confirm his significance in American music: the Guggenheim Fellowship in 1947; the New York Music Critics Award for his *'Cello Concerto*; most significantly, the Pulitzer Prize in music for his opera, *Vanessa*, libretto by Menotti.

The opera, Barber's first, was introduced by the Metropolitan Opera in New York on January 15, 1958. Later the same year, it was given at the Salzburg Festival— the first American opera to earn this distinction. The score combines Barber's well-known lyrical powers with dramatic strength and an uncanny gift for projecting mood and atmosphere. Here the Romanticist never sacrifices the traditional values of melody and harmony to attain his powerful theatrical effects. The setting is a Scandinavian city in 1905. In her baronial manor, the heroine, Vanessa, has been waiting twenty years for the return of her lover. But her lover is dead. His son, however, comes to visit Vanessa. Renouncing his own sweetheart, he substitutes for his father and runs off with Vanessa.

Among Barber's other works, mention should be made of the ballet *Cave of the Heart*, based on the legend of Medea and Jason. Introduced in 1946, it was extensively revised a year later. Other impressive achievements include a remarkable piano sonata in 1949 which the critic of the *New York Post* said "encompasses realism and fantasy, conflict and resolution, poetry and power"; the choral *Prayers for Kierkegaard;* and *Summer Music,* for wind quintet. He received the Pulitzer Prize a second time for his Piano Concerto, introduced in New York in 1962. When the Metropolitan Opera moved to its new auditorium at the Lincoln Center for the Performing Arts on September 16, 1966, its opening performance was Barber's opera *Antony and Cleopatra* which had been commissioned for this gala event.

CHAPTER 14

The Eclectics

THERE are many composers both in Europe and America whose style is a cloth of many colors and textures. Sometimes in different compositions, sometimes in the very same one, these composers travel with remarkable agility from one pole of expression to its very opposite: from the very old to the very new; from Romanticism to Neo-Classicism; from Impressionism to Expressionism; from austere Classicism to jazz. These composers like to take from each style that which best serves their artistic purpose at the moment. The composer's personality becomes the catalytic agent to combine these varied, often opposing, elements into a single compound.

Leonard Bernstein—whose *First Symphony,* "Jeremiah," has already been commented upon—is such an eclectic. Before he wrote "Jeremiah," he had produced a clarinet sonata in the Neo-Classical idiom of Hindemith. "Jeremiah," which followed, represented for Bernstein a completely different world. So did the music that succeeded "Jeremiah": the ballet, *Fancy Free,* with its jazz melodies, its bouncy rhythms, its jazz colors. Bernstein's *Second Symphony,* "The Age of Anxiety," fuses some of the elements found in his earlier works (Neo-Classicism, Romanticism, jazz) with polytonality, unresolved dissonances, and even the twelve-tone row. Yet so superb a technician is Bernstein, and so articulate is he in everything he is trying to say, that every style he undertakes becomes completely convincing.

II

Two of the most successful and significant opera composers to appear on the musical scene since the end of World War II are eclectics: Benjamin Britten in England, and Gian Carlo Menotti in the United States. Each is extremely sensitive to the demands of the stage and to the most exacting requirements of their text. Each composer never hesitates to use any musical equivalent to reflect every change of emotion, every nuance, every dramatic episode in their plays. Thus often within one and the same opera, Britten and Menotti continually change styles and techniques to invoke realism, mysticism, broad comedy, poetic moods, and grim and searing drama.

On several occasions, in preceding chapters, we had opportunities to remark some of the trends in opera since Wagner: notably, the Impressionism of Debussy's *Pelleas and Melisande,* the Expressionism of Alban Berg's *Wozzeck,* the Realism of Richard Strauss' *Salome,* the Primitivism of Carl Orff's *Trionfi,* the American folklorism of Gershwin's *Porgy and Bess,* and so on. But there were several other tendencies deserving mention. In Italy, at the close of the nineteenth century, opera was caught up in a movement known as Verismo. In Verismo, opera librettos departed from the costume plays or historical themes so greatly favored by earlier opera composers to relate everyday problems in familiar settings. Verismo became popular in 1890 with *Cavalleria Rusticana* by Pietro Mascagni (1863–1945); the movement gained further stimulus in 1892 from Ruggiero Leoncavallo (1858–1919), composer of *Pagliacci;* and it reached its zenith with Giacomo Puccini (1858–1919), whose *La Bohème* in 1896, *Tosca* in 1900, and *Madama Butterfly* in 1904 are the most important, and the most successful Italian operas since Verdi. Puccini's canvas may have been a limited one. He himself once said that "the only music I can make is of small things." But though he worked with miniatures, his creations are integrated masterworks—unforgettable for their sweet and personal lyricism; for their gentle and tender moods; for their subtlety of harmonic and orchestral writing; for their elegance of style and wonderful sense of the theater; and for their remarkable capacity to project three-dimensional female characters.

In France, a counterpart to Verismo could be found in 1900, in *Louise,* a naturalistic opera by Gustave Charpentier (1860–1956). With Montmartre in Paris as the setting (toward the close of the nineteenth century), and with its main characters drawn from seamstresses, other plebeians and Bohemian artists, *Louise* was filled with realistic touches of all kinds and socialist viewpoints. The central story concerns the love affair of Julien, a painter, and Louise, a seamstress. The idea the play tries to bring into the operatic theater for the first time is the right of a woman to live her own life without interference from parents or society.

III

The *Verismoists* and the naturalists produced a handful of genuine operatic masterworks in the twentieth century. The eclectics, of whom Britten is undoubtedly the most gifted and celebrated, made no less a contribution.

Born in Lowestoft, Suffolk, England, on November 22, 1913, Britten revealed such a remarkable childhood gift for music that comparison between his musical exploits and those of Mozart was inevitable. Britten was hardly more than two when he first became conscious that music could come from a piano. At seven he could read the scores of symphonies and operas as if they were fairy tales. He was only nine when he finally embarked upon composition with an adult seriousness of purpose, producing a string quartet and an oratorio. Nothing seemed capable of stemming the tide of his production. By the time he was sixteen he had written six quartets, ten piano sonatas, a symphony, and many shorter instrumental and vocal works. He used some of the thematic material from this *juvenilia* in 1934 for one of his earliest mature creations, *Simple Symphony*.

All this composing was done while he was deep in the study of all phases of his beloved art. While attending the Gresham School, in Holt, Norfolk, he studied composition with Frank Bridge; from 1930 to 1933 he attended the Royal College of Music, where his teachers included John Ireland and Arthur Benjamin.

As an avowed pacifist, Britten left Europe just before the outbreak of World War II and spent several years in the United States. Here he completed his first opera, *Paul Bunyan*, not a particularly impressive achievement; also an orchestral work that *was* impressive, the *Sinfonia da Requiem*, inspired by the death of his father. It was introduced by the New York Philharmonic under John Barbirolli in 1941.

By 1942, England was suffering devastation from the blitz attacks of the Nazis. Though still convinced of the futility of war—and still refusing to admit any validity for mass murder—Britten now felt impelled to go home and see what he could do to help his stricken countrymen in areas outside the battle front. He became an indefatigable morale force by giving concerts in hospitals, bomb-proof shelters, and villages ravaged by air attack. Despite the exacting demands made by these duties upon his time and energies—and despite the absence of serenity in time of war—Britten nevertheless managed to work upon a new opera commissioned by the Koussevitzky Foundation in the United States. He worked upon his opera through the war years, completing it several months before V-E day. It was this opera, *Peter Grimes,* that first made him a world figure in music.

Its world première at Sadler's Wells Theater in London on June 7, 1945 was a red-letter day in more ways than one. It marked the first reopening of a theater that had been bombed out of existence by the Nazis five years earlier. It was the first major artistic event in London since the end of the European phase of the conflict. It was the first important new opera by an Englishman since 1939. Long before the première, tickets for all scheduled performances were sold out; for the première itself, queues encircled the theater for cheap seats and standing room hours before curtain time. This event excited so much curiosity and interest that most of the world's leading newspapers had correspondents on hand to send in a report.

Perhaps anything less than a masterwork would have been anti-climactic. Fortunately, *Peter Grimes* was a masterwork whose dramatic thrust had a sledgehammer force. Between each act, flowers were showered upon the stage. After the final curtain the approval of the audience was a five-minute thunder. The curtain calls for the composer seemed endless. And the critics were as excited as the audience. Ernest Newman described the opera as "a work of great originality"; a correspondent for *The New York Times* called it "a milestone in the history of British music."

Peter Grimes soon traveled through most of the civilized world. In less than a year it had been given over a hundred performances in eight foreign translations, in Sweden, Denmark, Italy, Switzerland, Holland, Hungary, and Germany. Its American première took place at Tanglewood, in Lenox, Massachusetts, on August 6, 1946, Leonard Bernstein conducting. It was first performed at the Metropolitan Opera on February 12, 1948.

Based on a poem by George Crabbe, "The Borough" (adapted for the operatic stage by Montague Slater), *Peter Grimes* strongly reflects Britten's own pronounced social consciousness. The play pointed up the struggle of reason against hate and bigotry; the conflict of the individual against hostile masses. Peter Grimes, an English fisherman, is unjustly accused of having killed his apprentice. Though found innocent in the courts of law, Grimes is never completely cleared in the minds of his fellow villagers, who henceforth regard him with suspicion and malice. When Peter hires a new hand, his neighbors become convinced that in time this apprentice will also be murdered by his employer. To save the life of the boy, they descend in a mass upon Peter Grimes in his lonely hut. Seeing the mob approaching, Peter and his apprentice flee, and while running the apprentice stumbles, falls and meets a fatal injury. The mob, now convinced that Peter Grimes is a murderer, is determined to take justice in its own hands. Fear and anger unbalance Peter's mind to the point where he seeks escape from his neighbors in death. He goes out to sea to sink in his boat.

The elements in Britten's immensely effective score are many and varied. Dissonance and polytonality heighten the tensions and underscore the climactic scenes;

choral numbers in the style of sea chanteys provide the proper atmospheric background for a play about the sea and fishermen; orchestral tone painting is vivid in its realism in setting forth a program; beautiful arias accentuate emotion on the one hand while, on the other, stark lyricism almost simulates speech for the sake of dramatic effect; the most complicated harmonic and contrapuntal schemes alternate with many light moments. But here, as later, Britten proves himself to be a master craftsman who can fuse diverse material in a drama of inescapable power, yet for all that, a drama that also has compassion and tenderness.

Britten's eclecticism was proved not only by the varied means he employed in this opera, but also in the variety of subject, style and treatment of his later works for the stage. Where *Peter Grimes* was a work of Wagnerian dimensions, *The Rape of Lucretia* (Britten's next opera in 1946), was an economical work of chamber-music dimensions. The cast had only six principals; each of the two so-called "choruses" consists merely of a single person, one male, and one female, to interpret the action of the play. The harmonic and contrapuntal writing are reduced to essentials; scoring and the emotional pitch are subdued; the style is primarily lyrical. Then came *Albert Herring* in 1947 with still another approach, still another style. *Albert Herring* is witty to the point of burlesque; in format it is reminiscent of opera buffa, partial to formal arias, duets and ensemble numbers. *Albert Herring* was also of smaller size and scope as to cast, orchestra, and scenic requirements.

In his next important opera Britten returned to a large canvas. *Billy Budd*, in 1951, like *Peter Grimes*, was a story of the sea, and a bitter commentary on injustice and of man's capacity for cruelty. The story came

261

from Herman Melville's novel, adapted by E. M. Forster and Eric Crozier. The action takes place aboard an eighteenth-century British vessel. Billy Budd, a happy-go-lucky, lovable sailor, is hated by John Claggert, master-of-arms, to the point where the latter invents false charges of treason against his enemy. Aroused to blind and uncontrolled fury by this unjust charge, Billy attacks and kills Claggert. For this he is court-martialed and sentenced to hang. Only one officer, Captain Vere, is sympathetic, understanding full well the provocation that had led Billy to commit murder.

Billy Budd is an opera of the most ambitious structural dimensions, one enlisting extensive musical and stage forces. In this, as well as in its overall thesis of man's inhumanity to man, it bears a close kinship with *Peter Grimes*. But there are several technical details that set *Billy Budd* apart from the earlier opera. The melodic line is made up almost entirely of recitatives, song being virtually eliminated except for a few minor sections. The chorus is exclusively male. And the musical interest is subsidiary to the dramatic. Britten utilizes every resource at his command to further the movement of the plot and to strengthen the delineation of character; he is much less concerned with the interest or appeal of musical sound as such.

This greater interest in dramatic values than in musical ones is characteristic of *The Turn of the Screw*, written in 1954. The libretto by Mufanwy Piper is based on an eerie ghost story by Henry James in which a theme close to Britten's heart—the struggle between good and evil, with evil triumphant—is personified in two children. They are haunted by the ghosts of two former servants, and are attended to by a neurotic governess. The little

262

girl becomes a victim of uncontrolled terror, while the boy goes to his death.

The style is intimate; the opera requires only six voices and a chamber orchestra of only fifteen players. Nevertheless the score is sufficiently elastic to range from Impressionism to Expressionism, from the poetic to the realistic. An unusual feature of this opera is the introduction of an orchestral prelude preceding each of the sixteen scenes to comment upon what is happening on the stage. All these preludes are based on a twelve-note theme built from fourths and thirds.

A somewhat more romantic and lyrical approach can be found in *A Midsummer Night's Dream* in 1960. This opera demonstrates a remarkable capacity on Britten's part to find the proper musical equivalent for three different groups of characters: the fairies, the mechanicals, and the lovers. He preserves, as Eric Walter White has noted, "their musical identity while subordinating their development to the plan of the opera as a musical whole."

Britten has also been an eclectic in his orchestral music. The early composition, *Variations on a Theme by Frank Bridge*, for example, ranges in feeling and emotion from a funeral march to a gay waltz, from burlesque and parody to the sentimental and the dramatic, from lyricism to strident dissonances. In a similarly wide arc of mood and technique is his delightful *First Piano Concerto*, which opens with a classical toccata but in a modern idiom, continuing with a waltz and an impromptu, and ending with a march. In the song cycle *Les Illuminations*, for high voice and string orchestra, Britten adapts his style flexibly to meet the requirements of ten decadent poems by the French Symbolist, Rimbaud, with their delicate imagery and sensitive suggestions. In *A Ceremony of Carols,* for treble voices and harp obbligato, Britten tries to recreate in modern terminology the style of the medieval plain chant. In *Spring Symphony,* a large work for chorus, soloists and orchestra, we get a setting of fourteen English poems of past and present about Spring. In *A War Requiem,* which achieved world renown, we have one of the most eloquent anti-war testaments in all music.

Britten's most popular orchestral work, *The Young Person's Guide to the Orchestra,* is consistently tuneful. This composition describes the instruments of the orchestra, and for this purpose Britten uses a theme by Henry Purcell and subjects it to thirteen variations. In each of the variations, a different instrument, or group of instruments, is featured prominently. In the concluding fugue, these instruments reappear in the order in which they had first made their entry in the variations.

IV

Gian Carlo Menotti's eclecticism carries him from a Puccini-like lyricism to the most advanced avant-garde idioms. He can be romantic or mystic, esoteric or popular, lyrical or dissonant, impressionist or broadly satirical. Yet he never seems to sacrifice unity of concept, or coherence of dramatic or musical viewpoint. With his wonderful feeling for effective theater he always seems to find the *mot juste* for every stage requirement. His music in itself is rarely original, or for that matter consistently distinctive. But married to a play its emotional and dramatic force is irresistible. For Menotti above everything else is a man of the theater. He writes his own librettos, serves as his own stage and casting director, and is personally involved in every phase of the production. As a man of the theater he has made his operas not just a vehicle for musical invention, but a vibrant and pulsating stage experience. Perhaps for this reason he has commanded a larger and more varied audience than any other opera composer since 1900. This popularity is not confined to the opera house but extends to the Broadway theater, to television, to motion pictures, and recordings.

Menotti was born in Cadagliano, Italy, on July 7, 1911, to wealthy parents well able both by their financial and cultural backgrounds to nurse his immense musical precociousness. At four he started taking piano lessons; by the time he was six he was inventing his own melodies. When his mother presented him with a puppet theater on his ninth birthday he not only wrote his own plays for that little stage but also his own music. He also devised the sets and costumes, and contrived the stage effects. His first full-length opera for a more normal stage was written in 1922, when he was eleven.

His family moved to Milan where Gian Carlo pursued his academic education, and from 1923 to 1928 attended the conservatory. During this period he completed a second full-length opera besides making numerous appearances as pianist in the fashionable salons. In 1928 he came to the United States, enrolling in the Curtis Institute of Philadelphia as a pupil in composition of Rosario Scalero. He also had to learn a new language— English—and he did so by going to the movies four times a week.

His first mature opera was a one-act opera buffa, *Amelia Goes to the Ball*, produced in Philadelphia and New York by the forces of the Curtis Institute under Fritz Reiner in 1937. Menotti here wrote his libretto in Italian (subsequently translated into English by George

265

Mead); henceforth he would write his librettos in English. *Amelia* is a fluffy, witty diversion about a girl who is being delayed from going to a fashionable ball in Milan by a dispute between her husband and her lover. Upset by their refusal to come to terms, she throws a vase at her husband and calls to the police to arrest her lover. With the husband in hospital, and her lover in jail, Amelia can proceed to her ball—in the company of the police officer. The musical format is a traditional one with formal arias, romanzas, duets, trios, and recitatives; the style is consistently gay and tuneful, though at times piquantly spiced with the salt and pepper of discords and polytonality.

Menotti was visiting his native city in Italy during the summer of 1937 when the local postmistress came breathlessly to his door waving a telegram and yelling *"Il Metropolitano!"* She came bearing the news that the Metropolitan Opera had accepted *Amelia* for its 1937–8 season. Several years later, the Metropolitan commissioned Menotti to write a new opera; unfortunately, this opera, *The Island God,* produced on February 20, 1942, was a dismal failure.

Meanwhile, Menotti had written a second opera in the sprightly and light-hearted manner of *Amelia,* expressly for radio transmission. *The Old Maid and the Thief,* commissioned by the National Broadcasting Company, was a comic opera in a single act; it was first broadcast on April 22, 1939. A decade later it received in Philadelphia its first stage presentation. The subtitle gives a clue to the slight plot. It reads: "A virtuous woman makes a thief of an honest man." An old maid welcomes a tramp into her house as a permanent lodger, only to have him rob her of her most precious belongings and her attractive servant girl as well.

266

Thus far Menotti had proved that his gifts lay exclusively with comedy; his only tragic opera, *The Island God*, had been a stodgy and insufferably dull effort. With a new opera written on a commission from the Ditson Fund between 1945 and 1946, Menotti returned to a tragic libretto with a weighty and at times somber treatment—but this time with uncommon success. *The Medium*, first heard in New York on May 8, 1946, at Columbia University—later transferred to Broadway for an extended run in 1947—proved for the first time Menotti's far-reaching dramatic powers. The macabre play is built around a fake medium, Flora, who perpetrates her fraudulent seances with the assistance of a mute, Toby, and her daughter, Monica, with whom Toby is in love. During one of her sessions, Flora becomes panic-stricken when she feels a clammy hand gripping her throat; she shrieks out the confession that she is just a fake. Her terror leads her to excessive drinking. In one of her drunken stupors she suspects Toby of trying to do away with her, and kills him while he is hiding in a closet.

For such eerie, high-tensioned, and melodramatic proceedings, Menotti often had to alternate his Puccini-like lyricism with a severe kind of song-speech; his lighter moods had to make way for the harsh, strident sounds of dissonant chords and polytonal combinations.

When *The Medium* was transferred from Columbia University to Broadway, the audience response was initially negative despite the high opinion of the critics. Opera on Broadway had never done particularly well, and Broadway theatergoers avoided *The Medium*. But slowly, by word of mouth, the report began to spread that *The Medium* was superb theater and enthralling entertainment. Each time the producers announced a closing date, a sudden spurt at the box office impelled them to keep the opera running. At the end of that season it had had an impressive run and had made a sizable profit. Since then, *The Medium* has become one of the most frequently played American operas. It has been given over a thousand performances throughout the United States, semi-professional as well as professional. It has been seen in London, Paris, and Italy. It was also recorded in its entirety, and made into a stirring motion picture.

Perhaps as a temporary respite from the grimness of *The Medium,* Menotti briefly reverted to levity with *The Telephone* in 1946. This is a one-act trifle which the composer himself described most aptly as "a skit with music." Only two characters are involved: a young girl addicted to talking on the telephone, and her frantic lover who is trying to propose to her between telephone calls. He finally leaves her, rushes to the corner drug store, and proposes to her by phone. The whole thing is a tongue-in-the-cheek affair in which the sprightly descriptive music nimbly matches the wit and satire of the text.

Then, having caught his breath (so to speak), Menotti returned to tragedy with *The Consul,* an opera that brought him the Pulitzer Prize in music and the Drama Critics Circle Award for drama during its successful Broadway run beginning on March 15, 1950. *The Consul* is set in an unidentified European police state where a woman haunts the offices of the local consul trying to get a visa for a foreign free country so that she can join her husband. She never gets that visa, and ends up a suicide. The consul himself never appears as a character, but looms in the background as a foreboding *deus ex machina.* In most of the play, Menotti exploits to the full his leanings towards the macabre. Yet he fills both play

268

and music with a wonderful compassion which we do not encounter in *The Medium*. He writes with an overwhelming sense of pity for the inextricable forces that enmesh his principal characters and finally crush them. As Olin Downes wrote in his review in *The New York Times:* "He has produced an opera of eloquence, momentousness, and intensity of expression unequalled by any native composer . . . written from the heart, with a blazing sincerity and passion of human understanding."

While tragedy and the macabre continued to absorb Menotti's creative interest after *The Consul*, he has also tilled other fields with equal success. For television, Menotti completed in 1951 a radiant religious legend with music, *Amahl and the Night Visitors*, inspired by a Flemish painting by Hieronymus Bosch. Introduced over the NBC television network on Christmas Eve of 1951, *Amahl* has since become an annual Yuletide television feature. It tells in expressive recitatives, extended songs, and deeply affecting choral numbers, the story of a crippled boy at whose hovel arrive the Three Wise Men enroute to the Manger in Bethlehem. The crippled boy has only a single gift to bestow on the Holy Child— his crutches—and these he gives without hesitation. This generous gesture is rewarded when the child is cured miraculously. *Amahl* is the first opera written expressly for television, and the first opera commissioned by a commercial organization. Its first stage production took place at Indiana University on February 21, 1952, and it was successfully produced at the Florence May Music Festival in 1953.

In a similar category of fable and legend, lies *The Unicorn, The Gorgon and the Manticore* (1956). Here Menotti revived the age-old form of the madrigal se-

269

quence which often used to be staged in the seventeenth century. Menotti's "madrigal fable" consists of an introduction, six orchestral interludes, and twelve choral madrigals (some of them unaccompanied) in the style of Monteverdi, the seventeenth-century master. The required forces include ten dancers, nine instruments and a chorus. The "unicorn," the "gorgon," and the "manticore" are three animals—the pets of a lonely poet. When the poet takes now one, now the other, for a Sunday stroll, the women of the village are so stricken by envy that they demand from their husbands similar pets. At the poet's deathbed, he severely castigates his women neighbors for their petty envy and silly efforts to imitate him. The entire work is symbolic. The three animals represent the poet's youth, middle and old age; and his last address is intended to upbraid petty individuals for being the destroyers of a poet's dream.

In sharp contrast to *Amahl* and *The Unicorn, The Gorgon and the Manticore* are *The Saint of Bleecker Street* in 1954, and *Maria Golovin* in 1958. Both are compelling dramas on contemporary subjects with contemporary characters. *The Saint* takes place on Bleecker Street, in the Italian section of New York. Annina, a religious mystic, is a sickly girl who inspires the religious awe of her Catholic neighbors by receiving the stigmata on her palms. Michele, her brother, an agnostic, is singularly devoted to her. His sweetheart, Desideria, is aroused to such a pitch of jealousy over Michele's attachment to Annina, that she attacks him, and in the ensuing brawl is killed. Michele goes into hiding, but when Annina is accepted by the Church as the Bride, he emerges to witness the festive ceremony. Thus he is a spectator when Annina, in a frenzy of emotion and joy, falls dead.

Arias of both the florid and sentimental variety, religious chants, dramatic recitatives, dissonant harmonies and—as a welcome change of pace—humorous ditties and satirical songs are the varied means by which Menotti "dexterously underscores every word of dialogue and every instant of action," as Olin Downes wrote. One of the most powerful dramas of the theatrical season, *The Saint of Bleecker Street* received the Drama Critics Award as the season's best play together with the Pulitzer Prize in music.

The National Broadcasting Company commissioned *Maria Golovin* for the Brussels Exposition where it was introduced on August 20, 1958. The opera is set in a European frontier town, a few years after "the recent war." Maria's husband has been a prisoner of war for several years. While waiting for his release, she makes her home in a villa owned by Donato, a blind maker of bird cages. Their proximity to each other, combined with the emotional starvation each has suffered, draw Maria and Donato to each other. When Maria's husband is finally released from confinement, she comes to Donato to say good-bye. Donato, determined to have no other man possess Maria, shoots at her, but misses. Being blind, he is convinced he has killed her, and thus finds solace in the sad delusion that Maria and her husband can never again be reunited. Here, as in his earlier tragedies, the score continually underlines the emotional torment of the characters and enhances at every turn the dramatic conflicts of the play with realistic, programmatic, or lyrical writing.

Menotti's most important opera after *Maria Golovin* was *The Last Superman,* a satire on modern mores and customs, introduced in French in Paris on October 21, 1963, and in English at the Metropolitan Opera in New York on January 23, 1964. In 1958 he founded the "Festival of the Two Worlds" in Spoleto, Italy. As founder and president, he has been responsible for the presentation of several provocative contemporary operas.

V

In England, the mantle of Ralph Vaughan Williams fell on the shoulders of Sir William Walton. Walton is included among the eclectics, but not because he lacks a consistency of style in any single work. But, as Eric Blom once pointed out, each time Walton tackled a new composition "it turns out to be entirely different from the last."

Façade, the first work to bring Walton forcefully to the attention of the music world, indulges in burlesque, parody and satire, often in a jazz idiom. The orchestral overture, "Portsmouth Point," imitates the style of eighteenth-century English nautical songs. The cantata, *Belshazzar's Feast,* has the majesty of a Handel oratorio, but with modern overtones. The two symphonies, the *Violin Concerto,* the *Viola Concerto,* and the *Partita* for orchestra are essentially the work of a dedicated modernist. And in his opera, *Troilus and Cressida,* complex harmonic and rhythmic structures are supplemented by extended lyrical passages in which the composer permits his melodic line to soar.

Walton, a child of singing teachers, was born in Oldham, Lancashire, on March 29, 1902. Since his father was the choirmaster of the local church, the boy had an opportunity to sing in the choir. After attending the Choir School of Christ Church, he became the youngest student to receive his baccalaureate in music at Christ's Church, Oxford. At Oxford he was interested only in his classes in music, and completely indifferent to all other studies.

He was expelled before he could get his Bachelor of Arts degree.

Leaving Oxford, he came to London and for a while lived with the Sitwell family—its members (Edith, Osbert, and Sacheverell) were not only literary people of immense culture but also had formidable social station and wealth. Their guidance and encouragement led Walton to serious musical creation. In 1923, a string quartet was given at a modern-music festival in Salzburg; in 1924, a piano quartet was published with funds provided by the Carnegie Trust.

In both these chamber-music works Walton dabbled with experimental styles and techniques. Yet when he first became famous it was with a composition of far different character, one in which advanced writing made way for hilarity and mockery. This was *Façade*, a "melodrama" for reciting voice and seven instruments based on twenty-one abstractionist poems by Edith Sitwell written in 1922. Unusual and provocative as Walton's musical style was, the novelty of the composition was considerably enhanced by the way in which it was presented on June 12, 1923. Edith Sitwell recited her poems in sing-song fashion against an instrumental accompaniment. She was hidden from view (as were the instrumentalists), and her voice seemed to emerge from a huge megaphone-shaped mouth painted on the drawn curtain. The Sitwell poems were completely unintelligible, since they were concerned not with meaning but with rhythm and sound. Walton's music, on the other hand, was down to earth in its salty humor, in its jaunty tunes, sacrilegious parodies, calculated clichés. Rossini's *The Barber of Seville* and Mozart's *Don Giovanni* were gaily mocked through brief and hasty quotations; jazz was used to caricature the popular

273

song and the fox-trot; and the essential nature of such folk dances as the waltz, tarantella and polka were distorted in gay parodies. In 1923, this work aroused a good deal of comment and argument. But when it was revived about three years later with a revised and expanded score, it was nothing short of a triumph. The composer prepared two highly successful orchestral suites from this score for the concert stage, while the basic score was adapted in 1931 for a ballet, choreographed by Frederick Ashton.

After that Walton abandoned this note of levity for a style that was complex in texture and material. In this new style he assumed an imperial position in contemporary English music with the *Sinfonia concertante,* for orchestra with piano obbligato in 1927; the *Viola Concerto* in 1929; the monumental *Belshazzar's Feast* in 1931, probably the most successful choral work produced in England since Elgar's *The Dream of Gerontius;* the two symphonies; the *Violin* and *Cello Concertos;* the *A minor String Quartet;* the opera, *Troilus and Cressida;* the *Partita,* for orchestra.

Formal recognition of his formidable achievements came in 1951 when the government bestowed on him knighthood. When Vaughan Williams died in 1958, the opinion was universal that nobody deserved more than Walton to be now regarded as England's foremost living contemporary composer.

VI

In the United States, William Schuman and Walter Piston have been two composers with a pronounced individuality and a sufficiently varied style to warrant their inclusion among the eclectics.

For many years Schuman combined his activity as a composer with administrative duties as the President at the

274

Juilliard School of Music. In the future, creative work will be combined with his work at the Lincoln Center of Performing Arts, where he was appointed President in 1961. He was born in New York City, on August 4, 1910. After completing his academic education in the city public schools and Columbia University, he turned to intensive music study for the first time: privately with Max Persin and Charles Haubiel; then at the Mozarteum in Salzburg; finally with Roy Harris. Recognition first came to him with the *American Festival Overture* which Koussevitzky introduced in Boston in 1939, and with the *Third String Quartet* which received the Town Hall Composers Award. The *Third Symphony*, a work of compelling power and invention, advanced his reputation after the Boston Symphony under Koussevitzky had introduced it in 1941. A further giant stride in his career came two years later with the first Pulitzer Prize given in music, for the cantata *A Free Song*. After that came more symphonies and string quartets; the ballets *Undertow, Judith,* and *Night Journey;* a violin concerto; shorter works for orchestra; and a baseball opera, *Casey at the Bat.*

Most of Schuman's music is characterized by a motor energy combined with expressive counterpoint and lyricism. His eclecticism shows in the variety of his compositions. Some of his works are light and humorous or satirical: the *American Festival Overture, Newsreel, Circus Overture* and *Casey at the Bat.* Some have a pronounced dramatic or romantic bent: *Judith,* and the *Third* and *Sixth Symphonies.* Some draw their material from popular or folk sources: the *New England Triptych.* Some are filled with the most personal and original utterances: the *Violin Concerto.*

From 1926 to 1960 Walter Piston was professor of music at Harvard, from which he was graduated in 1924 *summa cum laude* in music. Born in Rockland, Maine, on January 20, 1894, Piston graduated from Normal Arts School. He studied music for a long time with private teachers. After World War I, and service in the Navy, he pursued music study more intensively at Harvard. Between 1924 and 1926 he was a pupil of Nadia Boulanger in Paris. Returning from Paris, he pursued the dual career of teacher and composer, the former at Harvard where he stayed thirty-five years. His debut as composer came with the *Symphonic Suite,* performed in 1928 by the Boston Symphony. After that he wrote a considerable amount of orchestral music which was performed by major orchestras, but most of all by the Boston Symphony. His *Second Symphony* received the New York Music Critics Circle Award in 1945; his *Third* and *Seventh Symphonies* earned the Pulitzer Prize in music in 1948 and 1961. In these and other compositions, Piston combines classical structures with Romantic viewpoints; but on more than one occasion he has wandered off into the world of dissonant harmonies and linear counterpoint. On the other hand a work like *The Incredible Flutist,* which originated as a ballet in 1938 but has become famous as a symphonic suite, is vividly programmatic, and generously spiced with the condiments of wit and burlesque. Eclecticism is particularly marked in a work like the *Concerto for Orchestra,* where the first and third movements are rooted in the eighteenth century both as to structure and style, while jazz makes a seemingly incongruous appearance in the middle movement.

CHAPTER 15

The Avant-Garde

MOST of the changes that took place in modern music discussed in the preceding chapters represent evolution. This remains true even of the twelve-tone technique which, after all, still owed a debt to the musical past by employing the chromatic scale, polyphonic processes (with particular emphasis on canonic writing) and often traditional structures.

But with the music of the avant-garde, which has so inundated the world of music, what we have is not evolution but revolution: a complete break with the past. Much more has been happening than just the invention of new techniques and idioms. What has been happening is that the whole concept of what the creative process, what the aim and direction of musical sound should be, has changed. A new notation has been devised consisting of lines, marks, curves, parabolas, so that many an avant-garde score looks like a design for a missile. A new vocabulary of musical terms has been created. Old structures, and old subservience to melody, harmony, counterpoint and rhythm, have been deserted for a completely free and fluid use of both *ordered* musical sound and—more revolutionary still—of sounds that are extra-musical, at times produced at random, at times produced electronically, and at all times comprising noise rather than ear-pleasing tones. Some avant-garde composers have come to regard the century-old way of presenting concerts as obsolete as the auditoriums in which

277

these concerts are being given—and have projected a completely new kind of performer-audience relationship in a new kind of hall where the music comes not from the stage exclusively, but from all sides and directions.

Before beginning a discussion of the avant-garde movement, one point should be made clear: Some of the most passionate proponents of our "new" music are extraordinary musicians, musicians with enviable backgrounds and scholarship, musicians of high ideals and purpose. These are not sensation or publicity seekers by any stretch of the imagination. They could, if they wished, write symphonies and concertos and operas in the traditional manner though in a twentieth-century language and could have undoubtedly produced important works. They refused to do this because they were driven by creative impulses far different from those experienced by their predecessors and their more traditional contemporaries. The well-schooled, immensely gifted composers of the avant-garde movement became adventurers in a new world out of artistic necessity.

Another point is perhaps worth making here and now, a point which, we hope, will be proved before this chapter is completed. Already we have evidence that some of the experiments of the avant-garde composers that at first had appeared so outlandish—so completely without rhyme or reason—have already proved their value both in the concert hall and in the opera house.

II

Many avant-garde composers have progressed through a single process of evolution. Once these composers had outgrown their apprenticeship they began by writing twelve-tone music. (A few outstanding avant-garde composers actually started from their beginnings to use this technique.) From twelve-tone music they proceeded to

278

serialism, from serialism to electronic music and aleatory (or "chance") music. Some went still one step further by entering the nonsense world of dadaism.

The most significant single tool of most avant-garde composers is serial music, or serialism. This is a method that has captured the imagination of composers the world over, and has already resulted in music of accepted significance. The concept of serialism sprang out of Anton von Webern's Symphony, Op. 21 (1928) which some musicologists consider as one of the most influential works of the twentieth century, and one of the major turning points in the entire history of music. Abstraction, objectivity, the absence of the human element, and brevity reach their ultimate destination in this Symphony—far beyond anything attempted by either Schoenberg or Alban Berg. In Webern's Symphony, melody and harmony are dispensed with. Isolated tones, without the slightest concern for sonority, become all important. Sometimes a theme is reduced to a single tone. What we have here is ideas reduced to fragments, ideas so pulverized that they have become atoms. Silences become as important as sound, the music being continually broken up by rests. The dynamics are reduced to the lowest possible level, so that the music is often spoken in a whisper. What we are left with are what René Leibowitz called "the bar bones. . . . A few notes seem scattered at random without any apparent reason."

Webern built his Symphony with the twelve-tone technique. But he went a step further. The twelve-tone technique governed pitch alone. By applying the twelve-tone technique to tone color as well as pitch, he added a new dimension. This gave rise to the possibility of using the discipline and restrictions of the twelve-tone technique not only to pitch and tone color but also to rhythm, dynamics, and timbre. Thus it was possible to establish a

279

series of twelve note values suggesting duration (eighth note, sixteenth note, quarter note, and so forth). A series of twelve dynamic markings and a series of twelve articulations could also be set forth (forte, crescendo, piano, diminuendo, staccato, spiccato, and so forth). Finally a series of tone colors could be concocted through the utilization of the sounds of twelve different instruments. Thus virtually total control dominates the creative process.

Serialism was developed almost simultaneously by two different composers on either side of the Atlantic. In the United States, Milton Babbitt (1916–   )—a member of the music faculty at Princeton—issued in 1946 the first published theoretical treatise on serialism, *The Function of Set Structure in the Twelve-Tone System*. He put theory into practice by writing *Three Compositions for Piano* (1947) and *Composition for Four Instruments* (1947)—the first pieces of music in America embodying a serial method. Almost at the same time, in France, Pierre Boulez (1925–   ) experimented with serialism, beginning with his *Second Piano Sonata* (1948). From that moment on, Boulez became such a confirmed serialist that he was led to say: "Since the discoveries of the Viennese school (he was referring specifically to Webern) all composition other than twelve-tones is useless." Boulez has since become one of France's most distinguished composers (as well as a world-famous conductor). One of his masterworks in the serial method is *Le Marteau sans maître* (*The Hammer Without a Master*), written in 1954. This is a nine-movement composition. Three of the movements are songs to texts by René Char. Six other movements are instrumental commentaries on the poems. "I have tried," Boulez said, "to find the deep roots of poetry in music, in the instrumental parts, even more than in the vocal sections." The nine movements are divided into three cycles of three movements each, one being sung, and two being instrumental. This composition also makes use of the "chance" method—but of this we shall have more to say later on.

Luigi Dallapiccola, who had been the first Italian composer to use the twelve-tone technique, passed on to serialism in 1950; one of his first distinguished works in this technique is the *Variations for Orchestra* (1954). Ernst Křenek, who evolved from jazz to romanticism to twelve-tone music, embraced serialism for the first time in *Sestina* (1957).

To mention all the composers who have become serialists—some of them adhering to this method with inflexible rigidity, while others used it with a certain amount of license—would almost be to list a "Who's Who" of avantgarde composers. These are a few significant representatives from Europe and the United States, some of them composers with established reputations, others come from the younger generation: Richard Rodney Bennett (1936–   ); Easley Blackwood (1933–   ); Karl-Birger Blomdahl (1916–1968); Alberto Ginastera (1916–   ); Hans Werner Henze (1926–   ); Luigi Nono (1924–   ); Goffredo Petrassi (1904–   ); the late Stravinsky; Gunther Schuller (1925–   ); Karlheinz Stockhausen (1928–   ), in his early compositions.

III

We had occasion to remark earlier in the book that a good many tendencies in modern music are the result of reaction to action. Serialism represents virtually total control. Many dedicated serialists, however, felt a compulsive need to go to an opposite extreme by going from total control to total freedom and license. This is the reason why so many serialists began writing aleatory music, or music of chance.

Actually, "chance" music had existed several centuries ago. In the seventeenth and early eighteenth centuries, composers such as Mozart and Beethoven used to delight their audiences by including on their concert programs extemporized music, made up at the spur of the moment. Famous virtuosos of those years used to improvise their own cadenzas to concertos by other composers; they, too, were indulging in "chance" music. Then, after Beethoven, extemporization and improvisation at public concerts went out of fashion. In the late nineteenth and early twentieth centuries, however, improvisation returned. Charles Ives, who had anticipated so many of the new methods of twentieth-century music, was one of the first serious composers introducing chance. As we have already noted in an earlier chapter, in one of his symphonic works he wrote the instruction that "from here on in the bassoon may play anything at all." Chance music was also resurrected by the great jazz men of New Orleans and Chicago where such masters as Joe "King" Oliver, Buddy Bolden, Bix Beiderbecke and Louis Armstrong would, in the midst of a performance, let loose their imagination and launch into solos that were thoroughly spontaneous, but based on some melodic or rhythmic detail in the composition they were performing.

Music of chance flourished with our present-day avant-garde composers. In Boulez' *Le Marteau sans maître* (which we already mentioned in connection with serialism) the performer must now follow the specific order of movements set down by the composer. The composer can, at will, use the instrumental commentary intended for one song for another song of his own choice. "The chronological order of composition," Boulez explained, "is not always the best way to hear a work. This way of working is fresher and more meaningful."

Boulez has made extensive use of chance methods. His *Third Piano Sonata* (1961) has five sections. The performer may omit any section he wishes, just as he may change the order of the sections. The *Improvisations on Mallarmé* (1958) is a work in strict serial technique with the addition of chance: At given points the singer is permitted to improvise.

Karlheinz Stockhausen, certainly one of the leading figures in the German avant-garde movement, has also made frequent use of chance. His *Klavierstuck XI* (1956) is made up of nineteen fragments which the performer can play in any order he wishes; even more, he can select any one of several designated tempi, dynamics, intensities and types of touch for each of the fragments. In Stockhausen's *Zeit-messe* (1956) the performer is allowed to change the tempo any way he desires besides being given the freedom of interpolating his own improvisations, but only with materials supplied by the composer. *Zyklus,* for percussion (1961), is a work for a single performer who goes from one percussion instrument to the next one until he has played every one called for in the score. The performer can begin on any page of the music he wishes. But he must run through the rest of the pages in the order set in the printed music and stop with the first stroke of the page with which he had begun.

John Cage, whose varied experiments and innovations have placed him in the vanguard of the American avant-garde movement, began using "chance" in a unique way. His method called for a pair of Chinese dice, and his process was entitled "I-Ching" (the Chinese Book of Changes). Under a prearranged system, Cage gets the pitch, note values, dynamics and instrumentation for a composition by throwing out the dice and employing those elements which the throw had indicated. Another method was one described in the Introduction of this book: Loose sheets of a manuscript are scattered on the floor, with the performer picking up one sheet at a time at random and playing it until all the sheets have been used. One of Cage's most complicated works in an aleatory style is the *Concert for Piano and Orchestra* (1958). In the published score he explained: "The *Concert for Piano and Orchestra* is without a master score, but each part is written in detail in a notation where space is relative to time determined by the performer and later altered by the conductor. Both specific directions and specific freedom are given to each player including the conductor. . . . The work can be performed in whole or part, any duration, any number of . . . performers, as a solo, chamber ensemble, symphony, concerto for piano and orchestra, aria, etc." The pianist need not play his instrument in the normal fashion, either. He can, at will, pluck the strings on the soundboard, or go under the piano and thump upon the wood. The *Concert* is made up of eighty-four different compositions, which the virtuoso can play in its complete version, or just in part, or in any sequence which interests him.

Another American composer, Lukas Foss (1922–   )— who first achieved recognition with works such as *The Prairie* (1943), in a highly neo-romantic style—has also been attracted to chance music in his later years. His most celebrated such work is the *Time Cycle* (1960)—four songs for soprano and orchestra. What is particularly unusual about this remarkable work is that it combines "composed" music with chance. The "composed" music is for the voice and orchestra. But between each song there is an instrumental interlude for piano, clarinet, cello and percussion—intended to comment upon the song just heard— whose music is created spontaneously during the performance. Thus every performance of *Time Cycle* is a different

284

one. The New York Music Critics Circle recognized the importance of this work by endowing it with its Award in 1961.

Three years before writing the *Time Cycle*, Foss founded an ensemble specializing in the presentation of "chance" music: Four members calling themselves "The Improvisation Chamber Ensemble." This ensemble makes up its music as it goes along during the concert proper, music which, in the composer's own description is "full of surprises for the listener and the performer as well. It is a music of which even the choices of pitch and duration are part of the act of performances." Foss wrote his *Concerto for Improvising Solo Instruments and Orchestra* (1960) for this group. This work suggests the broad outlines of the composer's intentions in a kind of chart through indications of germ motives, rhythmic patterns, the entrances and exits of the individual instruments, and other basic ideas. How this material is to be used is left to the discretion, and creative impulses, of the performing group.

IV

Directional music—or, as Karlheinz Stockhausen prefers to term it, "spatial dimension in music"—is an attempt to produce a stereophonic effect at public concerts. This is sometimes achieved by scattering parts of an orchestra or chorus in different sections of the auditorium; but the most significant use of directional music has come through electronic means, with loudspeakers placed in various points in a concert hall. In either instance, the aim is to have the musical sound converge on an audience from many different directions, rather than from a single place—the stage.

One of the earliest experiments in directional music came from an American, Henry Brant (1915–   ). In 1954 he wrote *December,* in which members of the orchestra and chorus were scattered all over Carnegie Hall. Trombones were placed in the second tier boxes; the tenor and soprano soloists, and some members of the chorus, sat on opposite sides in the dress circle. Some of the chorus and orchestra were found in the balcony. There was another chorus on the stage together with the brass instruments and a percussionist.

Stockhausen (who dreamed of the time when a concert hall would be spherical in design—the audience in dead center, with the music converging upon it from all directions through loudspeakers) experimented with directional music in *Gruppen* (1957). This is a composition for three orchestras, each with its own conductor, placed in three different parts of the auditorium, surrounding the audience, so to speak. Sometimes the three orchestras combined in a common tempo and rhythm, but just as often each of the orchestras went its own way where tempo and rhythm were concerned. Sometimes the music came from the left, sometimes from the right, sometimes from the front, sometimes from all three places.

Some of Stockhausen's later compositions, in which electronic devices are employed significantly, give prominence to directional music. In *Kontakte* (1960), for example, the sounds emerge from four loudspeakers coming from four different parts of the concert hall.

Remarkably effective use of directional music has been made in several avant-garde operas. In Alberto Ginastera's *Don Rodrigo* (1964), only six of the eighteen French horns found in the mammoth orchestra can be found in the pit; all the others are scattered over the balconies. In one part of the opera we find the hero searching for his beloved, who is fleeing in terror. A truly stunning stereophonic effect is realized when the twelve French horns pour down their sounds on the heads of the audience below. In

Gunther Schuller's opera, *The Visitation* (1966), directional music is also used with extraordinary dramatic impact: In the lynching scene the sounds come surging at the audience from all directions to create a shattering emotional impact.

V

In our Introduction (see page 5) we discussed Edgard Varèse's pioneer attempts to make artistic use of extra-musical sounds within serious compositions, that is, sounds from plain noisemakers of all sorts. We also talked about a similar attempt by George Antheil in the *Ballet mécanique* (see page 7). At that time—the 1920s, and with Varèse the early 1930s—such efforts inspired no end of ridicule and denunciations. During the end of Varèse's life, however (Varèse died in New York City on November 6, 1965), he was not only regarded by the avant-garde as occult and a prophet, but also was the recipient of numerous honors and awards from more conservative quarters. For by 1965, the use of disorganized, unordered sound had become one of the prime interests of the avant-garde movement.

In the early 1930s, Varèse had come to a standstill as a composer, since he had exhausted the possibilities of the materials for the making of non-musical sounds available to him. And so, creatively, he remained silent for almost two decades. Meanwhile, electronics had opened a new world of sound possibilities, far beyond the wildest dreams of men like Antheil and Varèse in the Twenties. With new resources now at hand, Varèse returned to composition by making extensive use of electronically produced sounds. He produced his first such work, *Deserts,* in 1957. Before he died he completed two more compositions enlisting the resources of electronics: the *Poème electronique* (projected through four hundred and twenty-five loudspeakers at the Brussels Exposition), and in 1960, *Nocturnal,* his last work.

It was perhaps inevitable for electronics, which has affected human life so profoundly in so many ways, to leave its influence upon musical creation. Since World War II an altogether new area has opened up with electronic music: music, or musical sounds, produced by electrophonic instruments through electromagnetic vibrations converted into sound waves by various electronic devices, or by means of a loudspeaker.

Experiments in this direction have been taking place since the turn of the present century. In 1906, a scientist, Cahill, devised the Telharmonium in which alternating current generators produced powerful tones. Later on, various instruments were devised, such as the Organova which transformed rays of light into sound waves.

What is perhaps the first significant achievement in electronic music came from Leon Theremin, a Russian scientist born in St. Petersburg in 1896. He was a student of both physics and music before becoming director of the Laboratory of Electrical Oscillations at the Physico-Technical Institute in Russia in 1919. It was there that a year later his first electronic instrument was produced. It was originally called "Aetherophone," since the sound was generated by the movement of the hands through ether (or "aether"); this instrument subsequently became famous as Thereminvox. In 1927, Theremin came to the United States where he obtained a patent for his ether instrument. On August 29, 1930, he gave a concert of electronic music through ten electronic instruments on the stage of Carnegie Hall. In 1932, he introduced in Carnegie Hall the first electronic orchestra (conducted by Albert Stoessel). The Thereminvox was also heard as a solo instrument with several major American orchestras. Joseph Schillinger wrote an *Airphonic Suite* for Thereminvox and orchestra which was introduced by the Cleveland Orchestra.

A significant technical advance over the Thereminvox was made in Paris by Maurice Martenot, conductor and professor at the École Normale de Musique. In 1928, he brought out the Ondes Musicales (now known as the Ondes Martenot) a radio-electric instrument which was equipped with a keyboard able to produce definite sounds in the tempered scale. He gave hundreds of concerts throughout Europe in collaboration with his sister. Many eminent French composers, including Milhaud and Honegger, have written compositions for this instrument; some of these works were given at the International Exhibition of Art and Technics in Paris in 1937, where the Ondes Martenot received the Grand Prix. Martenot was also the author of a textbook, *Méthode d'ondes musicales,* the first such instructional work on an electrophonic instrument.

VI

Since World War II, a new school of composers has sprung up whose art consists of drawing fantastic noises and sounds through electronic means. In Paris, on April 15, 1948, Pierre Schaeffer, an engineer for *Radiodiffusion française,* devised "concrete music." This consists of music produced from actual sounds recorded on tape, or distortions of those sounds. He recorded on tapes all kinds of street noises, radio commercials, conversations and other sounds. He then ran the tape backwards, sometimes increasing and sometimes decreasing the speed, and thus manufactured still other types of sound. These various sounds were combined into musical compositions. The first important composition using such a method was Pierre Schaeffer's *Symphonie pour un homme seul (Sym-*

phony for One Man Alone), a ten-movement composition in which sounds heard by a single man are reproduced on tape in rhythmic patterns.

It was "concrete music" that had brought Varèse back to creativity—he having come into contact with it during a visit to Paris. And it was "concrete music" that inspired Boulez and Stockhausen to use electronic sounds creatively. Boulez' first such composition was *Polyphonie X* (1951), which caused something of a sensation when it was heard for the first time—at the Donaueschingen Festival on October 6, 1951. Stockhausen's creative initiation into electronic music began with *Kontrapunt No. 1* (1953). In 1960 Stockhausen dramatized the conflict between electronic music and music produced by traditional instruments in a composition entitled *Contest Between Electronic Sound and Instruments.*

In his report from an international congress of experimental music in Venice, in 1961, Everett Helm provided a revealing description of the tonal art of "concrete music." He wrote: "Often the electronic music had certain resemblances to known sounds: whistles, the rushing of water, explosions, strong winds, or a dropped tray of china—even it must be added to Hollywood 'haunted house' music and dissonant chords played on an organ."

The capacity of electronically produced sounds to create unusual moods, extraordinary effects, and depths of emotion—in a way usual instruments are incapable of doing—has by now been proved. Already electronic sounds have become virtually an everyday tool for composers for motion pictures and television to create an eerie or fantastic atmosphere for mystery plays, or plays about schizophrenics, and so forth. Electronic sounds, for example, performed a major role in the background music for the motion picture *Freud,* in 1963—the electronic parts of an

290

otherwise regular musical score by another composer being the work of Henk Badings (1907–   ).

Already we have come to realize that electronic music can plunge to the profoundest depths of human emotion. A notable example is *Visage* (1961), by Luciano Berio (1923–   ). Only a single word is pronounced and repeated ("parole," Italian for "word"). Electronically reproduced and distorted—and supplemented by electronic sound backgrounds—this word is made to pass through a gamut of emotion without parallel in more formal music. As the composer explained: "The vocal events from inarticulated and articulated 'speech,' from laughter to crying and to singing, from patterns of inflections modeled upon specific languages to 'aphasia,' etc. are constantly related to electrically produced sounds." There are moments when the feeling reaches such an abyss of despair that it almost becomes intolerable to bear.

Unusual depths of emotion are achieved by Karlheinz Stockhausen by combining the soft, sweet, innocent voice of a boy soprano (produced naturally) with electronic sounds. He did this in the *Gesang der Junglinge,* or *Song of Youth* (1956), a setting of a text from the Book of Daniel. The poignancy of the boy's voice with the unorthodox timbres of electronic sounds produces an altogether unique quality, which becomes even more unusual and more effective when projected (as the score requires) stereophonically through a five-channel system.

The applicability of electronic music for a serious artistic endeavor was eloquently demonstrated by the opera *Aniara* by Karl-Birger Blomdahl (1916–1968). This is the first successful opera to use electronics; it has been produced successfully in numerous opera houses, has been recorded in its entirety, and was a feature at Expo 67 in Montreal in 1967. This is also the first successful opera about space travel. "Aniara" is a passenger space ship bound for Mars. It is thrown off course, is incapable of either reaching Mars or returning to earth. Thus it is doomed to follow an aimless course in space forever. Years of aimless space travel follow, the oppressiveness of space and time weighing down heavily on the passengers—strange voices emerging from outer space to contribute hypertension—until the passengers begin to lose mental balance. Curious sects, beliefs, religions spring up. In the end, the voice and spirit of a Blind Poetess is heard singing the praises of Death. Then the oscillating electronic sound depicts a scene of utter desolation such as no instruments could realize, as the curtain descends slowly. Blomdahl's music uses every means at his command: serial music, jazz, dance and church music. But the electronic element is the most significant of all in pointing up the tensions and anxieties of the passengers, to project an atmosphere of utter terror, to indicate the awesomeness of infinite space, to introduce the ghostly sounds of far-off voices in space. These electronic effects bring a new dimension to the opera, a totally new expressiveness. As the Boston critic, Harold Rogers, said: "Here is at least one instance when electronic music can be used to achieve dramatic effects not producible by the usual orchestral instruments."

Numerous operas after that have resorted to electronics for special effects. The list is now quite a formidable one. Of particular interest are Ginastera's *Don Rodrigo* (1964) and *Bomarzo* (1967) and Luigi Nono's *Intolleranza* (1960).

In concert music, too, electronics have proved their value and significance. If any evidence is necessary it was certainly provided by the fact that the Pulitzer Prize in music in 1967 and 1968 were both won by compositions with electronic sounds. In 1967, the prize went to Leon Kirchner (1919–   ) for his String Quartet No. 3, for four strings and electronic sounds. Here, as Peter G. Davis wrote in a review in *High Fidelity*, "the electronic element is used conservatively—discreet percussive accents and pitched 'woodwind' sounds mingle with the four strings, extending the textual range of the piece to almost orchestral proportions. At the end of the work's conclusion the two stage loudspeakers take over completely, wresting the thematic material from the human players and turning it into a breathtaking contrapuntal display that mere live performances could never hope to equal. Totally routed, the strings can only answer this outburst with a final pianissimo chord which sounds a knell of defeat."

In 1968, the Pulitzer Prize went to George Crumb (1933–   ) for *Echoes of Time and the River,* which had been commissioned by the University of Chicago. Here electronic devices assume even greater prominence than they do in Kirchner's quartet.

One of the by-products of the electronic age in music is the creation of music by means of computers. Where electronically made music produces new sounds by tape doctoring, computers are used to create the music itself by means of materials fed to it; this music is then performed on conventional instruments. The composer provides the computer with coded instructions about a variety of materials and styles which the computer selects and rejects. The computer produces compositions in the form of a code which is then deciphered into traditional notation. The first such successful attempt came in 1956 when Lejaren A. Hiller, Jr., and Leonard M. Isaacson fed various types of data on rhythm, melody, harmony, orchestration and style to a computer at the University of Illinois. The result was the *Iliac Suite,* for string quartet, which was then performed publicly.

One of the most significant creators today of music by

computer is Iannis Xenakis (1922–   ), who was born in Rumania of Greek parentage, and who makes his home in Paris. Xenakis is a trained mathematician and scientist as well as musician. He evolved a method all his own of feeding instructions to a computer known as IBM 7090 through which he has created numerous works that have received wide circulation, particularly in recordings. "Instead of thinking in terms of harmonies as musicians have for many years," explained Jan Maguire in the Paris *Herald Tribune,* in 1965, "Xenakis thinks in terms of sound entities, which possess the characteristics of pitch, intensity and duration as associated to each other by and within time. IBM 7090, whose routine schedule consists of planning movements for oil fleets, calculating the temperature of metal in furnaces and market research, is capable of ten decimal figures. It can accomplish 300,000 operations per second, or make 458,000 decisions per second. It is fed a 'program,' that is, a sheet of instructions codified in machine-language and registered on perforated cards. It will think, memorize and calculate anything. Xenakis writes programs for 7090 in his own personal philosophic parlance and asks it to give him back the laws of chance. He obtained figures to determine the length and sequence of sounds, their intensity and composition of the orchestra, as well as the moment of occurrence, pitch, speech, class of sound and instrument, and length and form of intensity. . . . If the listener makes the mistake of looking for form or structure as he has always known it in music, he finds himself quite at sea. The structure of this music is not by any means readily apparent. It requires either a profound knowledge of mathematical laws or a profoundly relaxed and detached attitude on the part of the listener." Xenakis has dubbed his works "stochastic music"—music based on the laws of probability. They in-

294

clude *Akrata,* for fifteen winds and vibraphone, which had been commissioned by the Koussevitzky Music Foundation; *Strategie,* for eighty instruments and two conductors; *Eonta,* described by one critic as "a violent stochastic combat between a piano and a sound-slab created by four trumpets and six trombones." Two of Xenakis' compositions—*Metastseis* and *Pithoprakta*—were used by George Balanchine for a modern ballet. All these compositions were completed in the 1960s.

Materials fed into the Mark II Sound Synthesizer also is an electronic process by which musical sounds are created. The Mark II Sound Synthesizer was produced by RCA which, in January of 1958, invited Milton Babbitt to acquaint himself with it and explore its musical potential. For many years Babbitt had been interested in the possibilities of electronically produced sounds, just as he had been deeply involved in the creation of serial music. The Mark II Sound Synthesizer gave him an opportunity to do not only research in the field of electronic music, but composition of electronic music as well. Babbitt's first work for Synthesizer was the *Composition for Synthesizer,* in 1961. This was followed the same year by the first composition ever written for a performer accompanied by synthesized music—*Vision and Prayer,* for soprano, based on a poem by Dylan Thomas. His *Ensembles for Synthesizer* was heard at the Ojai Festival in California in 1964, and in the same year *Philomela* (for soprano, recorded soprano, and synthesized accompaniment), which had been commissioned by the Ford Foundation, received a citation from the New York Music Critics Circle.

Here is how Richard Kostelanetz described the Synthesizer in the *New York Times Magazine:* "Some twenty feet long and seven feet high, the Synthesizer contains various sound-generating devices (tuning forks, oscillators, frequency multipliers, etc.) and about 1,700 tubes, all of which make it capable of producing sounds precisely to the composer's instructions. Potentially, Babbitt says, the machine can create any sound known to man. . . . On the face of the machine are switches that specify the following dimensions of a musical sound—frequency (pitch), octave, volume, timbre and envelope (degree of attack and decrease). When the composer assigns all the attributes of a note, the Synthesizer immediately produces the sound. If the composer finds that the result suits his intentions, he can affix it to the tape; if not, he can readjust the switches to make a new sound. . . . The composer can also place one sound atop another (as is standard in tape doctoring), transform live sounds and even program wholly original scales. . . . In short, unlike the tape laboratories, which require that sound be transferred from one machine to another, the Synthesizer does all its work itself."

To all these adventurers in the world of electronics even the most advanced methods and systems of twentieth-century music are obsolete. They feel that the music of the future lies solely with the sounds produced by electronic means. "My guess," sums up Faubion Bowers in the *Saturday Review,* "is that they are right. The fact of their music is with us, whether we oppose or proclaim it. Electronic music is here to stay, for too many serious people are working on it, too many rockets are shrieking up into the skies, too many children are watching TV, too many people have stood at the corner of 42nd Street and 8th Avenue and listened to noonday traffic, heard an electronic recording and recognized the closeness in the sounds of our times. If something has to give, it probably won't be electronic music; it will have to be our sensitive attitudes towards the unfamiliar, our fear of being adrift in a sea of sound where we don't know how to feel, whether to cry or laugh or nod our heads in time to the beat, or even when the composition has ended so that we may applaud or boo and hiss. . . . Well, rich or poor, young or old, the fact stands. The noise of the world is soon in our concert halls—controlled and organized, if not always premeditated—and a new aesthetic is evolving. All of it has the sound of this new music in it: electronic."

VII

Probably no composer has gone to the extremes that John Cage has gone in experimenting with noises and other non-musical sounds—whether produced electronically or by any other means his fertile imagination can contrive. Even before electronics provided him with hitherto unexplored sounds, sonorities and tone qualities, he had followed the lead of Edgard Varèse (with whom he had studied for a while) in trying to produce "organized sound." In 1940, Cage's *Living Room* for percussion and speech quartet simulated sounds heard in a normal household, such as the banging of doors, the moving of furniture, and so forth. With *Imaginary Landscapes,* Nos. 1 and 2 (1941–42) Cage embarked on a technique he identified as "rhythmed sound." The first *Landscape* is scored for percussion instruments and such items as tin cans, buzzers, a metal wastebasket, an amplified coil of wire capable of producing unusual noises. The second *Landscape* included electronic as well as mechanical devices: audio-frequency oscillators, and a variable speed turntable for the performance of recordings of sounds. In *Imaginary Landscape No. 4* (1951) twelve radios are manipulated by twenty-four performers (two performers for each radio). One man manipulates the tuning dial, while the other one adjusts the dynamics. Cage's score indicates wave lengths and time values. Otherwise the element of chance plays an important role, since the sounds produced by the radios at any given performance depend upon the kind of static that is then heard through the loudspeakers, or the material that is being tuned in from the stations. The work is an amalgamation of music, speech, static, squeals, and silences. *Water Music* (1952) consists of sounds created by pouring water from a full container into an empty one and from the shuffling of a deck of cards. In explaining his curious procedures, Cage has said: "I don't hear noise. I hear music."

With the development of electronic music, Cage's ingenuity and daring seemed to recognize no limits. Though *Fontana Mix* (1958) is, loosely speaking a work for the piano, hitherto untested sounds are introduced: the electronic amplification of the process of writing a letter, or putting on and removing a pair of eyeglasses, or flipping ashes from a cigarette into an ashtray. The performing pianist and his partner have microphones attached to their throats to amplify the sounds of smoking a cigarette, the swallowing of water, coughing, grunting, and so forth. The climax of this work comes by turning the amplification to full strength as the microphones are being scraped over sheets of metal.

Compositions such as these bring us close to the world of dadaism. Dadaism—the expression of nihilism in art, literature and music through the glorification of sheer nonsense—had come into existence in Zurich during World War I. Through escape into absurdity, artists were expressing their contempt for a world willing to accept death, war and destruction. The aim of dadaism, as one of its disciples explained was "to spit in the eye of the world." Dadaism, an attack against reason, became a kind of cult with the arch-cynic.

Post World War I dadaism produced a number of interesting compositions, the most significant of which was William Walton's *Façade* (see page 273).

The revival of dadaism in the avant-garde movement of the 1950s and 1960s was probably the result of the same kind of cynicism, frustration, contempt with the political and social realities of the time, and rejection of war that helped to bring dadaism into existence in the first place. Of all the trends produced by the present-day avant-garde school of our times, that of neo-dadaism is perhaps the most difficult to understand as an artistic potential. For what the neo-dadaist is doing is transforming a temple of art into a shabby honky tonk, reducing sublimity to the ridiculous.

John Cage is a leading figure in the neo-dadaist movement of today. *Variations V* (1965), presented at the Lincoln Center for the Performing Arts, requires dancers, electronic equipment, and a screen on which can be flashed distorted images from TV and motion picture clips. One of the principal dancers wears red pants and a gray shirt. He rides a bicycle through a mass of electronic transmitters, the movements of his bicycle encouraging the electronic equipment to produce a cacophony of noises which then is relayed throughout the auditorium by loudspeakers.

Theatre Piece (1965) requires a man to hang upside down wrapped up in a black plastic cocoon. A female cellist plays a Cage composition while the composer places a cigar in her mouth, and removes it from her lips from time to time. A tiny Japanese waves silken banners from atop a huge bamboo pole. An oil drum is rolled down the stairs—*outside* the auditorium. As the work progresses, blown-up balloons are punctured, buzzers are sounded, and all kinds of screeching and squealing sounds come from electronic equipment.

In his Piano Concerto (1965) Cage requires the men of the orchestra to whistle into bottle openings, to blow up paper bags and then explode them by puncturing them with a pin. One of the violinists is called upon to use a ham bone as his bow. The assistant concertmaster has to fire a toy machine gun.

Maurice Klagel, an Argentine, has written compositions during the performance of which one of the musicians is required to bounce a rubber ball, or two musicians are instructed to engage in a loud conversation.

Perhaps the final word in neo-dadaism has been spoken by Nam Jun Paik, a Korean, in a composition entitled *Action Music* given at a festival of avant-garde music in New York in 1965. Here is how Howard Klein described in *The New York Times* what happened during the performance of this work: "The opening consisted of the composer doing an action painting with black paint applied by both hands and hair entitled 'Homage to Cage.' After that one of the upright pianos was smashed, eggs were broken, and roars came from loudspeakers through electronic means. This was followed by nails being driven into one of the pianos, with Mr. Paik cutting his hair, bedecking several men and women with strips of shaving cream, with cutting off the tie and shirt of one man with a scissors. The high point of the performance came when Charlotte Moorman played the cello. She played *Variations on a Theme of Saint-Saëns*, wearing a costume consisting solely of a cellophane sheath. While she played, the composer held the end pin of the cello in his teeth. Midway in the performance of Saint-Saëns' *The Swan*, Miss Moorman climbed a six-foot ladder and immersed herself in an oil drum filled with water. Then she climbed out, her cellophane sheath clinging to her body, to complete playing *The Swan*."

300

Perhaps this is the way the music of tomorrow will go. Or, if the pendulum of music history continues to swing away from extremes, it is just as likely that music will revert to the greatest art of all, the art of simplicity, in which a world of sentiment and thought and experience is caught within the simple lines of a beautiful melody.

12/30/72

Index

309

313

Muradeli, 229 (RUSS.)
Music After the War, 128
Music for a Scene from Shelley, 252
Music for Strings, 166
Music for the Theater, 181–182, 220
Musical America, 109, 198
Musik, Die, 150
Mussorgsky, 18, 83, 132, 155
Mutual Life Insurance Company, 52
Mystery Chord, 39

Napoleon, 235
National Broadcasting Company, 252, 266, 269, 271
National Dances of Moravia, 176
National Institute of Arts and Letters, 116
National Institute of Arts and Sciences, 54
Nationalists, 155–177
   American, 178–197
Natoma, 180
Negro ballet, 87
Negro melodies, 178–180, 189, 207, 217–218
Negro Rhapsody, 92, 180
Neo-Classicists, 142–154
Neue Freie Presse, 123
Neues vom Tage, 95, 220
New England Triptych, 191, 275
New Fire, 197
New Orleans, Louisiana, 208–209
New York City Opera, 124, 185
New York City Symphony, 103, 181, 214
New York Drama Critics, 268, 271
New York Metropolitan Opera, 34, 124, 251, 253, 260, 266

New York Music Critics Circle, 54, 93, 184, 203, 204, 217, 253, 276, 285, 295
New York Philharmonic, 94, 124, 188, 214, 252, 258
New York Post, 254
New York Times, The, 32, 34, 36, 50, 138, 217, 222, 259, 269, 295, 300
New York Tribune, 139
New York University, 220
New York World, 139
Newman, Cardinal, 247
Newman, Ernest, 122, 259
News of the Day, 95
News of the Season, 138
Newsreel, 275
Nietzsche, 42
Night Journey, 275
Nights in the Gardens of Spain, 174
Nijinsky, 129, 132
Nineteenth century music, 14–17
Ninth String Quartet (Miaskovsky), 240
Ninth Symphony (Shostakovich), 229
No for an Answer, 103
Noblissima visione, 152
Noces, Les, 144
Nocturnal, 286
Noise-making devices, 4
Nono, Luigi, 281, 282
Norfolk, Connecticut, 162
Norfolk Rhapsodies, 169, 170
North and West, 249
Northwestern University, 250
Norwegian music, 156
Nose, The, 226

O, Bury Me Not, 183
O for a Thousand Tongues, 190
O'Casey, Sean, 104

314

318

DAVID EWEN

is the most widely read living writer on music. Since 1931 there has hardly been a year when one of his books on music was not on the lists, and as *Music Journal* once said, it was usually "the cream of the crop." His more than three score of books have been on best-seller lists, on the permanent reference shelf throughout the civilized world, have been translated into seventeen foreign languages (including Chinese, Japanese, Vietnamese, and Hebrew), and have been promoted by the leading book clubs, and the Metropolitan Opera broadcasts for a full season. He is, as *Time* once said of him, "music's interpreter to the American people." Among his books are *Encyclopedia of the Opera, Encyclopedia of Concert Music, The Story of America's Popular Music, The New Book of Modern Composers,* and *Leonard Bernstein.* He is the authorized and definitive biographer of George Gershwin, Richard Rodgers, and Jerome Kern. In 1961–62 he was contracted by the Office of Information in Washington, D.C., to write and co-produce fifty-two broadcasts on the history of American popular music to be beamed throughout the free world by the Voice of America.

13 ✓
38 ✓
41 ✓
76 ✓
78 ✓
129 ✓
133 ✓
134 ✓
135 ✓
147 ✓
173 ✓
174 ✓
186 ✓
192 ✓
207 ✓
212 ✓
214 ✓
239 ✓
250 ✓
266 ✓
279 ✓
282 ✓
311 ✓
310 ✓